TRIUMPH OVER THE TALIBAN

•••

THE UNTOLD STORY OF US MARINES' COURAGEOUS FIGHT TO SAVE
CAMP BASTION

JEANNE McKINNEY

Triumph Over the Taliban

The Untold Story of US Marines' Courageous Fight to Save
Camp Bastion

Jeanne McKinney

Published by Patriot Profiles Productions
ISBN 979-8-9896809-0-0
Library of Congress Control Number 2024903687

Cover illustration: Anhar Hawari
Cover and interior design: Karl Hunt
Editing: Howard VanEs and Joshua Price
Back cover photo: DVIDS by Cpl Gregory Moore

TRIUMPH OVER THE TALIBAN

Truth lives in silence . . . until it is set free.

FOREWORD

By Lieutenant General (Retired) James Terry, U.S. Army, Commander ISAF Joint Command

Triumph Over the Taliban is a riveting story about United States Marines fighting for each other, civilian contractors, and their aircraft and facilities in order to accomplish the mission. It also demonstrates the ethos imbued in every Marine from boot camp until death that was individually and collectively displayed during the night of fierce battle against the Taliban on September 14, 2012, at Camp Bastion, Afghanistan. Through exhaustive research, interviews, and exacting details, author Jeanne McKinney has captured their story—masterfully outlining and revealing what others have not recognized—an important military battle that has not been fully chronicled until now. She brings to life the selfless courage,

CAMP LEATHERNECK, Afghanistan, April 22, 2013. U.S. Army LTG James L. Terry, commander of International Security Assistance Force Joint Command, presents a challenge coin to U.S. Marine Corps Sgt Jason Stewart, assigned to Headquarters Company, Regimental Combat Team (RCT) 7. Terry visited RCT-7 during a battlefield circulation of various bases in the area of operation. (USMC photo by Cpl. Alejandro Pena)

personal initiative, and values that every Marine holds dear, culminating in one of those rare books that you will read from cover to cover before putting it on the shelf . . . and then pulling it back down to re-read.

Located in the southwest corner of Afghanistan, in a massive expanse of mostly wide-open arid desert, the combined expeditionary megaplex consisting of Camp Bastion (U.K.)/Camp Leatherneck (U.S.), and Camp Shorabak (ANA) was part of Regional Command (Southwest) RC(SW)'s area of responsibility (AOR). The huge military forward operating base was included in the International Security Assistance Force's (ISAF) coalition of security forces deployed across regional commands. Geographically, the AOR encompassed over 38,000 square miles (nearly the size of Kentucky) in the Helmand and Nimruz Provinces and included 196 combat outposts and forward operating bases with 19 districts. This was one of the most volatile areas in Afghanistan, primarily due to the poppy grown there, which was central to the Taliban economy. Securing Camp Bastion (forty square miles and twenty-five miles of fence line) was a monumental challenge as force protection tasks were exponentially more difficult in combat.

From June 2012 to May 2013 in Afghanistan, I was the ISAF Joint Command Commander and helped to coordinate the ISAF plan to put Afghan National Security Forces (ANSF) in a lead counterinsurgency role as coalition forces transitioned to an assist/advisor role, all while conducting a directed surge recovery of U.S. troops. At all echelons, commanders were balancing forces and capabilities while putting ANSF in charge of their own security and protecting our own forces, still flying critical air missions. In March 2012, there were 17,000 United States Marine personnel in RC(SW). Six months later, there were only 7,400.

The Marine campaign in RC(SW) achieved operational success by wreaking havoc on Taliban infiltration lanes and sanctuaries while disrupting critical financing. At the center of U.S. Marine operations was the Air-Ground Team. The Taliban, ever determined to disrupt that team, sent a suicide squad to destroy the Air Component and obstruct the Marine mission on that fateful night.

As the ISAF Joint Command Commander, I had witnessed the challenges of fighting and withdrawing, along with transitioning ANSF. The 3rd MAW Marines played an essential role in setting conditions for this period of transition, as Taliban operations, attacks, and violence were very present in the region. This period encompassed some of the most violent fighting faced by U.S. forces during Operation Enduring Freedom. It was a pivotal period that made unrelenting demands on Marines and their aircraft, pushing them to the outer limits of endurance.

As outlined by Jeanne McKinney in this book, RC(SW) met roadblocks to making the airfield more secure, at odds with British partners who built Camp Bastion originally. The coalition of nations that came to Afghanistan was essential to the counterinsurgency mission. The integration of these forces was complicated by the fact that contributing nations set their own limitations and constraints for when they can engage and how they approach security and command. Collaboration, focused effort, and relationship management were especially challenging during a fighting season with reduced manpower.

The announced timeline of the withdrawal provided opportunities for the Taliban to regenerate in sanctuary and conduct operations to keep their presence known to locals living in the volatile Helmand Province region. This presented daily Troops in Contact (TIC) calls for close air support from 3rd MAW Marines protecting U.S. ground forces and, ultimately, the Afghan people subject to Taliban rule.

The Taliban actively recruited for insider attacks and suicide missions to continue to kill and disrupt U.S. forces while cementing lasting fear in the Afghan people. Afghan National Security Forces were not as proficient or as well equipped as U.S. forces and, at times, were easily influenced and coerced by the Taliban. The shift motivated and emboldened the Taliban to attack ISAF forces inside their bases, often a suicide mission, as was the attack on Camp Bastion/Leatherneck.

The night of the enemy attack on Camp Bastion/Leatherneck, the ACE did exactly what Marines have learned to do at USMC training grounds across our nation. Their readiness to win in battle, along with their ingrained training, paid off when 3rd MAW Marines put down their tools, picked up their weapons, and secured the base in order to continue the mission.

Thanks to exceptional small unit leadership, courage, skill, and the desire to accomplish the mission, they succeeded in repelling that violent suicide attack. That night, they lived their ethos, rose up aggressively and in concert to the call of battle, and proved the adage: *Every Marine is a rifleman!* As you will see in this book, there are many stories of extraordinary heroism and valor from that night that need to be told.

DEDICATION

This book is dedicated to all aviation Marines who served at Camp Bastion, Afghanistan, in a legacy fight to defeat their attackers on September 14, 2012. A special thanks and dedication go out to LtCol Christopher Raible and Sgt Bradley Atwell for leading and fighting alongside their Marine brothers, giving their last full measure of devotion.

CONTENTS

TERMS

For easy reference, the following is a list of terms and their abbreviations that you will see throughout this book.

3rd MAW (FWD)	3rd Marine Aircraft Wing (Forward)
AAMO	Assistant Aviation Maintenance Officer
ACE	Aviation Combat Element
AGL	Above Ground Level
AGSOC	Air Ground Special Operations Command
al-Qaeda (FTO)	Islamic Foreign Terrorist Organization
AMOF	Authorized Military Overhaul Facility
ANA	Afghan National Army
ANDSF	Afghan National Defense Security Forces
AOA	Airfield Operating Authority
AOBW	Area of Operation Belleau Wood
AOIC	Acting Official in Charge
AOR	Area of Operations
APKWS	Advanced Precision Kill Weapons System
ARG	Amphibious Ready Group
AT/FP	Anti-Terrorism and Force Protection
BLS	Bastion Leatherneck Shorabak
C2	Command and Control
CAOC	Combined Air Operations Center
CAS	Close Air Support

CASEVAC	Casualty Evacuations
CJO	Chief of Joint Operations
CJOC	Combined Joint Operations Command
CO	Commanding Officer
COIN	Counterinsurgency
COP	Combat Outpost
CWO	Chief Warrant Officer
DASC	Direct Air Support Center
DOSS	Director of Safety and Standardization
DTRA	Defense Threat Reduction Agency
EAW	Expeditionary Air Wing
ECP	Entry Control Point
ESG	Executive Steering Group
FAC	Forward Air Controller
FAC/A	Forward Air Controller/Airborne
FARP	Forward Army Refueling Point
FLIR	Forward-Looking Infrared
FML	Force Management Level
GCE	Ground Combat Element
Haqqani Network (SDGT) (FTO)	Islamic Specially Designated Global Terrorists, Foreign Terrorist Organization
HMH	Marine Heavy Helicopter Squadron
HMLA	Marine Light Attack Helicopter Squadron
HUD	Heads-Up Display
IED	Improvised Explosive Device
IJC	ISAF Joint Command
IMEF (FWD)	I Marine Expeditionary Force (Forward)
ISAF	International Security Assistance Forces
ISC	International Shipping Container
ISIS (FTO)	Islamic Foreign Terrorist Organization
ISR	Intelligence, Surveillance, Reconnaissance
JDAM	Joint Direct Attack Munitions
JHF	Joint Helicopter Force

TERMS

JSIVA	Joint Staff Integrated Vulnerability Assessment
JTAC	Joint Terminal Attack Controller
LAR	Light Armored Reconnaissance
LP/OP	Listening Post/Observation Post
LSA	Logistics Support Area
MACG (FWD)	Marine Air Control Group (Forward)
MALS	Marine Aviation Logistics Squadron
MARSOC	Marine Special Operations Command
MCT	Marine Combat Training
MEF	Marine Expeditionary Forces
MIRC	Military Internet Relay Chat
MOD	Ministry of Defense (British)
MOU	Memorandum of Understanding
MRAP	Mine Resistant Ambush Protected (Vehicle)
MWHS	Marine Wing Headquarters Squadron
MWSS	Marine Wing Support Squadron
NGZ	Northern Green Zone
NVD	Night Vision Device
ODO	Operations Duty Officer
OEF	Operation Enduring Freedom
OIF	Operation Iraqi Freedom
PJHQ	Permanent Joint Headquarters
PKM	Pulemyot Kalashnikova Modernizirovany (Russian Rifle)
POG	Personnel Other than Grunt
POO	Point of Origin
PPV	Protected Patrol Vehicle
PRI	Immediate Priority
PSO	Personal Security Officer
QRF	Quick Reaction Force
RC(SW)	Regional Command (Southwest)
ROE	Rules of Engagement
SAPHEI	Semi-Armor Piercing High-Explosive Incendiaries

SECFOR	Security Forces
SFA	Security Force Assistance
SOC	Special Operations Capable
STOVL	Short Take-Off and Vertical Landing
TAAC	Tactical Air Command Center
Taliban (SDGTs)	Islamic Specially Designated Global Terrorists
TAU	Twin Agent Unit (Firefighting)
TCN	Third Country National
TFBW	Task Force Belleau Wood
TIC	Troops in Contact
UAS	Unmanned Aerial Systems
VMA	Marine Fighter Attack Squadron
VMGR	Marine Aerial Refueler Transport Squadron
VMM	Marine Medium Tiltrotor Squadron
VMU	Marine Unmanned Aerial Vehicle Squadron
WTI	Weapons and Tactics Instructor
XO	Executive Officer

PROLOGUE

LITTLE DID MOST AMERICANS know that three days after the September 11, 2012, attack on the U.S. diplomatic compound in Benghazi, Libya, that another attack would be occurring on a massive forward operating base called Camp Bastion in Afghanistan. Originally built and operated by the British, the base expanded to include a U.S. headquarters called Camp Leatherneck, and a section for the Afghan National Army camp. Coalition troops who rotated through this overseas expeditionary hub knew it as the Bastion/Leatherneck/Shorabak (BLS) complex. BLS served as a temporary home for those involved in counterinsurgency operations, projecting power throughout Southern Afghanistan and specifically in Helmand Province, a poppy-growing empire. They were fighting an entrenched active insurgency, creating chaos for local populations and upending security and local governments. The Taliban's campaign included control, extortion, and coercion by violence.

The Taliban, in an uncharacteristic move, planned to attack U.S. Marines in their own work and living spaces on an unusually dark night (2 percent illumination) on September 14, 2012—not their usual mode of shooting from murder holes and compounds. They prepared to leverage former President Obama's mandated drawdown of troops, while they had no intent to draw down their insurgent fighters.

The 3rd Marine Aircraft Wing (MAW) was sent to Bastion and ordered to reduce 4,500 Marines to 1,723 in less than six months while still maintaining full offensive combat capability. The aviation combat element (ACE) alone had 3,772 personnel in February 2012 and was reduced to 1,920 personnel in September 2012. This drawdown was part of the greater reduction of strength in Regional Command Southwest RC(SW) from 17,000 to 7,400 Marines from March until September 2012.

Despite the massive reduction, the ACE still had the mission to provide aviation support to USMC/Coalition/Afghan forces. Their role to deter and disrupt Taliban plans (24/7) was beset with dwindling manpower over a quickened period of mere months, while facing blaring security gaps at the Bastion airfield not of their making.

In comparison, two years previously, Obama had ramped up the number of U.S. troops in Afghanistan from 30,000 to more than 100,000 in 2010, a majority of them in Helmand Province.

On September 14, 2012, it had only been a little over seventy-two hours since the world was dished out a story from the White House that an anti-Islamic video caused protestors to storm and set fire to the Benghazi compound, killing Ambassador J. Christopher Stevens, Information Officer Sean Smith, and CIA security contractors Tyrone Woods and Glen Doherty (both former SEALS). No one in the media was focused on the concerning challenges going on at Bastion for 3rd MAW facing the same type of hardened terrorists planning to kill Americans. Whether it is the Taliban or al-Qaeda, as in the case of the Benghazi attack, they all ooze vengeance. Their goals were to send Americans home with flags draped around their coffins or missing body parts, and make the U.S. know who they were.

In the smoke and mirrors of lies about Benghazi, the Taliban attack on an American airbase on the night of September 14, 2012, was hardly on anyone's radar. The news media was generally cold to it, and what the press did come out with was skimmed over quickly. A random small number of reports contained errors about who really engaged the enemy and what was at stake.

The tactical element of surprise cannot be underestimated, as the Taliban proved over and over again. Late at night, Marines scattered all over the airfield heard ground-shaking blasts from explosions. They quickly assessed an enemy was inside the wire on their home turf. Without comms or situational awareness, Marines immediately began mobilizing, arming, creating defenses, and protecting each other and civilians in their midst. Their ingrained response to a violent storm of bullets, bombs, and catastrophic arson culminated in a night of fiery battle deserving of a distinguished legacy, not unlike legacies established by Marine Aviation predecessors during battles such as those at Henderson Field, Guadalcanal. The Taliban would learn in a harsh, unforgiving way they miscalculated U.S. Aviation Marines.

Why didn't we hear about this? Because it was covered up and misrepresented by both the U.S. and U.K. governments in the interest of political ends. The Bastion base itself was touted to be "impregnable," but 3rd MAW leaders soon found out that was far from the case. High officials in Washington took the briar patch to explain how a group of fifteen Taliban breached the wire. Facts were ignored and accusations were levied that were untrue.

As post-attack investigations evolved, a night of victory became a source of pain to many in a political move to save face. What became highly public was finger-pointing and blame towards the very Marine generals driven to fix the security problems they saw even before the arrival of 3rd MAW. The generals' hands were tied, and requests to make critical improvements to do away with threats to base security were repeatedly turned down. A once-trusted British ally, Lt. Gen. David Capewell, turned his back on owning accountability to secure the Bastion airfield, which his British personnel down the chain were assigned distinct responsibility for.

Yet it was war, and if there is a will, a determined enemy will find a way to execute a plan. The Taliban aptly leveraged the British complacency to security, as they'd been probing by close observation opportunities for months while building a plan to attack the base. Seventeen months later, on April 16, 2014, the U.K. House of Commons Defense Committee published, "Oral and written evidence" compiled by Defense Committee members who unraveled Capewell's deception to get to the bottom of what really happened and why.

The spell-binding fight to save lives, aircraft, and property was not the focus of U.S. military investigators. Unfortunately, they tarnished the reputations of 3rd MAW personnel, with irrevocable damage done. Their brave fight at Camp Bastion went sorely under-recognized.

The book was written to repair some of that damage and restore the legacy earned by 3rd MAW Marines for their actions against the Taliban that night. Sadly, nothing of real substance was ever officially documented of these Aviation Marines' efforts, who had to pick up their rifles and act as infantrymen. The Marine Corps is the only service branch requiring all personnel to qualify on a rifle range regardless of their occupational specialty. Without that, the battle for Camp Bastion would have had a very different outcome. On that dark night, the true character of U.S. Marines shone brighter than the hellish enemy fires.

In my journalistic pursuit of truth, I provide overwhelming evidence that the battle of Bastion was not about the failure of any one person, especially longtime career generals. They put dedication and care for their forces first—while also under the crushing weight of their dual-sided mission to conduct an uncompromising fight against the Taliban and prepare to leave Bastion.

Opposite to how governments labeled the attack on Camp Bastion—I offer a much different light, showcasing success when Marine Corps training was put to the ultimate test, going above and beyond to save hundreds of lives, and according to MajGen Gregg Sturdevant, "5.1 billion dollars worth of aircraft, and approximately $400 million in spare parts, yellow gear (special equipment) and fuel." Through a series of in-depth interviews over nine years, thirteen Marines share what happened on the ground and in the air in mind-blowing detail. It's not the same story that those at the top of the Marine Corps or British military and defense circles told. This account is not about who should be blamed, but it is about what really happened and who should be honored.

As you read through the book, you will meet Marine heroes who fought with valor, determination, grit, and exceptional skill. Marines such as (former Capt) LtCol Adam Coker, who flew a UH-1Y Huey into danger close configurations to get targets on Taliban hiding below, shooting at him and his crew. Or (former Maj) Col Robb T. McDonald, who came face to face with the Taliban in a gunfight showdown. Or Fuels Marines fighting multiple 50,000-gallon jet fuel bags that were on fire while getting shot at from Taliban rifles and RPGs flying around them.

This is the true and remarkable story of the Battle for Camp Bastion.

•••

Triumph Over the Taliban is largely based on thirteen 3rd MAW Marines who shared their battle experiences during in-depth interviews for the purpose of writing this book. You'll read (with their permission) what happened to them woven in the context of the entire battle throughout this book. Also included is information from USMC summary reports, various personal emails, and additional conversations given/afforded to the author from the Marines (in the book) for factual authenticity. Official U.S. and U.K. investigations and news stories are footnoted for easy reference.

The U.S. Marines who contributed to this book are:

Major General (MajGen) Charles Mark Gurganus, Major General (MajGen) Gregg A. Sturdevant, Brigadier General (BGen) Stephen Lightfoot, Colonel (Col) Robb T. McDonald, Colonel (Col) Richard Bew, Lieutenant Colonel (LtCol) Adam Coker, Chief Warrant Officer 3 (CW 3) Timothy Killebrew, Major (Maj) Kevin Smalley, Major (Maj) Brian Jordan, Major (Maj) Matthew McBride, Captain (Capt) Bryan Yerger, Sergeant (Sgt) Jon Cudo, Sergeant (Sgt) Mike Doman.

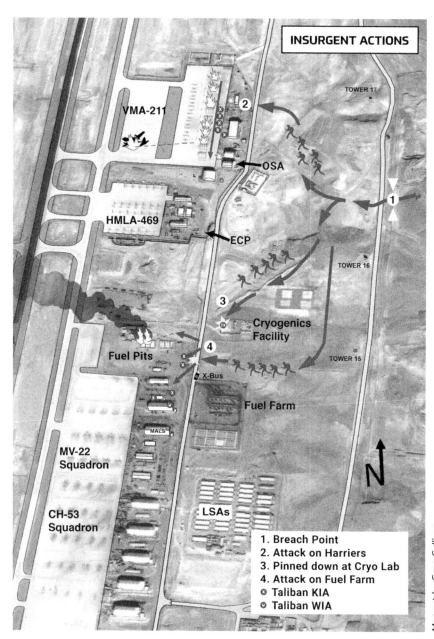

INSURGENT ACTIONS

TOWER 17

VMA-211

OSA

HMLA-469

ECP

TOWER 16

Cryogenics Facility

Fuel Pits

X-Bus

Fuel Farm

TOWER 15

MALS

MV-22 Squadron

CH-53 Squadron

LSAs

N

1. Breach Point
2. Attack on Harriers
3. Pinned down at Cryo Lab
4. Attack on Fuel Farm
⊘ Taliban KIA
⊘ Taliban WIA

Map art by Sean Sullivan

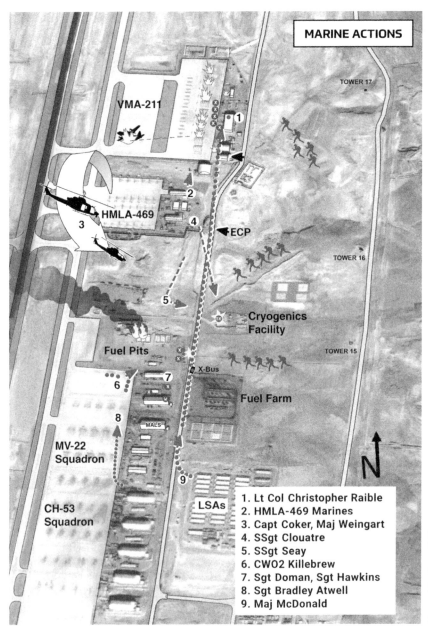

MARINE ACTIONS

1. Lt Col Christopher Raible
2. HMLA-469 Marines
3. Capt Coker, Maj Weingart
4. SSgt Clouatre
5. SSgt Seay
6. CWO2 Killebrew
7. Sgt Doman, Sgt Hawkins
8. Sgt Bradley Atwell
9. Maj McDonald

Map art by Sean Sullivan

1

A VULNERABLE FORTRESS

ON SEPTEMBER 14, 2012, a USMC Harrier jump jet, finished with its airborne combat mission of the day, noisily approached its home base airfield, always aware of the danger in Taliban country. Taliban rifle shots would, at times, spray out from beyond the chain link fence, topped with concertina wire, that wrapped around the eastern airfield perimeter. The jet-powered attack aircraft, capable of short take-off and vertical landing (STOVL), comprised Marine Fighter Attack Squadron 211 (VMA-211). Known as the "Wake Island Avengers," they had only arrived weeks before to augment air support operations against embedded Taliban executing their campaign of violence in the Helmand Province region.

Harriers were a bane to the Taliban; they hated the noisy sky demons that would make them run upon hearing their approach and showed no mercy. Now, the USMC fiery beasts were occupying the most northern flight line at the Bastion/Leatherneck/Shorabak (BLS) forward operating base (FOB), a massive hub of counterinsurgency operations in the middle of the southern Afghanistan desert. The British had originally built Bastion in 2006, with the intention of making it an impregnable fortress.

BLS expanded to base U.S. Marines, who set up their own hub of counterinsurgency operations in southern Afghanistan. Construction on Camp Leatherneck, the U.S. headquarters compound, commenced in 2008 and finished in 2009. The job of the United States Marines deployed there was to distribute units out to the hinterlands to clear insurgents terrorizing the local populations, deter movement of fighters and weapons, block mobilization and bomb-making, and make waste of illegal opium that funded rampant terrorism. Historically, over the years, sending U.S. Marines to Helmand Province amounted to stabilizing the region so the economies could grow, kids could go to school, and people could live without fear. No one, not even the Afghan locals, were spared Taliban brutality and murders in the embattled region, rife with poppy fields in the notorious Northern Green Zone (NGZ). Afghan forces were also housed in Camp Shorabak in the northwest corner of the Bastion complex. Hundreds of people came in and went off the base daily. They all worked under the umbrella authority of the International Security Assistance Forces (ISAF)—a NATO-formed coalition created for the Operation Enduring Freedom (OEF) counterterrorism campaign throughout Afghanistan.

The Third Marine Aircraft Wing (3rd MAW) had arrived a couple of months earlier for what would be their last deployment there as forces were ordered to draw down by then-President Barack Obama, making good on a campaign promise. Upon arrival, they saw the Brits had allowed the villages of Sheikabad and Nawabad to spring up to the east and southeast of the airfield's eastern perimeter. Farmers in those towns increasingly grew poppies right up to the fence line. It was a given that if there were poppies, there were Taliban, and where there were Taliban, there were poppies. For illogical reasons in Taliban country, the Brits trusted the local governor Mohammed Daoud (who controlled the valley) for "security" in those villages right next door to Bastion's grand central station of counterinsurgency forward power. The Taliban had endless opportunities to blend into the poppy fields, pretending to be local farmers, able to surveil the base's round-the-clock close air support operations.

Taliban caused chaos wherever they went, like a storm moving in on the locals, never leaving. The Taliban killed and overran local Afghan security forces trying to enforce the law and maintain stability. Malevolent insurgents killed their families, too, or anyone who crossed them.

Farm Progress news reported in 2013 that, as battles came and went in Afghanistan after the Taliban fell from power in 2001, their cash cow crop, opium, remained.[1] In 2012, the opium trade thrived, bringing in tens of millions. For poor farmers in Afghanistan, opium meant currency to support their families. The surge of poppy acreage added up to make Afghanistan one of the world's top suppliers of heroin. Both the U.S. and U.K. had spent millions trying to get farmers to plant corn, wheat, cotton, and other legal crops.

So, it didn't make any sense to allow poppy fields to thrive right next to the very forces trying to eradicate them. British overseers at Bastion turned their heads away as poppies reached for the life-giving sun—not the case for the Americans due to arrive.

The insurgents sought to control the towns and villages and extort and profit from the locals' labor, growing the illegal crops. They squeezed them throughout Helmand Province, becoming this narco-state, appearing to be benevolent, supplying seed, fertilizer, and advance payments only to rule over them, requiring a tax and *submission*. Failure to submit meant violence—even death. The Afghan forces alone were not equipped or strong enough to hold the Taliban back.

Farm Progress reports, "As Ghulam Muhammad Woror, director of narcotics control in Afghanistan's Helmand province, told

---

1 Bennett, Coop, "Bull market, bitter legacy for opium farmers," *Farm Progress*, August 5, 2013, https://www.farmprogress.com/business/bull-market-bitter-legacy-for-opium-farmers.

Newsweek, "Drugs are ultimately providing the money, food, weapons, and suicide bombers to the insurgency and the good life to Taliban leaders . . ."[2]

The eastern sector of the base that housed the Bastion airfield presented this blaring security gap prior to 3rd MAW's arrival. Top USMC officers Major General Mark Gurganus, Commander Regional Command Southwest RC(SW), and Major General Gregg Sturdevant, Commanding General, 3rd Marine Aircraft Wing (Forward), were alarmed upon their arrival seeing the poppy cultivation so near the airfield. Local construction was ongoing to build multiple compounds lining the area near the airfield perimeter with no one to stop them. The British facilitated co-existence with the budding villages, though Bastion was originally intended to be a remote desert fortress, housing highly-trained expeditionary forces.

No mote surrounded this installation, only open ground except for the poppy fields that grew right up to the perimeter fence line, providing a relative degree of safety from anyone's line of sight. The prolific flowering plants grown in Afghanistan provided illicit opium protected by insurgents and in great demand. A significant amount of the drug was converted to heroin to be trafficked internationally, with profits feeding and arming the insurgencies. The colorful fields blocked a clear, open view to the east, required to defend it from an attack. The British were irrigating the poppy fields with base runoff and protecting the harvests, according to the observations of a British tower guard at the time who preferred to remain anonymous.

Gurganus and Sturdevant did not take the unsettling discoveries sitting down. They both assessed the base was continually being probed. Gurganus made multiple requests to bulldoze the poppy

2 Bennett, Coop, "Bull market, bitter legacy for opium farmers," *Farm Progress*, August 5, 2013, https://www.farmprogress.com/business/bull-market-bitter-legacy-for-opium-farmers.

fields to eliminate the enemy using the farmer's fields for cover and concealment. This would be a critical line of defense to unobstruct the field of view. Gurganus was met with strong resistance from higher headquarters for a host of reasons, saying, "Wait for the harvest," "Too late, a new crop had been planted," and that an Afghan face had to lead the way to bulldoze the fields. From the start of their time there, they were sharply elbowed by their British counterparts, saying, "This is our bit of the base. We are in charge here—our rules."

Yet it was American lives Gurganus was protecting, and British "rules" were not enough. Additional second line of defense fortifications were placed around the airfield in the form of T-walls, HESCO barriers, berms, manned checkpoints, etc. Not every inch of ground on the airfield compound and multiple flight lines could be covered with a wall, as it was a lot of geography. So, the British "rules" had better include denying would-be attackers from inside access through any part of the perimeter. The British played host to the USMC aircraft squadrons, and a host protected his tenant units. Ultimately, 3rd MAW Marines were the last line of defense, and they were properly trained and ready. This would be conveniently forgotten when the government went after Gurganus and Sturdevant like heat-seeking missiles.

The Taliban had no care for international politics and planned simply to seize the opportunity before all the U.S. forces were removed from the country. They were friends and allies with al-Qaeda, the Haqqani network, and other offshoot terrorist groups that seemed to spin off regularly. They all connected in some form of jihad similar to each other. Death was welcomed to gain standing when their bodies would be ripped to pieces and their sacrifice a legend. The night, forecast moonless, had arrived. The Taliban had two effective weapons: constant surveillance and patience. They picked the time to pay back the thrashing U.S. Marines had given them, causing them to scurry back to their murderous planning dens. They'd later emerge to plant more bombs in secret and establish firing positions, blending into the urban landscape where Afghan people worked and lived—but they were nonetheless teeth-gnashing and full of uncompromising reprisal.

The newly arrived air crews had their hands full, trying to both fight and remove themselves from the combat theater. September 14 was busy like any other day, with no real hiccups to speak of. Behind the scenes, Gurganus and Sturdevant had made no haste to address the security gaps, which were largely aggravated by a split command established by an outdated security contract, which hung over their heads like a ceiling with holes.

• • •

As stated in the Dept. of the Army Bastion Attack Investigation: "MajGen Gurganus and RC(SW) inherited the BLS Complex [Anti-Terrorism and Force Protection] (AT/FP) [Command and Control] (C2) arrangement, established by a January 2011 Memorandum of Understanding (MOU) between USCENTCOM and the UK Permanent Joint Headquarters (PJHQ), titled 'The Command and Support Arrangements for UK/US Forces Based at Bastion/Leatherneck Combined Operating Base Afghanistan.'"[3]

The 2011 MOU arrangement was confusing with gaps—a challenge to enforce. It amounted to having to trust the British forces to provide security for U.S. Marines in the event of an insider assault on the airfield. This was due to the MOU's designation of Camp Leatherneck (USMC headquarters) and U.K. Camp Bastion as two separate camps. The Brits were assigned force protection responsibility for the airfield.

---

3 Garrett, William B., Murray, Thomas M., "Army Regulation (AR) 15-6 Report (Final)," Dept. of the Army Bastion Attack Investigation, August 19, 2013, Pg. 8, https://www.hqmc.marines.mil/Portals/142/USCENTCOM%20Bastion%20Attack%20Investigation%20Redacted%2015-6%20Report.pdf.

The U.S. CENTCOM Bastion Attack Investigation Executive Summary clearly stated: "Although the boundaries between Camps Leatherneck and Bastion were not clearly demarcated, there was a sense that the US was completely in charge of Camp Leatherneck, and the U.K. was completely in charge of Camp Bastion. The 2011 MOU clearly established the separate camps in addition to the Bastion airfield, which was a U.K.-U.S. shared airfield located on Camp Bastion and operated by the U.K. 903d Expeditionary Air Wing (EAW) as the Airfield Operating Authority (AOA).

"The 2011 MOU further specified that the US would protect Camp Leatherneck and conduct security operations in Area of Operation Belleau Wood (AOBW), which included the area surrounding the BLS Complex. The MOU specified that the UK was responsible for protection of Camp Bastion, including the airfield, and that they would provide security patrols to assist US security operations in AOBW."[4]

The most concerning area was right outside the base (mainly in the Washir District), encompassing settlements on most sides. The area was laid out to take out the threat ring from mortars, rockets, and anti-air missiles that could impact the airfield and approaches. Those threats were monitored daily, with U.S. forces able to saturate that area regularly before the drawdown. Afterwards, U.S. forces did not have the necessary manpower—a concern Gurganus voiced loudly to ISAF Joint Command (IJC).

Dept. of the Army Camp Bastion Attack Investigation:

"The MOU stated that the US and UK force protection standards would be in accordance with national command element

---

4 Garrett, William B., Murray, Thomas M., "USCENTCOM Bastion Attack Investigation Executive Summary," The United States Central Command (USCENTCOM), Accessed November 29, 2023, Pg. 2, https://www.hqmc.marines.mil/Portals/142/Docs/USCENTCOM%20Bastion%20Attack%20Investigation%20Executive%20Summary.pdf.

requirements, but did not specify those standards. This arrangement effectively created two different camps with two different protection standards . . . the MOU did not discuss integration of Camp Shorabak, the Afghan National Army (ANA) installation, into a comprehensive force protection plan for the entire BLS complex."[5]

And why not? Our allies occupied a portion of the base. The Taliban did not show favoritism to Afghan forces—quite the opposite. Force protection responsibilities were shared by the commander of the 215th ANA Corps for Camp Shorabak. So, three separate militaries were working under different commands, different watches, and different security and response protocols. How was this all supposed to mesh together in the event of an insider attack on any one part of the BLS complex, when no clear camp boundaries existed?

"The end result of the CENTCOM-PJHQ MOU was what Lt. Gen. [Adrian] Bradshaw, Deputy Commander ISAF, characterized as a 'suboptimal C2 solution.'"[6]

It wasn't hard to see why Lt. Gen. Bradshaw saw it that way and why it would be more than problematic to U.S. generals Gurganus and Sturdevant.

The Taliban didn't give a rip about a *suboptimal* split command arrangement. They already knew they could hide in the neighboring populations and not be easily detected. The 2004 Constitution of Afghanistan was the supreme law of the Islamic Republic of Afghanistan, and the Taliban opposed it with their own system of *Islamic* justice. That is why the NATO forces were there—to help the Afghan government root out and control the criminal violence perpetrated against the government by networks of insurgents plaguing the country.

---

5 "Army Regulation (AR) 15-6 Report (Final)," Pg. 8.
6 "Army Regulation (AR) 15-6 Report (Final)," Pg. 8.

In 2012, *France 24* reported that "Afghan civilian deaths rose for a fifth consecutive year to a record 3,021 fatalities in 2011," as reported by the UN. "Most civilians die in attacks by Taliban insurgents."[7]

The Taliban had activists, journalists, and civil servants on hit lists. They claimed to be bringing law and order by Sharia law to the people, but violated both, clearly without conscience, as they continued to rape and murder. The Afghan people were not human shields, but human sacrifices to spread fear and gain control. And so was the nature of embedded neighbors harvesting poppy immediately outside Bastion.

The Marines of 3rd MAW expected the British airfield, their new temporary home, to be secure. U.S. Camp Leatherneck was located in the southwest section of Bastion opposite the British airfield. The incoming 3rd MAW Marines, however, lived and worked on or near the airfield.

Ten months earlier, the safety and well-being of over three thousand Leatherneck Marines and a myriad of NATO personnel was a mission not taken lightly for one battalion in particular. Marines of the 1st Battalion, 25th (1/25) Marine Regiment patrolled the base and the outlying desert perimeter in extreme heat and cold to maintain the security of the U.S. forces housed there.

DVIDS News reported:[8] "'We have Marines on the perimeter 24 hours a day, manning the towers and entry points,' said LtCol Brian O'Leary, commanding officer of 1/25."

"'We maintain a constant presence in the battle space, engaging in full spectrum [counterinsurgency] COIN operations designed to provide (International Security Assistance Force) freedom of movement and deter any threats against the camp.'"

---

7 "Afghan civilian deaths reached record high in 2011," *France 24*, April 02, 2012, https://www.france24.com/en/20120204-afghan-civilian-deaths-reached-record-high-2011-un-report-insurgents-taliban.

8 Cpl. Solano, Timothy, "What is Task Force Belleau Wood," *DVIDS News*, December 23, 2011, https://www.dvidshub.net/news/81718/task-forcebelleau-wood.

Insuring observation and control over thousands of people who moved in and out of the base daily was an "unglamorous duty" but one of unequivocal importance that helped people sleep better at night.

"The United Nations Office on Drugs and Crime released in their '2011 Afghan Opium Survey' that opium poppy-crop cultivation in Afghanistan reached about 323,570 acres this year, a seven percent increase in production since 2010."

The Taliban used opium to fuel their years-long campaign to retake Afghanistan. Opium is the essential ingredient for manufacturing the street drug heroin. One only had to look under bridges and homeless camps for addicts, some tripping out in tents and some lying in the dirt amid garbage, oblivious to a dead person next to them. Poverty and years of war left its scars.

The Brits were supposed to help man security patrols in AOBW with the Americans. Yet they created a conflict of interest with their "hands off" towards the locals living in AOBW, and that was a blaring red flag. To patrol or not patrol was a dangerous compromise for busy airfield combat operations. The Taliban knew what those aircraft were doing to their fighters during air support missions. Since the first U.S. troops made boot prints in Afghanistan in 2001, the Taliban proved, over the years, that these generational tribal warriors were a patient enemy.

●●●

"They could visually see the aircraft all day long, and they could sit out there, and we couldn't really do anything if they weren't holding a weapon. So absolutely, they could observe everything that we were doing," said Maj Matthew McBride, Operations Officer for Marine Wing Support Squadron MWSS-273. His east coast unit arrived prior to 3rd MAW, responsible for all things airfield—including matting, fueling, fire protection, aircraft recovery . . . and making it secure.

It took time, but they were able to bounce 10,000 meters of wire

AFGHANISTAN, January 2012. Maj Matthew McBride, MWSS-273, on a reconnaissance ("leaders recon") convoy to check out the area of operations and responsibilities from their predecessors' pre-deployment of his unit to Camp Bastion. (Photo courtesy of Maj Matthew McBride)

to reinforce an exterior wire with an interior wire the length of the runway, adding some barriers. They rerouted civilian contractor traffic away from the flight line.

McBride knew the base was vulnerable. He observed that there wasn't enough effort in a combat mindset from the Brits to put enough people on the towers. However, McBride could afford to send out good security vehicles to support the guard towers with very good optics. So, if the airfield were attacked, there would be enough immediate response available.

He wanted to push the vehicles on the outside of the wire, but it became a conflict between the responsibilities of battlespace. McBride asked numerous times to patrol out there because Task Force Belleau Wood (TFBW) didn't have the assets to do it.

TFBW was the Leatherneck Security force on hand at Bastion, assigned to conduct external patrols and provide the quick reaction force. They were not infantry in their entirety. They were comprised of rotational units under the command of the Marine Expeditionary Force (MEF) HQ Group Commander.

McBride felt that battlefield coordination measures should have been taken because Marine Corps aircraft were taking enemy rounds on approach some days.

Two days leading up to a changeover of east and west coast squadrons, McBride had no backfill for security except for a company called Triple Canopy. This private security contractor was supposed to know what Marine MPs would do in the event of threats on the airfield and combatants trying to get inside access.

Berms, vehicle ditches, and extra sentries were needed, but cost and resources were obstacles. Especially vulnerable were the fuel pits. It was, after all, a British base.

The drawdown put a countdown on how much damage and death the Taliban could inflict on American forces before they were gone. How much intelligence the enemy had on Obama's drawdown reduction of force was not measurable. They tended to pass information, plans, and movements back and forth through runners, avoiding using phones and computers that could be traced by intelligence and surveillance technology. Any slip of the tongue put the enemy's plans at risk as the night of retribution encroached still, but sure, over the battle-torn land. The Taliban welcomed the darkness.

•••

Gurganus and Sturdevant took their roles seriously and worked actively to reduce risk to their Marines. Gurganus had a million thoughts swirling in his mind. He knew his guys were going out to some really shitty spots. He'd ask himself, *How do we reduce the*

KAJAKI, Afghanistan, May 17, 2012. MajGen Charles M. Gurganus, commanding general of Regional Command (Southwest), commends the Marines with 1st Battalion, 8th Marine Regiment, Regimental Combat Team 6 on their accomplishments in the Kajaki area, Helmand province, Afghanistan.
(DVIDS photo Sgt Albert Carls)

pressure on these guys? What operations do we need to do now? Do we need to reinforce them or cut down in size, because they are doing so well?

The Taliban had come into the Helmand Valley and promised the farmers a quick profit turnover to grow opium poppies instead of pomegranates, dates, and cotton. If the farmers grew fruit, they had to send it to Pakistan for cold storage and then buy their own fruit back again for much more money. Fighting at the Afghanistan-Pakistan border prevented the fruit from getting to cold storage, so it would sit there and rot.

"Those people weren't looking to get rich; they just wanted to be able to provide, but were not allowed to," said Gurganus, who threw on a flak jacket and went out to talk to the farmers in the fields himself about sustainable crops. The Taliban destroyed infrastructure that threatened the farmers.

Gurganus discovered it was a broken system, and he was stuck moderating it as best he could. He knew the Marines were experts in fighting lethal enemies, not managing Afghanistan's economic issues, which all tied into Taliban crime and illegal opium—a problem wherever poppies grew. At the Bastion airfield perimeter, poppies flourished without British impairment. Gurganus was not able to change that by his command alone. The British Commander in charge of logistics and Bastion security did not report to Gurganus, but instead reported to someone back in the U.K.

Both Gurganus and Sturdevant knew that nothing was off limits to forms of attack where this enemy was concerned. No one wanted them getting through to their Marines on their own turf. And yet the handcuffs were on by higher authorities who turned down Gurganus' requests for much-needed manpower, the ability to follow USMC doctrine in a unified command, infrastructure additions to make the airfield less vulnerable, and the approval to remove the compound threats that provided enemy surveillance.

It became Gurganus' job to make sure those Marines had every advantage when out there fighting. He relied on his team, his logisticians, to make magic happen when the odds were against them during the drastic reduction of forces.

The Dept. of the Army Bastion Attack Investigation went on to say: "From March-September 2012, RC(SW) reduced its strength from approximately 17,800 to 7,400 Marines. [This drawdown] occurred during the middle of the fighting season, during a period of increased insider attacks, and during a period of ANA growth, which produced numerous adjustments in force posture across the regional commands. . . . As commanders across Afghanistan adapted to achieve the mission with fewer forces, MajGen Gurganus requested an FML increase to augment his security forces (SECFOR). Although LTG Terry supported the request for an FML increase, it was disapproved by Gen John Allen, the commander of ISAF/ USFOR-A."[9]

The Brits didn't make Gurganus' job any easier. Shantytown clusters of people were allowed to set up their tents right up to the main Entry Control Point (ECP) so much that they blocked military vehicle traffic using the main access road to enter and exit the base. A plan was conceived by TFBW Commander Col Steve Hansen to push the shantytown to the north side of the east-west road that ran a mile north of the main Bastion ECP (on the north end of the BLS Complex). Gurganus approved the plan, and it was done. Yet, the same effort to eradicate Afghan poppy fields and structures that came right up to the Bastion eastern perimeter was met with British and ISAF resistance.

The regional command mission was expansive, especially during a drawdown when every building, piece of equipment, every foot of airfield matting, and each nail had to be crated up and sent back to the states. Not only were Gurganus and Sturdevant there to protect the Afghan people under siege by the Taliban, but they also had to develop Afghan National Defence Security Forces (ANDSF) capabilities and support improved governance and economic development in conjunction with the government of Afghanistan. The lack of adequate security they inherited put all that at risk. Any disruption at the airfield could impede aviation operations flying close air support (CAS) missions, which translates into gaps in overhead protection for U.S. troops fighting in Helmand Province.

Despair was the last thing Gurganus and Sturdevant wanted their Marines trapped in a Taliban gun battle to experience.

Inherent to the mission was the requirement to protect the force. When Gurganus set about unifying command and clarifying roles

9 Garrett, William B., Murray, Thomas M., "Army Regulation (AR) 15-6 Report (Final)," Dept. of the Army Bastion Attack Investigation, August 19, 2013, Pg. 7, https:// www.hqmc.marines.mil/Portals/142/USCENTCOM%20Bastion%20Attack%20 Investigation%20Redacted%2015-6%20Report.pdf.

and responsibilities, it evolved into a consequential rejection for him and his staff. They were turned away by both British and U.S. officials who had approval power. Decisions, not to his liking or comfort, set the stage for potentially dire consequences.

As RC(SW) commander, Gurganus had tactical control over the fighting forces (the British Brigade). National caveats imposed restrictions on the employment of those forces outside of a given set of districts. National caveats can restrict a wide array of operations within any military mission, including limiting a troop-contributing country's rules of engagement and ability to perform certain tasks, missions, or maneuvers. Anything that went against these national caveats had to be referred up the chain of command and back to Britain for approval.

"Interoperating at the tactical level is not easy. Even seemingly simple tasks bring myriad challenges in blending our procedures, our technology, and our cognitive approach to operations," states the *Multinational Interoperability Reference Guide*.[10]

What was clear was that the British Support Forces (logistics, airfield, admin, security personnel, etc.) remained under the command and control of a British commander on the ground aboard Bastion. Gurganus had no command authority over these forces.

International Security Assistance Force commander Gen John Allen's headquarters was in Kabul. He was responsible not only for the fight, but a myriad of other functions, such as building facets of the Afghan National Army and Police Forces, coordinating with various Afghan government agencies, and arming and equipping the Afghan Forces. Allen was also in charge of coordinating all aspects of NATO forces in the Coalition. Everyone had responsibilities to protect the forces, not just one or two USMC officers. It was

---

10 Decker, Marvin K., "Multinational Interoperability Reference Guide," Fort Leavenworth, KS: Center for Army Lessons Learned, 2016, https://usacac.army.mil/sites/default/files/publications/16-18.pdf.

a bigger picture than anyone outside Gurganus cared to admit when the enemy showed up at Bastion's perimeter prepared to destroy.

•••

The Harriers had been at Kandahar a couple of months prior to September 14, and a ramp extension was built at Bastion to facilitate their placement there. The air wing moved a gate and a list of other things. That wasn't all.

A senior officer at USMC headquarters seemed surprised that Sturdevant planned to provide documentation on the force improvements made in his command history. Sturdevant assured him that even though they weren't getting what they asked for and needed, they were improving measures in their control every single month.

Quick Reaction Force (QRF) exercises with the Brits took place each month. No Marine sat around doing nothing when it came to force protection.

CAMP BASTION, Afghanistan, 2012. AV-8B Harrier deployed to conduct counter-insurgency operations, Helmand province. (DVIDS photo Sgt Keonaona Paulo)

2

SECURITY SHORTCOMINGS

THE TALIBAN CAME AND went in the settlements, butting up to Camp Bastion's perimeter. They kept a low profile, although suspicious criminal activities were observed and reported by tower guard personnel, only to be told by their British overseers, "Don't worry about it."

On a base covering 712 square miles, it's impossible to monitor every square inch of ground.

Camp Bastion's perimeter consisted of a single-strand concertina wire, a thirty-foot chain link fence, and twenty-four concrete guard towers at varying setback distances from each other and from the fence line.

According to the CENTCOM Bastion Attack Summary, the terrain surrounding the BLS Complex was mostly desert, yet the area just outside the eastern perimeter fence consisted of "undulating terrain with hills and shallow wadis." This undulating terrain in front of the guard towers provided a dismounted enemy with covered and concealed avenues of approach that led directly to the fence line. "The UK 5 FP Wing did not employ a dedicated security force on the Camp Bastion perimeter." Instead, they relied on tasking to provide guards from various U.K. tenant units to augment (third party)

Tonga Defence Services. Although the manning of the towers was rotated to avoid predictability while still maintaining interlocking fields of fire and observation, the terrain made accurate and timely observation difficult on the eastern perimeter.

"Very few barriers and obstacles existed between the perimeter and the airfield, and the area behind the towers was not under persistent surveillance."[11]

Reports from both Marines and British soldiers complained of a "relaxed," even "sleepy" atmosphere of Tongan guards in the guard towers.

According to private evidence submitted to the Greater Manchester Police provided by an anonymous source (reference 0717/130917), Guards were "observed by one anonymous soldier to 'be watching a movie' while on duty." The same source was informed by another "about soldiers caught sleeping on guard duty going unpunished per senior British commanders' instructions."

An independent investigation later revealed through a security contractor working in Camp Bastion, "Sleeping on sentry was a topic raised by the Royal Military Police Company Sergeant Major almost weekly, him being of the opinion that offenders should be subject to court martial. The Garrison Sergeant Major, however, thought a 'stern talking to' would sort the problem."

Random surveillance observations directed towards the villages of Sheikabad and Nawabad, approximately several hundred meters to the east of the perimeter fence line, had limited line of sight due to hills and shallow wadis. The central wadi or depression, the main north-to-south arterial route, was only one kilometer from the perimeter.

---

11 Garrett, William B., Murray, Thomas M., "USCENTCOM Bastion Attack Investigation Executive Summary," The United States Central Command (USCENTCOM), Accessed November 29, 2023, Pgs. 4-5, https://www.hqmc.marines.mil/Portals/142/Docs/USCENTCOM%20Bastion%20Attack%20Investigation%20Executive%20Summary.pdf.

Regular scrapping activity developed around the fence line due to a large scrapping economy operating in Nawabad and Boldak. Outsiders would try to come near the base to take or steal metal to sell. Sometimes, they would get through unmanned guard posts.

The Dept. of the Army Bastion Attack Investigation reported that U.K. personnel on patrol identified three unobserved breaches in the Camp Bastion perimeter after they had occurred in the July-August 2012 timeframe.

". . . two of the breaches took place near Tower 8. There were also two nighttime surveillance videos capturing Camp Bastion breaches. On one occasion, two individuals entered the perimeter fence through a breach, moved near the cryogenics lab by the airfield, and then departed out of the same breach."

Another nighttime surveillance video recorded an individual who breached the perimeter wire, looked inside a guard tower that was empty and left.[12]

Local criminals had set up illegal checkpoints periodically to extort the people of Nawabad and Sheikabad. This all could be observed by anyone looking before 3rd MAW arrived. It was obvious that the fence was the only barrier between the outside of the base and the inside. Sturdevant did not know every other tower was manned, a critical omission by his hosts. It wasn't Sturdevant's job to babysit the Brits. Manning the towers was their task and an important responsibility to take seriously. Sturdevant didn't have time to guess *who's in the tower*. With so many tasks to manage, he had to rely on his allies or man them himself. That was not in the 2011 MOU agreement. His aircraft squadrons were saving their

---

12 Garrett, William B., Murray, Thomas M., "Army Regulation (AR) 15-6 Report (Final)," Dept. of the Army Bastion Attack Investigation, August 19, 2013, Pg. 7, https://www.hqmc.marines.mil/Portals/142/USCENTCOM%20Bastion%20Attack%20Investigation%20Redacted%2015-6%20Report.pdf.

brothers on the ground, clashing with well-armed Taliban, all while U.S. forces were getting the hell out of Dodge, never to return to that piece of hellish, bloodstained ground.

•••

The suboptimal C2 command and control role would unravel as a group of fifteen Taliban moved quietly under the cover of an inky black night. They could easily track through the wadis that provided cover-up to the perimeter, unseen and undetected by tower personnel who were unequipped for nighttime surveillance any further than their own immediate area. Guards were unable to see down in the wadis and were too far from the Taliban's intended destination to spot anything on the unusually dark (2 percent illumination) night of September 14, 2012. They were not given night vision devices (NVDs)—a mistake admitted to by a tower guard, aghast at the British inadequacies to do the job.

•••

Thirteen months later, on December 17, 2013, an appointed evidence session took place in the U.K. House of Commons. A well-rounded U.K. Defence Committee set forth to ask some dogged questions directed to witnesses in attendance. The witnesses included:

- Lieutenant-General David Capewell, Chief of Joint Operations, Ministry of Defence (MOD)
- Mr. Paul Rimmer, Chief of Staff (Policy and Finance) Permanent Joint Headquarters MOD
- Dr. John Noble, with Operations Directorate, MOD

Defence Committee members had done their homework and could not be content until they secured evidence of British actions or inactions regarding Bastion security. They knew there were previous security breaches that led up to September 14.

●●●

As Capewell testified before the nine-member official body, he quickly painted a picture of the British being completely void of security accountability or responsibility, rejecting the fact that the overall airfield protection fell under British command purview, according to the previously delegated 2011 MOU.

●●●

The unraveling of Capewell, the wolf in sheep's clothing, begins on that fateful December day when he finds himself in the hot seat from his own countrymen in a future *battle for truth* that would shake up the House of Commons floor. The opening remarks of the Defence Committee targeted to the Camp Bastion attack show a genuine drive to get to the facts behind the actions or inactions that led up to September 14, 2012. They are clearly burdened with a lack of transparency from U.K. military counterparts in charge, who have wiped their hands of blame even though they had a large share of responsibility for securing the base and protecting the forces housed there. Capewell immediately tries to remove himself from the equation, promoting the lies levied on two of his former allies.

> *(Q2) Chair:* "During the course of this evidence session we will need to get at a few things . . . the attack took place in an area of the camp that was subject to British control. There were a number of unmanned towers. The Ministry of Defence agreed a week or so ago that there were 11 unmanned towers. There had been a number of incursions for scrap, or it was thought that they were for scrap. A number of questions have been

asked about responsibilities for these vulnerabilities. The question that we will need to get at is whether there was any British responsibility for these vulnerabilities . . .?"

(Q3) Chair: "And you said that there had never been a direct ground attack on Camp Bastion before and that there was no intelligence that this sort of thing was coming. It shows the limitations on intelligence but does it also show a lack of imagination, in other words fighting the last attack rather than the coming attack?"

Lt. Gen. Capewell: "I don't think I can comment on the imagination of the commanders at the time. What I would say is that there were most certainly shortcomings, which were identified, as you are well aware, in the US investigation. That is why two of their commanders were, in my view, held to account. They were held to account for a range of causal issues that contributed to the vulnerabilities that were discovered by the insurgency."[13]

The U.K. Defence Committee remained dogged, having done their homework. What Capewell would say at the beginning of the inquiry would be inconsistent, inconclusive, and come unraveled as they dug deeper. Capewell hid efforts both Gurganus and Sturdevant made while pointing a damning finger. And why?

•••

---

13 House of Commons Defence Committee, "Afghanistan—Camp Bastion Attack," *The Stationery Office,* April 16, 2014, Ev. 4, https://publications.parliament.uk/pa/cm201314/cmselect/cmdfence/830/830vw.pdf.

September 2012, Camp Bastion

Fifteen Taliban fighters had trained for months for their moment of glory. What was going through their heads was unknown. Perhaps the promise of martyrdom suppressed the risk—perhaps opium drugs gave false courage. They knew the Marines well enough to know they were a force to fear. But in the distance, their first target awaited; they were hungry to reach it.

The small terrorist group seemed an unlikely threat against an expansive base that was the Taj Mahal compared to all the other FOBs scattered throughout Afghanistan. The air power lineup deployed there was massive, ready, and lethal. The British forces hosted 3rd MAW (Fwd), Marine Air Control Group 38 (MACG 38) (Fwd) and Marine Aviation Logistics Squadron 16 (MALS 16) (Fwd).

Did the enemy care how much or how many were housed there? No, they only wanted to destroy their enemy, a final "fuck you" before everyone went home. They were sick of being governed by American airpower overhead, a terrible threat they could not escape from.

A sense of calm or complacency was not the atmosphere running round-the-clock air support for combat operations in a war zone. A lot of moving parts had to click together . . . and they did in the impressive collective of U.S. air power. Included in the air wing were the following squadrons: Marine Heavy Helicopter Squadron 361 (HMH-361), HMH-362, Marine Light Attack Helicopter Squadron 469 (HMLA-469), Marine Wing Support Squadron 273 (MWSS-273), MWSS-373, Marine Fighter Attack Squadron 211 (VMA-211), Marine Medium Tiltrotor Squadron 161 (VMM-161), Marine Aerial Refueler Transport Squadron 352 (VMGR-352) (Detachment), Marine Unmanned Aerial Vehicle Training Squadron 2 (VMUT-2), and Marine Wing Headquarters Squadron 3 (MWHS-3) (Detachment 3). Also on the base was the British Aviation Unit: JHF(A), Joint Helicopter Force, Afghanistan.

Uncertainty shadowed pilots, crews, maintenance personnel, and airfield support operators, including fuelers, firefighters, civilian contractors, and third-country nationals (TCNs) brought in to augment a massive array of duties. Fulfilling the mission was on the minds of everyday activities. The Taliban were in a constant state of recruitment for fighters who flocked to the call to kill the foreigners in their land. The watch should have been on for any kind of terrorist plan.

Only eleven of the twenty-four guard towers (called "sangers" by U.K. personnel) were manned by the British the night of September 14, 2012, when only three days prior, four Americans had been overrun and killed and another injured in Benghazi, Libya, in a surprise attack on an American diplomatic compound and secret CIA facility. One successful terror attack will embolden another; if anyone knew that well—it was troops familiar with terrorist fighting tactics.

The Dept. of the Army Bastion Attack Investigation described how, of these guard towers,[14] ". . . only Tower 16 (unmanned) or Tower 17 (manned) could have detected [an approaching enemy] on the night of 14 September 2012."

"Even with significant engineering work to reduce some of the terrain outside of the perimeter, and with new lighting to illuminate the terrain, it would still be a questionable decision today to only man Tower 15 and Tower 17 on the eastern perimeter."

In addition, Camp Bastion lacked intelligence, surveillance, and reconnaissance (ISR) capabilities "to provide redundant observation of the eastern perimeter from the Combined Joint Operations Command (CJOC)."

---

14 Garrett, William B., Murray, Thomas M., "Army Regulation (AR) 15-6 Report (Final)," Dept. of the Army Bastion Attack Investigation, August 19, 2013, Pgs. 21-23, https://www.hqmc.marines.mil/Portals/142/USCENTCOM%20Bastion%20Attack%20Investigation%20Redacted%2015-6%20Report.pdf.

"Camp Bastion lacked persistent observation of the roughly 550 meters of terrain between the perimeter fence and the airfield. Due to this vulnerability, the 3rd MAW (FWD) AT/FP Officer at the time of the attack, described the perimeter fence as the 'single point of failure.' The tower guards could not observe the dead space behind the towers. If an enemy force could breach the Camp Bastion perimeter fence and move past the guard towers, there was unimpeded access all the way to the hard surface road abutting the eastern side of the airfield."

Although the British built the towers, randomly manned the towers with third-party Tongans, and were responsible for airfield security as well as patrols in TFBW, the U.S. Dept. of the Army would levy (in the future) all the blame on Major Generals Gurganus and Sturdevant for not mitigating British-made vulnerabilities and the lack of British planning for unobstructed tower observation at the eastern perimeter fence. In the Dept. of the Army's words, they did "not appropriately recognize and mitigate the risk of inadequate observation outside and inside of Camp Bastion, or the unobstructed freedom of movement once past the perimeter fence guard towers."

The truth was personnel under Major Generals Gurganus and Sturdevant's command did identify the perimeter fence as "the single point of failure." The generals were literally pushed back when they voiced their security concerns to the British, to ISAF, to the ESG. The truth is that 3rd MAW personnel were left hanging and with gaps, not by the inactions of their commanders, but by the British themselves. Instead of receiving steel-clad assurance of proper tower manning with all appropriate night vision tools, lighted and open fields of observation, the generals were strapped under an ineffective command and authority structure with hands tied to change vulnerabilities that threatened their aviation Marines from Day 1 of their arrival. This paved the way for the inevitable to happen . . . and it was coming fast and furious. While the two generals' concerns and efforts were relegated to a back room to be later replaced with lies about their conduct as commanders.

3

MAJOR MCDONALD – FROM HEARTACHE TO HELL

MOHAMMED NAZEER WAS RECRUITED by a Taliban commander for a "big important mission" approximately four months before September 14, 2012.

Nazeer was in charge of a group of fifteen militants who planned to get inside the Bastion airfield, a dramatically dangerous diversion from the Taliban's mode of operation to fight from the shadows.

Yet, the Taliban were capable of strategic planning and coordinated action. They learned to adapt to U.S.-led Coalition moves, but the Coalition also adapted to theirs. They would create a new IED, and it was only a matter of time before the Marines would figure it out. If they changed their tactics, the Marines found a way to overcome them to win in counter moves. Although the Taliban appeared to have an efficient leadership, it wasn't without force and coercion. One indisputable trait of the Taliban was that they were quick to exploit their adversaries' weaknesses.

The unusual move to expose themselves on open ground to hundreds of Marines who all know how to shoot a rifle was ballsy on the one hand and a death wish on the other. No one would expect that, except those who knew the Taliban weren't afraid of dying, taking as many as they could with them.

The only question was how much destruction could they inflict before that happened?

The Dept. of the Army Bastion Attack Investigation was a conflicted narrative listing blaring statements of the Bastion airfield's threat liabilities only the British could have controlled as it was their base. Was 3rd MAW supposed to come in and rebuild the eastern part of the base (on the U.S. dime) when they were ordered to tear down their footprint in Afghanistan in mere weeks, by then-president Barack Obama? Impossible, as the Brits welcomed their neighbor's encroachment right up to the fenceline with blind trust, uncharacteristic of a military mindset, calculating the enemy's future moves. That British complacency signaled this thinking adversary of lax concern about what was happening along their perimeter. The Army Regulation (AR) 15-6 Report (Final) did not include what (if any) intelligence was gained about any future Taliban attack plans, but managed to lay down some details about the September 14 attack:

> "The first group's objective was to destroy the jets and hangars; the second group's objective was to destroy the helicopters and what they thought were tents near the helicopters; and the third group, led by [Nazeer], planned to kill inhabitants in tents located across the airfield."[15]

Nazeer and other insurgents were prepared to reach a breach point along the airfield's eastern perimeter wire, equipped with simple wire cutters, spray paint cans and cigarette lighters (to serve as mini

---

15 Garrett, William B., Murray, Thomas M., "Army Regulation (AR) 15-6 Report (Final)," Dept. of the Army Bastion Attack Investigation, August 19, 2013, Pg. 6, https://www.hqmc.marines.mil/Portals/142/USCENTCOM%20Bastion%20Attack%20Investigation%20Redacted%2015-6%20Report.pdf.

CAMP BASTION, Afghanistan, 2012. Taliban breach point looking towards VMA-211 line on Bastion airfield. (HMLA/VMA Bastion Attack Presentation 2015)

blow torches), F-1 anti-personnel grenades, assault rifles, RPGs, and ammo.

Previously, Nazeer attended training at a village believed to be on the southern border of Helmand Province and Pakistan seventeen days before a dismounted assault would be set in motion. The location was due south of Lashkar Gah, the capital of Helmand Province, in a remote region called Bahrām Chāh. The Bahrām Chāh complex earned the reputation as "the most trafficked import and export point for insurgent opium and logistics in southern Afghanistan's Helmand province," as II MEF News reported in March 2011,[16] when 3rd Light Armored Reconnaissance (LAR) with II Marine Expeditionary Force (MEF) launched strikes during Operation Rawhide II to destroy this major insurgent border hub.

16 Sgt Ross, Jeremy, "3rd LAR Strikes Key Insurgent Border Hub During Operation Raw Hide II," II MEF NEWS, March 19, 2011, https://www.iimef.marines.mil/News/Article/528814/3rd-lar-strikes-key-insurgent-border-hub-during-operation-raw-hide-ii/.

"'The area had long been a favorite staging and distribution point for insurgent activity, and a hotbed for the opium processing and exporting that serves as the financial lifeblood of the insurgency,' said LtCol Kenneth Kassner, 3rd LAR commanding officer.

"'For the enemy, Bahrām Chāh is isolated from much of the coalition's activity,' Kassner said. 'They know it takes effort for us to conduct operations this far south.'"

Operation Rawhide II targeted structures harboring insurgents, weapons, bomb-making materials, and facilities for narcotics production. Much was destroyed, and surprise and deception rendered the insurgents' defenses too little too late. Assessments of time and resources to rebuild the hub may have been underestimated, as training was up and running a little over a year later, and fighters were flowing in, some with eyes on Camp Bastion. The enemy never sleeps or quits.

The Dept. of the Army Bastion Attack Investigation established that training included "weapons training, physical training, communications, individual movement techniques, and chain link fence breaching, among other things." Nazeer did not know the others, but knew they were from Afghanistan or Pakistan. "An unknown individual responsible for briefing the attackers went to Helmand and returned the next day with a sketch map of Camp Bastion, which he used to brief the group on their approach route and perimeter breach point." The attackers were incorrectly briefed that Tower 17, 250 meters directly northwest of the breach, would be unmanned.[17]

Someone had not only synchronized the plan but kept it guarded and under intelligence radar. Launching an assault on USMC home turf against some of the most highly-trained warfighters in the world was no small objective. The Taliban did not typically engage in man-to-man combat. An open assault was way out of their comfort

---

17 "Army Regulation (AR) 15-6 Report (Final)," Pgs. 4-5.

zone of hiding and shooting. The Taliban brought high-energy food in their backpacks, believed to have been eaten prior to commencing their attack. Paint was sprayed on their face masks, believed to keep them high and likely impervious to pain when wounded. What awaited these dupable insurgent recruits on a "kill and destroy" assignment was more fearsome than they could prepare for.

•••

In September 2012, Maj Robb T. McDonald, call sign "Wachee," showed up a little bit late on deployment to Helmand Province, Afghanistan. As an AV-8B Harrier pilot, McDonald had flown combat missions in Iraq and experienced ground fighting in three tours

Al ASAD, Iraq, 2005. Capt Robb McDonald stands by AV-8B Harrier II loaded with a 500 lb. laser-guided bomb (not pictured). A 25mm Gatling gun is fixed to the underside of aircraft with an AIM-9 air-to-air missile on outboard side of the left wing. (Photo courtesy Col Robb T. McDonald)

in Afghanistan. He was familiar with the enemy shooting at him and him shooting back, with no hesitation or regrets. Leadership was in his blood, and patriotism surged through his veins.

McDonald grew up with the legacy of military achievers going back to the Civil War. He believed "that to be an American man, one should serve in the military." This way of thinking remained ingrained, and in 1996, he enlisted in the Marine Corps, where he learned to jump out of planes, dive, and shoot. He opted for reconnaissance until he found something he saw as "more cool." In 2000, he was discharged as enlisted and rejoined as a 2nd Lieutenant in flight school.

The Corps assigned him to the Harrier AV-8B jet, the STOVL light attack aircraft that acted like a helicopter, affording Marines support in austere conditions during expeditionary warfare. With no need for a runway, the Harrier could conduct deep air support, reconnaissance, and air interdiction in both offensive and defensive anti-air warfare. It was a powerful asset as one of the most heavily armed attack aircraft of its time. It carried a five-barreled cannon and other positions able to attach munitions to include rockets, missiles, and bombs—up to 9,200 pounds of ordnance payload. No wonder the Taliban hated Harriers, and ground forces loved them.

McDonald was sent to gun squadron VMA-211. He took a forward air controller (FAC) tour with the Marine Special Operations Command (MARSOC) and completed two trips to Iraq in 2006 and 2007, living and working at al-Asad Airbase. While on a routine air patrol over Fallujah, his intelligence, reconnaissance, and surveillance mission turned into close air support. His buddy Kirby radioed over tactical frequency, "Hey Wachee, you gotta get over here! Something's going down over Ramadi." McDonald checked out with his Fallujah FAC and flew to Ramadi.

"The guys down lower are in some kind of gunfight. Okay, we're trying to get the tunnel set up to . . . let's see, we didn't get approval to strike . . . we can do a show of force," rattled off a new FAC.

MUSA QALA, Afghanistan, 2007. Capt Robb McDonald in the desert outside Musa Qala while deployed with elements of 2nd Marine Raider Battalion, Marine Special Operations Command. AH-64 Apache gunship in far background sky. (Photo courtesy Col Robb T. McDonald)

Firefights were common in subsequent missions, as was dropping ordnance to support ground troops. McDonald's Harrier squadron dropped a lot of bombs, including 500-pound laser-guided bombs, using the Joint Direct Attack Munitions (JDAMs) attached guidance systems.

Afghanistan was the next hotspot, and that gave him the idea to do a FAC tour with the new MARSOC based on the east coast. He went to Tactical Air Control Party (TACP) school to learn how to direct combat-strike aircraft against enemy targets. As a Joint Tactical Air Controller (JTAC), he would embed with Special Forces teams often on high-risk missions, likely to engage with the enemy.

After two flight tours that kicked off his thirst for action, McDonald was getting to know remote Afghanistan, where no one in the media really knew or cared what the American ground forces were doing.

Eventually, special operators partnered with the Afghan Commandos and the Afghan National Army, advising them how to fight the bad guys, shape the operations, and collect actionable intelligence.

Trouble was, in 2007, the Afghans smoked a lot of pot and showed up high for missions. Some would smoke opium. They never had their equipment—didn't want to put NVDs on and would drive off the road and get lost, even roll their vehicles. They'd run away. It was a mess. They'd often leak mission information to the Taliban, and bad things would happen. In 2008 and 2009, it got better, especially with the better-trained commandos.

McDonald believed there was a culture gap—theirs was tribal, ancient. The values they had and the way they looked at things were different. Yet, they were a warrior culture. And the U.S. was trying to teach them the American way of fighting. A guy McDonald knew put it really well, "You know these guys suck, but they probably wouldn't suck so bad if we just let 'em fight like Afghans."

Just before McDonald was set to ship out for another deployment to Afghanistan, his pregnant wife, Jen, went into labor two and a half months early. Their first son was born with a life-threatening condition called Potter's Syndrome. He was incomplete on the inside and had a lot of surgeries right away. It was *touch and go* whether he would live. Most babies born with this abnormality don't survive more than a few days.

At the same time, LtCol Christopher Raible, Commanding Officer (CO) of VMA-211 Harrier Squadron, was preparing to go to Camp Bastion. Raible was a friend and served with McDonald during his first deployment to Iraq. U.S. troops were drawing down, packing up, and moving from the offensive to more of a support role. This, thanks to Barack Obama's presidential campaign promises. However, insurgent activity remained high.

"You just stay in Phoenix at the hospital with your son and wife until he's stable. We're all going to deploy. I don't care if it's the last day of the deployment; we're going to fly you out," Raible told McDonald.

Raible made McDonald feel valuable to the squadron, something McDonald will never forget. Several months later, when his son was stabilized, and mom and dad were sure "he wasn't going to die," McDonald was on his way via military transport to Camp Bastion to join Raible, VMA-211, and the rest of 3rd MAW without a clue about the next crisis he would step into. Vital intelligence had slipped right through British fingers.

•••

In the House of Commons Defence Committee's December 17, 2013, evidence session, Mrs. Madeleine Moon was a star interrogator, intent to own British force protection responsibility where it lived in the shadows, omitted, lied about, or unclear in previous U.S. and U.K. post-attack narratives and reports. She continued to grill Lt. Gen. Capewell, who felt the opposite.

> *(Q4)* "... can you confirm to the Committee that the UK knew nothing about the July 2012 intelligence report of a Taliban attack on a base in Helmand that had been avoided owing to the premature explosion of an IED that killed several of the attackers? Are you saying that the UK knew nothing of that?"

Capewell seemed pressed for an answer and acted like he didn't know which report Moon was referencing, "There are a thousand intelligence reports, so you would have to be very specific."

Moon hammered back:

> *(Q5)* "It is the one that is repeated several times throughout all the documents mentioned in the US report. If you had read the US report, you would be aware of that."

Capewell, struck dumb, asked, "Could you therefore repeat your question?"

The British had gained intelligence two months earlier, in July, of a potential attack.

> *(Q6) Mrs. Moon (repeating question):* ". . . intelligence reports were circulated about a Taliban attack that was due to take place on a base in Helmand but had been avoided because there had been a premature explosion of an IED that killed several of the attackers."

Capewell eventually conceded, "Yes, we knew about that."[18]

Yet Capewell, in his opening statement to the House of Commons Defense Committee before questioning began, stood up and insisted, that the focus of U.K. commanders on the ground was outside BLS, in Task Force Helmand's area of operations (AOR). He alluded to no intelligence reports of imminent threats to the BLS complex, because up to September 14, BLS "had never been subject to ground attack."[19]

Capewell must have missed the news reports of the day as real and present warning signs.

Reuters reported on the August 27, 2012, insider attack:

> "During [Army Specialist Mabry Anders] six-month tour the Taliban staged a major attack at his base; a suicide bomber had killed one of his brigade's most revered leaders, and an Afghan villager threw a fire-bomb at a vehicle he was traveling in.

18 House of Commons Defence Committee, "Afghanistan—Camp Bastion Attack," *The Stationery Office*, April 16, 2014, Ev. 4, https://publications.parliament.uk/pa/cm201314/cmselect/cmdfence/830/830vw.pdf.
19 U.K. Defence Committee, "Afghanistan—Camp Bastion Attack," Ev. 2.

"Insider attacks accounted for one in every five combat deaths suffered by NATO-led forces in Afghanistan, and sixteen percent of all American combat casualties, according to 2012 data."[20]

Roll forward a little over two weeks to September 14, Camp Bastion, when another Taliban insider operation was in its final stages. For Capewell, eleven years of Taliban attacks (commencing with the war on terror) was not enough to imagine or prepare for their next move. Everyone knew this enemy had, many times, leveraged the art of surprise. Their inner drive was unstoppable. It wasn't just the Taliban the U.S. was up against. It was any jihadist fighter, even those from different terror groups like al-Qaeda, who wanted to take a shot at their bitter enemies.

•••

Mrs. Moon's questioning of Capewell continued after mentioning the intelligence reports of a brewing Taliban attack that ended badly in training when an IED exploded prematurely:

(Q7) "And it did not lead you to see that Camp Bastion could be attacked?" Mrs. Moon asked:

Lt. Gen. Capewell: "I don't believe it led the commanders on the ground to make that judgment. This is a really important point: what I do not do is command that operation from 6,000 miles away."

---

20 Stewart, Phil, Shalizi, Hamid, "Insight—In U.S. soldier's death, a window into Afghan insider killings," *Reuters*, September 27, 2012, https://www.reuters.com/article/uk-usa-afghanistaninsider-attacks/insight-in-u-s-soldiers-death-a-windowinto-afghan-insider-killings-idUKBRE88P1TG20120926.

Capewell skirting being involved in command authority was a real stretch, as there was always a higher chain of command all the way to the top. Assuming threats to personnel inside the wire in Afghanistan did not exist or were not on his radar questioned his ability to protect his forces.

"In my view, the judgments that they made at the time about what was going on were addressed at the right threats, which were the threats to life in the Helmand River valley area."[21]

There was nowhere in Helmand Valley, where the enemy was entrenched, that was off limits to the Taliban. Bastion, a big target, was alluring to strike a sweeping blow.

•••

With no absolute authority for decisions made in regard to Coalition base operations and force security, Gurganus worked with a team. His deputy commander from the British Army was Brig. Gen. Stuart Skeates. The primary RC(SW) staff had deployed with I Marine Expeditionary Force (IMEF) (Fwd) out of Camp Pendleton, California. Coalition partners rounded out the rest of the staff, primarily from the U.K. Gurganus' team had access to in-theater operations and intelligence reporting. What Gurganus knew was shared with Skeates daily.

These top commanders had decision-makers above them back in their home countries. For a range of Coalition issues, they were also subject to the Executive Steering Group (ESG) on the base itself. The ESG had colonel-level representation from each Bastion area constituency and made judgments about issues inside Bastion, from force protections to resourcing. It had the authority to make recommendations. The same ESG group denied Gurganus' attempt to

---

21 U.K. Defence Committee, "Afghanistan—Camp Bastion Attack," Ev. 4.

provide a new MOU that provided one commander for the base and one for security forces.

The older 2011 MOU placed the Marines under a split U.S./U.K. command arrangement, which not only breached the established USMC unified command requirement, but lacked USMC battle-tested command structure to count on. As a top leader in the USMC, with many years of experience, Gurganus voiced his deep concern over this only to be overridden by those outside his command.

Gurganus and Sturdevant were also vocal about an insider threat posed by over 6,000 U.S. local, national, and third-country national contractors that performed duties on the BLS Complex.

U.S. CENTCOM Bastion Attack Summary stated,

> "Gurganus' command RC(SW) significantly increased efforts to improve vetting, badging control measures, and contractor accountability. TFBW and the RC(SW) C2X counterintelligence (CI) Officer led a large effort to combine the US and UK vetting and badging procedures [signifying a current position or role on base] out of a common location near the CJOC, to identify and account for all contractors on Camp Leatherneck, and to ramp up random inspections of contractor living areas to search for illegal activity and restricted items like cell phones, cameras, and other electronics."[22]

Yet, the CENTCOM Summary failed to compile a list of the many security measures RC(SW) under Gurganus' command took or tried to take. They did not weigh those hard-fought efforts against the ominous charges in the wings that would be naked fabrications exposed on a public stage.

---

22 Garrett, William B., Murray, Thomas M., "USCENTCOM Bastion Attack Investigation Executive Summary," Accessed November 29, 2023, Pgs. 6-7, https://www. hqmc.marines.mil/Portals/142/Docs/USCENTCOM%20Bastion%20Attack%20 Investigation%20Executive%20Summary.pdf.

According to the Dept. of the Army Bastion Attack Investigation, the TFBW Anti-Terrorism Plan in place before September 14 stated, "The possibility existed that a determined terrorist force may be successful in breaching the security perimeter of the base and executing an attack."[23]

Had Capewell even read it before presenting a blasé attitude about Bastion getting attacked? There lie a blatant warning to all in the theater.

The evidence session between Mrs. Moon and Capewell continued:

> *(Q8) Mrs. Moon:* "We understand that the decision about the control of Camp Bastion was subject to a memorandum of understanding that had been signed in 2011. After the 'burning man' incident—I do think that that is a horrible description—"

"Me too," Capewell concurred.[24]

• • •

The Dept. of the Army Bastion Attack Investigation described, in part, what happened March 14, 2012, at Camp Bastion that became known as "the burning man" incident:

> ". . . two days after Major General Gurganus took command of RC(SW), he, and other members of the RC(SW) staff were waiting on the airfield for the arrival of Secretary of Defense Leon

23 Garrett, William B., Murray, Thomas M., "Army Regulation (AR) 15-6 Report (Final)," Dept. of the Army Bastion Attack Investigation, August 19, 2013, Pg. 3, https://www.hqmc.marines.mil/Portals/142/USCENTCOM%20Bastion%20Attack%20Investigation%20Redacted%2015-6%20Report.pdf.

24 House of Commons Defence Committee, "Afghanistan—Camp Bastion Attack," *The Stationery Office*, April 16, 2014, Ev. 5, https://publications.parliament.uk/pa/cm201314/cmselect/cmdfence/830/830vw.pdf.

Panetta. At the same time, a disgruntled local national inter-preter working for coalition forces commandeered a vehicle and drove onto the airfield. He narrowly missed Major General Gurganus and his party before being pursued into a ditch. The individual set himself on fire and exited the vehicle, dying of his wounds that evening."[25]

Gurganus and RC(SW) were able to determine that the Taliban had threatened this individual and his entire family. His task was to kill as many American and British forces on base as possible. Unbeknownst to Gurganus and his staff, before he drove past them and on to the tarmac, he had been riding around looking for large groups of troops gathered together. He was successful in finding a newly-arrived group of Brits who were going through their initial familiarization training. As they were all walking away from the area, he sped into the group and was successful in actually hitting one Brit soldier before speeding off to find another group.

Mrs. Moon was taken aback by the term *burning man* (calling it "quite offensive") in reference to the insider breach on March 14, 2012; nevertheless, the interview continued:

> *(Q9) Mrs. Moon:* "After that incident, we are told by the Americans that they sought a new memorandum of understanding that would have given the commander of Leatherneck overall con-trol of both their part of the base and the UK part of the base, but that that was turned down by the Bastion, Leatherneck and Shorabak steering group. Who was on that steering group and what were their nationalities? Did the UK repre-sentatives on the steering group refuse to ratify and approve the new MOU, and did Permanent Joint Headquarters in the UK play any role in that at all?"

25 "Army Regulation (AR) 15-6 Report (Final)," Pg. 14.

The ESG, Capewell claimed, was the appropriate apparatus to be used, even though funding played a great role. Resource thresholds were at £500,000 for in-theatre decisions . . . "I have no evidence whatever that there was any exclusion or any sort," quipped Capewell, who conveniently stated in his testimony that Gurganus was *not rejected* by the ESG for a new MOU.

Capewell admitted it wasn't a perfect system, "When you are in a coalition, some compromises have to be made."

When Mrs. Moon asked why a new MOU (the Americans put forward post-March 2012) wasn't signed or why the Americans said it had not been ratified by the ESG, he then acted as if he didn't know what Mrs. Moon was talking about.[26]

26 House of Commons Defence Committee, "Afghanistan—Camp Bastion Attack," *The Stationery Office*, April 16, 2014, Ev. 5, https://publications.parliament.uk/pa/cm201314/cmselect/cmdfence/830/830vw.pdf.

4

MAJOR GENERAL GREGG STURDEVANT, INHERITING A MINEFIELD OF TROUBLE

A TEMPORARY HOME, THE airfield housed Marine aircraft main-tenance workstations, a cryogenics facility, aircraft squadrons on respective flight lines, a runway and fueling area, and other stor-age and logistical 3rd MAW air operations components. Airwing support personnel worked in the fuels compound, including the fuel pits (housing six 50,000-gallon fuel bags), the Fleet Readiness Building (FRB), the fuels testing lab, a small gym, a hangar called the Clamshell, shipping boxes, the fuel ramp and skids (an area where the tactical airfield fuel dispensing system was located). The fuel bags had hoses and pumps that went to the fuel points at the edge of the fuel ramp, where the Cobras and Hueys lined up on the Skids, aptly named because of the helicopter landing gear.

All was the central hub for Fuels Marines (fueling the aircraft) and Aircraft Rescue and Fire Fighting (ARFF) Marines (tasked with

LASHKAR GAH, Afghanistan. November 22, 2012. MajGen Gregg A. Sturdevant, commanding general, 3rd Marine Aircraft Wing (Forward), conducts a battlefield circulation to wish Marines and Sailors a Happy Thanksgiving. (DVIDS Photo Sgt Keonaona Paulo)

fighting, aircraft recovery, and airfield maintenance). There was also a bulk fuel installation (BFI) located at the fuel farm on the east side of the X-bus access road, along with the cryogenics or cryo lab and HAZMAT storage lockers. The cryo lab (on the east side) was on elevated terrain as well as the fuel ramp on the west side, while the fuel bags (also on the west side) had dirt berms surrounding them at a lower elevation. This high-low terrain mapping would come to play, in the cataclysmic events to come.

A motor pool parking area adjacent to the BFI housed P19 fire-fighting/fuel trucks. Marine living quarters were located on the southeast end of the airfield, near the fence perimeter.

Although outdated and inadequate, the old 2011 MOU wasn't the only problem that threatened a breach of the OEF operations hub in the desert. Camp Leatherneck was like a modern city compared to the more remote and austere outposts Marines would ship out to.

Every new troop rotation into Bastion had a variety of battalions, companies, and platoons, uniquely trained Marines in those units, and specific missions. One umbrella agreement could not be expected to cover the wide scope of operations and the fluctuating levels of manpower. Gurganus had to juggle a staggered reduction of manpower order for the 2011-2012 withdrawal of troops while still running 24/7 air operations for ground forces still fighting outside the wire. Thirty-three thousand troops were being withdrawn in a fifteen-month period to be completed by end of September 2012. Nearly a third of those troops were "surge" forces.

Some frontline troops complained the logistical rollback from bases and packing up of military equipment was getting in the way of NATO-led operations against insurgents, reported *Reuters*, August 2012.[27]

"The pullout of more than $60 billion worth of war-fighting equipment from Afghanistan is expected to be one of the most complicated logistical exercises in recent history, much more difficult than the pullout from Iraq."

"'It's a nightmare. We barely have enough guys to cover our area, let alone get ready to pack up,' a U.S. officer recently told *Reuters* in volatile eastern Kunar province ahead of a pullout from several bases and transition to Afghan control."

Incoming troops like 3rd MAW were reduced in size, faced with cutting even more. The British's quick reaction force (that would normally respond to any ground invasion on the base) was located on the west side of the airfield, which left the aviation Marines on the east side in the direct line of any potential enemy fire. Luckily, all Marines knew how to shoot a rifle and had the chain of command all figured out. If the top officer was taken down in a fight,

---

27 Taylor, Rob, "NATO says combat operations unaffected by pullout logistics," *Reuters*, August 26, 2012, https://www.reuters.com/article/us-afghanistanbases/nato-says-combat-operations-unaffected-bypullout-logistics-idUSBRE87P03S20120826/.

the next highest rank would step up, all the way down to a lance corporal if that was the last man standing. No one knew that better than the generals and the men they put in charge.

The Taliban had a simple plan to get close enough to the aircraft on the flight lines undetected, and to roll Soviet-made grenades underneath multimillion-dollar aircraft. The attackers moved in civilian clothing across the Afghanistan/Pakistan border on September 13, 2012, to meet in Kandahar City. From there, they were transported to the safe house in Shah Pusta, Washir District, about an hour away from the BLS complex. Here, weapons, ammunition, clothing, and radios were dropped off in the pitch-black night.

They then moved out on foot to the airfield fence approaching eastward through a wadi, and then low-crawled the last bit of distance to a hide-site behind a pile of sand, short of the fence line. After cutting the wire, they crossed the boundary road and formed a defensive position on the west side of the road.

Tower 17 was located approximately 250 meters northwest of their intended destination, manned by Tonga Defense Services personnel. The Taliban armed group saw Tower 17 train a light towards them once inside the perimeter wire, but they moved to hide in a wadi. Tower 17 did not react further. Why this was not investigated further by tower guards is a mystery. Someone must have seen or heard something for them to have trained the light.

"Tower 16, which was approximately 150 meters southwest of the breach point, was unmanned based on the tower manning rotation set by the U.K. commander responsible for force protection."

Tower 15, 400 meters southwest of the breach point, was also manned by Tongan Defense Services but did not have a direct line of sight to the breach point.[28]

---

28 Garrett, William B., Murray, Thomas M., "Army Regulation (AR) 15-6 Report (Final)," Dept. of the Army Bastion Attack Investigation, August 19, 2013, Pgs. 5, https://www.hqmc.marines.mil/Portals/142/USCENTCOM%20Bastion%20Attack%20Investigation%20Redacted%2015-6%20Report.pdf.

Undulating terrain masked a critical vantage point. The question remained: why, in the original positioning of eastern airfield guard towers, was nothing done to mitigate disadvantaged natural terrain to ensure tower guards open fields of view that crossed over each other?

There was no indication of any permanent airfield perimeter lights. Permanent lights would have had adverse effects on NVDs used in airfield operations.

The Taliban attackers were split into three groups and dispersed.

•••

The U.K. Defense Committee remained tenacious and coy trying to get straight answers from Capewell as to why the new MOU was not signed at the Americans' request.[29] They must have seen the need as well as the flawed logic presented by Capewell. They surely weren't content to believe his word alone, claiming the U.K. had "no culpability" in what happened on September 14, 2012.

> *(Q18) Ms. Stuart:* ". . . I want to come back to the MOU because I am assuming that you have enough on your plate not to do anything unless it serves a purpose. I would not have thought that at that time you would indulge yourself in reviewing an MOU just because it gave you something to do. Presumably, that exercise was to achieve something. Can you tell me what it was trying to achieve?"

Then Capewell launched into how the Afghan footprint changes with forces that come and go and "that everybody has a fair share of both the risk and the resources."

---

29 House of Commons Defence Committee, "Afghanistan—Camp Bastion Attack," *The Stationery Office*, April 16, 2014, Ev. 6, https://publications.parliament.uk/pa/cm201314/cmselect/cmdfence/830/830vw.pdf.

(Q19) Ms. Stuart: "So it is a risk and resource sharing?"

"It is absolutely about risk and resource," Capewell said, somehow forgetting the U.K.-owned responsibility for the Bastion airfield security. The *sharing* was an incorrect term when it came to the separation of camps in the 2011 MOU. Each had their own assignments. Gurganus tried to unify that into a better-oiled force protection machine.

> *(Q20) Ms. Stuart:* "So would you like to speculate why the Americans use the word 'reject?'"
> *Lt. Gen Capewell:* "I think that is an erroneous remark in-theatre at the times. Remember, of course, that there is a lot of emotion in this—"
> *(Q21) Ms. Stuart:* "On both sides."

Capewell tried to sidetrack the Defence Committee, saying the Americans (i.e., Gurganus) used the word *reject* as an *emotional response* for the turndown to create a new, optimal MOU that would serve the forces best when it came to protection from a lethal enemy inside the Bastion wire. He absolutely assured the development of the MOU was a "measured and balanced" equitable process examined by a "range of parties."

Yet was the need to protect the forces in a combat zone meant to be fair or impartial or, instead, effective, comprehensive, and bulletproof? Not to be delayed by indecision and time delays. When in July 2012, "intelligence reports were circulated about a Taliban attack that was due to take place on a base in Helmand." Ms. Stuart wasn't buying Capewell's diversions and levied more questions.

> *(Q22) Ms. Stuart:* "So would the Committee be right to conclude, because this is quite a key issue, that if the Americans use the word 'reject' while you are quite adamant that that is

an inappropriate description, in the process of negotiation, which is about resources and responsibilities, the British side was a still thinking we were talking while the Americans thought we had already rejected?"

"No, I don't think that is right . . ." Capewell said. "This is a dynamic negotiation so words like 'reject' could refer to anything."

(Q23) Ms. Stuart: "Which words would you use?"

Capewell, in the hot seat, continues to divert towards answering Ms. Stuart directly, "I think it comes back to this question of operating within a coalition."

(Q24) Ms. Stuart: "No, that is not sufficient. Could you give me a word that describes that outcome? An MOU is a negotiation. You say we are still negotiating; the Americans say reject. Could you give me a couple of words that satisfactorily describe that state of affairs?"

Could the British investigators have surmised that if it was a matter of shared risk and resources with a split command, how do you come to a meeting of the minds when it is obvious only one party is worried about the perimeter security threats?

● ● ●

September 14, Camp Bastion

The Taliban began to disperse in the darkness. One group of five headed towards the VMA-211 flight line. One group of five moved south and west to the fuel pits area. One group of five advanced towards the cryo lab. The chain link fence fell short of offering any real deterrence. The towers manned by Tongan Defense Services and the key tower left unmanned fell short of detecting the approaching attackers. Once the crisis hit—the old MOU fell woefully short, lacking unified command. Those unmitigated shortcomings were now threatening unsuspecting Marines.

•••

During the evidence session, Capewell continued to answer questions:[30]

(Q27) *Chair:* "I am sorry, but I am getting completely confused. It [the new MOU] was either very adequate, or it was not up to the job."

Lt. Gen. Capewell: "Let me correct you. I said it was adequate. It was described as adequate for the job at the time. They subsequently found out, from the 'burning man' incident and a range of other incidents, that it fell short in a number of areas. That is a fact of tactical life."

(Q28) *Mrs. Moon:* "But if it was so short, why was it not ratified by the ESG? You just said it fell short."

Lt. Gen. Capewell: "It clearly did fall short. I don't think I can add anything more to this debate."

(Q31) *Chair:* "It is very easy, I know, to look at attacks like this with the benefit of hindsight. Nevertheless, I hope you will accept that this does not sound good."

30 U.K. Defense Committee, "Afghanistan—Camp Bastion Attack," Ev. 7.

September 2012, Camp Bastion

It was the Marines and their flying machines that were mitigating those deaths in Helmand Province, and so if the Marines weren't safe on base—no one was safe outside the wire in the gnarly battle fray. The British Apaches also provided a level of lethality to the fight, taking off on that same Camp Bastion airfield at risk to unguarded threats. The Marines' aircraft, with the exception of the KC-130s, were on the east ramp, and the British aircraft and American KC-130s were on the west ramp. The Taliban were going to prove the British wrong in their casual assessments, or lack of, in very short order.

• • •

October, 2011, Camp Bastion

A year before the Taliban's attack on Camp Bastion, U.S. Marine commanders would question the handling of boots on the ground, air defense tactics, and base security, but it was ignored.

MajGen Sturdevant visited Camp Bastion for a pre-deployment survey focused on the future of aviation combat. He soon discovered someone had decided to strip out the C-130s and transfer responsibility to a *function of boots on the ground.*

"That was the wrong answer," Sturdevant concluded, because he knew the C-130s were the heavy lifters for the MEF commander. Sturdevant's subsequent visits to outlying FOBs gave him a *feel* for the combat theater.

February, 2012 Camp Bastion

Sturdevant took over authority, and over twelve months (Sturdevant's command tenure at Bastion), twenty-four squadrons rotated through, did time, and went home. In total, there were approximately 10,000 people spread over twenty-four units, 3,500 at any one time, paired with 130 aircraft. That's a lot of flight operations during a draw-down, which indicated the fight was far from over.

Sturdevant observed what worked and didn't work in different units among various styles of leadership. A good Marine commander knows his leaders and lets them lead because he can't always be on the ground or in the air.

He was a two-star wing commander who'd normally have a one-star assistant wing commander. However, in Afghanistan, it was Sturdevant and twelve squadron commanders and no assistant wing commander. Also, no colonel air group commander was stationed at BLS. He had two colonels, one as chief of staff and one as operations officer.

●●●

Colonel Richard "Otter" Bew was Sturdevant's Chief of Staff. He was responsible for planning for the air wing, running the staff, and overseeing a drawdown from over 4,000 to 1,723 in less than six months. Given that the ACE still had to maintain offensive combat capability, working it out with higher headquarters inevitably became a tug of war as well as a risky decision about who would stay and who would go. Reducing manpower so drastically, yet still maintaining combat capability and performing all the other functions of the air wing, meant accepting risk.

Bew knew they'd have to carry risk in multiple places. He believed if one tried to achieve the best balance of risk they could, and then explained it further up the chain of command where they accepted that risk, ultimately, the higher-ups would be okay with it. Then those who endorsed the decisions, owned them.

This came into play in a competition for resources. Gurganus' command was in the process of digging an anti-vehicle ditch around

IRAQ. 2008. Iraq Squadron Commander LtCol Richard "Otter" Bew walks to his EA-6B Prowler to launch a mission to support a six-hour convoy. (Photo courtesy of Col Richard "Otter" Bew)

the base to prevent high-speed vehicle advances. It could not be completed because RC(SW) had limited engineering equipment left, as the drawdown was in full swing. The ditch competed with the requirement to close numerous combat outposts, which took most of their engineering assets. Although the ditch may not have prevented an attack on foot, it was known the Taliban and al-Qaeda smuggled vehicle-borne improvised explosive devices (VBIED) onto U.S. bases. One of the deadliest attacks in CIA history was a result of a VBIED.

On December 30, 2009, Humam Khalil Abu-Mulal al Balawi conducted a suicide attack inside the CIA facility inside Camp Chapman, southeast of Khost, Afghanistan. Seven American CIA officers and contractors were killed, along with a Jordanian intelligence officer and an Afghan ally, when al-Balawi detonated a bomb in his suicide vest. The attack was a major setback to the agency's operations in

Afghanistan and Pakistan and the second-largest single-day loss for the CIA.[31]

Bew knew the British manning of the towers were spread thin, and visual observation was limited. Both Gurganus and Sturdevant were well aware of the risk that invited. They weren't sending false reports up the chain that *everything was okay*. Instead, they were saying in so many words, "This is a tough situation. We've got a lot of real estate here." After all, the Americans did build Leatherneck at Bastion. Yet, they did not choose to surround it with poppy fields and unknown locals who easily trained their eyes on airfield business going up and down on the eastern perimeter.

NATO stated that the U.S. was part of the ISAF Coalition, one of the biggest and most challenging in history, and worked under ISAF's mission. The force was more than 130,000 strong at the peak of the war in Afghanistan, combining troops from fifty-one NATO and partner nations. "The primary objective was to enable the Afghan government to provide effective security across the country and develop new Afghan security forces to ensure Afghanistan would never again become a safe haven for terrorists."[32]

For 3rd MAW and other air wings like them, their days of air support for U.S. ground troops were numbered as the ISAF mission was shifting from a combat role to training, advising, and assisting the Afghan forces to take the lead in reducing the Taliban or any insurgent capability. The Afghans weren't ready when the drawdown was kicked off, and the ground combat was not over. You can't fight for eleven years and then, in a matter of months, expect the enemy to back down or go home. Those ordering the drawdown knew they were leaving Afghan forces vulnerable by prematurely stripping off their training wheels and giving them a shove on the bike.

31 Wikipedia Contributors, "Camp Chapman Attack," *Wikipedia, Wikimedia Foundation*, Accessed December 24, 2023, https://en.wikipedia.org/wiki/Camp_Chapman_attack.

32 "ISAF's mission in Afghanistan (2001-2014)," NATO, May 30, 2022, https://www.nato.int/cps/en/natolive/topics_69366.htm.

Sure, Bagram Air Base in the north would remain open for a time, also with reduced manpower, but Afghanistan was a big country. Helmand in the south was always the problem child because of its rich farmland and Taliban coercion to grow poppies.

•••

One of the greatest risks for 3rd MAW was they had to engender support from the people who worked underfoot. TCNs drove 5,000-gallon fuel trucks delicately in between rows of helicopters to refuel them every day.

"We had to make sure we had a reliable trust," stated Bew to those ignorant of their dilemma.

Bew didn't trust the fence bordering the perimeter. Anyone could see generally where the Harriers were located. Any nefarious or simply curious person could see them approach, hear them taxiing, and hear the aircraft runups (a series of last-minute engine checks before take-off) from outside the wire. From outside of the base gate, one could get some idea of where the aircraft were located. The helicopters lifted out of the same spot all the time. Bew believed a persistent voyeur mapping the base would be aware of the flight line road, the single most significant geographic feature on the base. It went around the south end of the airfield and then turned north and ran up the east side of the airfield, along the hangar spaces.

A recommendation ensued to send the Harrier squadron home. Not because the Harriers were unimportant or incapable; rather, they represented the heaviest force end of the spectrum, augmenting rotary wing fires with might and lethal capability. The decision to maintain a high level of offensive power meant that trade-offs came elsewhere—including security. Both Sturdevant and Gurganus' years of experience and knowledge of the character of insurgents and their activities helped them see the writing on the wall was not good and they wanted solutions. The personnel conducting daily combat flight operations and all air and ground tasks aboard Bastion were part of the larger Marine Corps family.

They went about their business as ordered. Over the course of the twelve months that 3rd MAW (Fwd) served in Afghanistan, they successfully supported 61,000 flight hours during 47,691 combat sorties, including support to 1,035 named operations as stated in an April 4th, 2014 letter from LtGen Rick Tyron, the Commander, U.S. Marine Forces Command to the Secretary of the Navy. The indomitable and persevering ACE, based out of Bastion, also conducted 230 combat operations, delivered 513 tons of ordnance, and moved over 300,000 personnel. They carried nearly 25 million pounds of cargo, and provided 16,000 hours of U.S./U.K. intelligence, surveillance, and reconnaissance support.

All that in the year of a major drawdown begged the question, *what will hold the region together when it's all gone?*

Bew was an EA-6B Prowler pilot, and what Bew brought to Operation Enduring Freedom was eight combat deployments, including Deny Flight (Iraq), Decisive Endeavor (Bosnia), Deliberate Guard (Bosnia/Herzegovina), Northern Watch (Iraq), Southern Watch (Iraq), Allied Force (Serbia), and Iraqi Freedom 1 and 2 (Iraq).

What brought Bew to Enduring Freedom in Afghanistan was something else.

Bew ended up at the Pentagon for his second time in 2008, working as a legislative aid for the Chairman and Vice Chairman of the Joint Chiefs. Bew was coming up on orders when he asked James "Hoss" Cartwright, the eighth vice chairman at the time, what he thought Bew should do.

"Look, you know, you're successful in the Pentagon; you want to go back to the operating forces," said Hoss, where Bew could make a seasoned difference. Mixing in with troops beat a desk job and was something Bew loved.

One of the options was doing a rotation to Afghanistan to serve with Sturdevant, who chose Bew based on his reputation alone.

IRAQ. 2008. LtCol Bew (center-right) provides feedback and guidance to his maintenance officer. EA-6B Prowler in background. (Photo courtesy Col Richard "Otter" Bew)

However, there were no EA-6Bs on the Bastion airfield. The good ole' days had faded too fast. So, after arriving at Bastion, Bew would climb in the back of the C-130s and push cargo because he didn't have an aircraft.

Sturdevant was surrounded by men of character in 3rd MAW—Marines who took their job seriously. That was something he could not have imagined the day a pushy USMC recruiter grabbed him by the shoulder on his way to join the Air Force.

●●●

As a young man, Sturdevant had watched the Air Force recruiting commercials calling out to "the young, the brave, and the adventurous to find a great way of life." In contrast, the Marines' commercials pictured a short drill instructor wearing a campaign cover (hat), poking a recruit in the face, saying, "We don't promise you a rose garden. The only thing we promise is we'll make you a Marine."

Little did the pushy USMC recruiter know that young man would become a devoted naval aviator. Sturdevant trained, developed impeccable skills, and passed all the tests to earn his wings as a USMC pilot in 1984. There were no promises of an easy life as he prepared to hunt down America's enemies in both Operation Iraqi Freedom (OIF) and OEF in Afghanistan. Sturdevant rose in the ranks to Major General, commanding air squadrons and air wings. He gladly took on terrorists, rebels, criminals, and other war-worthy adversaries from across the sandbox (Middle East). Insurgency urban warfare presented a completely different set of challenges than that of massive national armies fighting each other in WWII. Insurgents would travel long distances just to shout "Allahu Akbar" before they detonated a bomb or fired off a machine gun towards unsuspecting civilians or foreign troops protecting them.

The day was coming when Sturdevant would not only face this lethal nest of tribal warfighters wreaking havoc in the Helmand Valley, outside the wire, but also find a shocking revelation inside the wire about trusted allies.

5
THE THREAT IS REAL

THE U.K. DEFENSE COMMITTEE demanded to know where the boundaries lay between Task Force Belleau Wood and RC(SW) areas of operations as well as U.K. Bastion operations.[33] Trying to get a picture of where all the security incidents like "burning man" occurred. They asked about a slide showing yellow dots depicting "incidents" that were taking place along the perimeter fence, trying to determine if the British had control of that area. Capewell tried to water down the incidents, claiming they were not attacks.

Colonel Fox: "I would say from looking at this slide, within our area of responsibility. But I think the point, as the CJO is making, is the issue about—when you say 'critical incidents,' these are security incidents."

(Q117) Mrs. Moon: ". . . surely, if you have this many security incidents—albeit they can be a man having a fight, a disagreement between individuals, a carjacking, or anything—it

---

33 U.K. Defense Committee, "Afghanistan—Camp Bastion Attack," *The Stationery Office*, Ev. 24, https://publications.parliament.uk/pa/cm201314/cmselect/cmdfence/830/830vw.pdf.

shows us that areas of tension and security concern were largely focused in the area where we had responsibility."

Lt. Gen. Capewell: "No. This looks beyond the wire. This could be indirect fire (IDF) [a firing of ammunition without relying on any direct line of sight between the weapon and the target]. I can't live with the contention that there are some security incidents, so you can say that we are responsible for them. They are outside the perimeter of Camp Bastion, of course, because they were in Task Force Belleau Wood, this is local policing."

Capewell inadvertently admits to leaving security in the TFBW area of operations to local police, who have very different means and standards than NATO forces. The Taliban could get to them with threats because the illegal poppy trade started there in the fields. Casual trust in local police added to major gaps in 24/7 security in TFBW surrounding the Bastion airfield.

Mrs. Moon: "You are missing my point—"

(Q118) Chair: "The point to get at is this. . . . The main concern of some members of this Committee is that this incident happened in an area under the control of British forces."

Lt. Gen. Capewell: "No, it is under coalition control. It is Task Force Belleau Wood."

(Q119) Chair: "Yes, but this area was surely where the British part of the coalition was."

Colonel Fox: "If you're asking about the perimeter element, or in other words which part of the perimeter we manned and was used by ourselves, then it is correct that we effectively manned the area from that southern point up around on the eastern side to the north. We were responsible for that perimeter."

The Chair expresses Committee concerns that the fallout for Bastion's gaps in security was attributed solely to two American generals.

> (Q 94) *Derek Twigg:* "My question to you: did any of the British commanders raise any concerns about security at Bastion?"[34]
>
> *Lt. Gen. Capewell:* "To whom?"
>
> *Derek Twigg:* "To command. To you. To your command."
>
> *Lt. Gen. Capewell:* "Not to me, because they were abiding by the protocols of coalition chain of command."

Capewell remained insistent on taking his command role in the U.K. Ministry of Defense out of the equation when it came to operations at Camp Bastion. Important matters like dealing with threats to U.K. deployed personnel would have been fielded up the chain by officers on the ground. Passing the buck or distancing oneself obliterated trust from those depending on British command at the top. Surely, from the highest realms of the U.K. MOD, monitoring the pulse on British deployed troops, battlefield operations in a combat zone is more than critical—it's lifesaving.

> (Q95) *Derek Twigg:* "Did they raise it with the American general?"
>
> *Lt. Gen Capewell:* "They would have raised it on a daily basis."
>
> (Q96) *Derek Twigg:* "No, did they? I am asking not would they, but did they? Have you got evidence?"
>
> *Lt. Gen. Capewell:* "I think there is always a conversation of, 'We're a little concerned about this.'"
>
> (Q97) *Derek Twigg:* "Have you got evidence that the British commander—the person who was in charge of Bastion, or parts of Bastion—or his deputy raised concerns about the future threat, or the security of their part of Bastion?"
>
> *Lt. Gen. Capewell:* "I would be very surprised if he did not raise concerns."

34 U.K. Defense Committee, "Afghanistan—Camp Bastion Attack," Ev. 22.

(Q98) Derek Twigg: "I want to be clear. So you don't actually know, Sir. Could you find out for us and let us know?"

• • •

(Q103) Chair: "If a decision had been taken to reduce that poppy field, whose responsibility would it have been to take that decision?"

Lt. Gen. Capewell: "That would have had to go in to the local shura, because in a counterinsurgency, of course, this is the civilian leadership lead. There would have been a very clear view expressed, I think, if you had asked the provincial governor or the man in charge of the village to take that poppy field down. There would have been a reaction. These things are very difficult in counterinsurgency. You cannot preclude people . . ."

(Q104) Ms. Stuart: "I am slightly puzzled. . . . I find the *well-being* of the local population a curious expression to use, in terms of allowing them to grow poppy even closer to the fence. Were we not supposed to eradicate the wretched things?"

Lt. Gen. Capewell: "That is other government departments' business, not mine."

Capewell would ultimately testify that poppy cultivation so close to the perimeter fence was a "minor tactical error."[35]

• • •

---

35 U.K. Defense Committee, "Afghanistan—Camp Bastion Attack," Ev. 22.

September 2012, Camp Bastion

Why didn't the wire perimeter have a warning system? So, if anyone tried to breach—it would trip an alarm? Ignoring this simple security solution would later become a painful afterthought. Overall, ignored signs and a lack of imagination had caused dominoes to fall and empires to collide, bringing U.S. troops to Taliban country, where they were not wanted.

A few short months after al-Qaeda terrorists attacked the World Trade Center, the Pentagon, and crashed a plane full of trapped Americans fighting for their lives over Shanksville, PA, the 13th Marine Expeditionary Unit (MEU) Special Operations Capable (SOC) departed San Diego, California. It was December 1, 2001. Deployed with the MEU was Sturdevant (then a LtCol) in command of Marine Medium Helicopter Squadron 165 (HMM-165) (Rein).

On board with the MEU were helicopters, AV-8B Harrier jets, landing craft, and amphibious vehicles. The USS Bonhomme Richard Amphibious Ready Group sailed their way to the southern coast of Pakistan, where the Bonhomme Richard, a Wasp-class amphibious assault ship, served as a launching site for the Harriers flown in to support operations in Afghanistan.

American forces had mobilized under NATO on the hunt for the world's most-wanted terrorist, al-Qaeda leader and 9/11 mastermind Osama bin Laden. From day one in Afghanistan—it was going to be a difficult task as the Taliban gave Osama bin Laden, an Arab, safe harbor. He had once helped the Afghan Mujahideen fight against their pro-Soviet government. After the Soviets were expelled from Afghanistan, bin Laden radicalized.

During March 2002, HMM-165 and Task Force 165 (a detachment of AH-1W attack helicopters and CH-53E heavy lift helicopters forward deployed to Bagram Airfield) performed close air support (CAS), aerial reconnaissance, logistics support, and a list of other tasks to support the 10th Mountain Division. They effectively

AFGHANISTAN. 2002. LtCol Sturdevant (center) in the back of an Army Blackhawk on an Air Mission Commander mission. (On right) 2 Brigade, 10th Mountain Division commander, Col Wilkenson. (Photo courtesy of MajGen Gregg Sturdevant)

destroyed insurgent mortar positions and hide-sites in Khost and the Shah-i-Kot Valley.

It was no small feat, given most of the fighting took place a hundred miles southeast of Bagram at 10,000 feet above sea level. A 200-mile round trip required some adjustments in order to maximize time on station to better support the U.S. Army and Canadian soldiers fighting on the ground.

The Federation of American Scientists Intelligence Resource Program published a statement from Osama bin Laden as part of evidence linking the bin Laden network to the September 11 terrorist attacks; the murderous terrorist mastermind issued a religious ruling (fatwa), declaring war on other countries and specifically the U.S. requiring the killing of Americans, both civilian and military.[36]

---

36 Bin Laden, Osama, "Jihad Against Jews and Crusaders," Federation of American Scientists, February 23, 1998, https://irp.fas.org/world/para/docs/980223-fatwa.htm.

America's longest war against hate-filled jihadists kicked off. We became entangled with resistance guerilla fighters driven to install a global Islamic state under strict Sharia law. A new kind of warfare shook the ground and began to leave trails of American and Coalition blood.

Sturdevant would also face a different kind of foe at Camp Bastion—a foe who sought to pin the blame on him and fellow officers, who would find themselves under the accusing eye of their own government.

•••

Camp Bastion air traffic managed 600 flights a day, making it, at that time, Britain's fifth-busiest airport. It was a freeway of air traffic. The newcomer Harriers' roar could be heard from a distance while taking off and landing, boasting a max speed of 585 knots, able to carry a 25mm five-barrel Gatling cannon, four rocket pods carrying nineteen rockets (70mm), and up to four laser-guided 500-pound bombs.

Taking off daily were AH-1W Super Cobras, UH-1Y Venoms, MV-22 Ospreys, and C-130s. With the air wing greatly reduced, available flights were a non-stop operation. Maintenance Marines did their checks and plied their wrenches, Explosive Ordnance Disposal (EOD) Marines loaded weapons on the aircraft with pinpoint accuracy, and pilots suited up on a carousel of twelve-hour shifts. No rest for the Taliban from Marines who uprooted them out of their hiding places to stop their regional chaos.

•••

High traffic in and out of the base was a management nightmare. Gurganus had his Marines remove all cell phones from TCNs that were contracted support for the wing. TCNs helped on the flight line with fueling and other assorted tasks. Some were denied entry to the base if their credentials didn't match up. Who to trust was a daily concern when you were the one in charge.

Gurganus wore no crown, nor wanted to, and set about each day to watch over the guys who did the heavy lifting. Those on the patrols and in the fights, those in the air supporting them, and those making sure they had what they needed to survive the rigors of combat. There were so many working parts grinding away to mission success.

Gurganus worried all the time about the safety of his Marines, Sailors, and partners.

He'd say, "When you're the guy in charge, and you're delivering orders that are going to put people in combat, you want to give everybody the best chance they have."

U.S. air power based at Bastion threatened to eradicate the revenue gained from the local opium trade in Washir District and others in and around Helmand that had supported poppy growing. To that end, the local Taliban could not let that go.

•••

McDonald had been at Camp Bastion for a couple of months, got in the rotation, and flew air support missions. The fighting never let up, even though U.S. deterrence was thinning as personnel were shipped back home. He'd moved into the two-story Logistics Support Area (LSA) building with the other Marines. Yet they were transitioning out to a smaller one-story building with internet that worked and was surrounded by concrete barricades. McDonald refused to move out of his second-floor "penthouse suite" that consisted of a little more than stark base accommodations. On the night of September 14, he went to bed early because he had to get up at 0400 for an early flight. Raible, call sign "Otis," and some other guys had the late flight shift.

He was the only one left when Marines Matt Martinez and Brett Ackerbauer came around pounding on doors. Ackerbauer stopped to knock on McDonald's door and woke him up. McDonald threw a big dip of tobacco in his mouth and, while standing at the door in his green silk skivvies, was informed:

"Hey, we're under attack," said Ackerbauer on edge.

Reverberations, explosions, and gunfire assaulted his ears. McDonald's door looked north, and he could see the VMA-211 flight line on fire.
"Oh, shit!" McDonald yelled.
Huge fires from the fuel pits to the west met his shocked eyes. McDonald saw rifle tracer fire and heard the familiar sound of RPG explosions. Battle-tested, he went for his pistol.

•••

Meanwhile, Raible was at the LSA 13 barracks, about a mile south and across the X-bus road from his squadron, when the first Harrier exploded. The LSA was approximately a half mile from HMLA-469's compound and VMA-211 (his unit) north of that. Raible and Maj Greer Chambless were moving gear, when interrupted by the sound of explosions. He craned his neck to peer over a berm to the North and saw a Harrier go up in a fireball, roughly a mile away. He ordered Marines to grab their battle gear and directed SgtMaj Cayer to establish a defensive position. Then he grabbed his flak, Kevlar helmet, and a pistol and got in his vehicle, a privilege of a commander. Chambless and Cpl Warren joined him, and Raible drove north towards VMA-211, his boot hard on the accelerator.

MARINE CORPS AIR STATION YUMA, Arizona. August 27, 2012. LtCol Chris K. Raible, Commanding Officer of Marine Attack Squadron VMA 211. (DVIDS photo by Cpl Ken Kalemkarian)

•••

Headquarters for 3rd MAW had a compound inside Leatherneck that housed about 250 Marines who worked day and night shifts. There were T-walls around the command element where Sturdevant worked and a manned access gate.

Sturdevant normally worked in his office until midnight, before retiring to his can, the sleeping quarters, about thirty yards from his office and the TACC (Tactical Air Command Center). The close living/working proximity gave the air wing commander the ability to react quickly if something bad happened. Sturdevant led a strong team, hard to beat in an era of counterinsurgency where USMC aircraft dominated the skies over Afghanistan.

•••

LtCol Stephen "Beast" Lightfoot was one of the best squadron commanders Sturdevant ever had the pleasure to serve with. Lightfoot was a superbly qualified Marine leading day-to-day combat operations for HMLA-469—commanding a fleet of AH-1W (Whiskey) Super Cobra attack helicopters and UH-1Y (Yankee) Huey light utility helicopters.

HMLA-469 Vengeance provided life-saving close air support for ground forces in the surrounding provinces. The squadron also served to move/insert Marines, conduct casualty evacuations (CASEVACs), resupply, and other tasks in the wildly kinetic combat zone. HMLA-469 was one of many squadrons serving throughout Afghanistan, swept up into full-fledged ground war, like no other in history.

While political battles intensified, the Afghan government was under attack, and terror threatened every citizen—Lightfoot put

AFGHANISTAN. 2012. Initial combat aircrew pairing for HMLA-469 OEF deployment: (Right to left) LtCol Stephen "Beast" Lightfoot (pilot), Capt Frank Jablonski (copilot). (Photo courtesy of BGen Stephen L. Lightfoot)

on the uniform each day. He stepped out to his aircraft, mission-focused like Marines do. There were no time-outs, no replays in this theater of war. It was crucial to do it right the first time. Marines, like Lightfoot, had a way about them, doing just that. Equipment trouble, weather upsets, and unconventional guerilla fighting all went into the mix, and the blades of freedom still lifted off under Lightfoot's command. The security blanket Lightfoot and his attack helicopter crews provided kept U.S. troops fighting and . . . winning in the Helmand Province region, especially during a drawdown, when manpower was thin.

"Marines know you care—even if they don't like what you are telling them to do—they're going to do it, because they trust you," believed Lightfoot.

Lightfoot always liked the idea of a challenge and heard (before joining) that the Marines enjoyed the reputation of being the hardest of the four service branches. He always wanted to fly and discovered at flight school he wanted to fly the AH-1W.

Upon seeing the signature aircraft, he thought, *This thing looks deadly.* One person sat in the front and one in the back—tandem style. With a huge canopy, one could see everything in a Cobra. A Cobra didn't carry extra people; instead, it carried extra weapons. The pilot in the front typically shot laser-guided Hellfire missiles, rockets, or a 20mm cannon attached underneath him.

In 2012, night vision devices helped Lightfoot and his Dash 2 section aircraft see anti-aircraft artillery rounds roughly the size of softballs coming at them on a distant trip to an objective in Helmand Province. The massive rounds flew between their aircraft, narrowly missing them.

Experience built nerves of steel in the dark-haired leader with chiseled, eye-catching facial features. Confidence led to calmness under fire.

Self-control under extreme duress was a non-negotiable skill to fly HMX-1 Marine One (official helicopter transport for U.S.

THE WHITE HOUSE, United States. December, 2022. Capt Lightfoot ready to depart the White House south lawn in "Marine One" with President G.W. Bush on board. (Photo courtesy of BGen Stephen Lightfoot)

presidents)—a job Lightfoot had prior to deploying to Afghanistan. Former Commander-in-Chief George W. Bush would enter HMX-1 and slap Lightfoot on the shoulder, saying, "How's it going, Tex?" and then go back to his seat. Bush always thanked his pilots and aircrew for their assistance and service to the nation.

Former President Bush launched the war on terror, which quickly rolled in the Taliban harboring 9/11 mastermind and al-Qaeda leader Osama bin Laden on Afghanistan's soil. Then it was al-Qaeda, the Taliban, Haqqani, and any foreign insurgent recruit crossing the border into Afghanistan, disrupting life and crushing freedoms for Afghan citizens.

> "Our war on terror begins with al-Qaeda, but it does not end there. It will not end until every terrorist group of global reach has been found, stopped and defeated."
>
> *- President George W. Bush, September 20, 2001 (National Archives)*[37]

Lightfoot always thanked his Marines under his command, knowing success depended on them and how far they would go. As flames licked the dark night sky on the Harrier flight line, he sprung to action to get aircraft launched, out of reach of the unseen enemy now in full assault on 3rd MAW's turf.

---

37 Bush, George W., "Global War on Terror," National Archives, October 11, 2001, https://www.georgewbushlibrary.gov/research/topic-guides/global-war-terror.

6
ENEMIES INSIDE THE WIRE

LIGHTFOOT THEN PROCEEDED to his office to call his Commanding General. He knew time was of the essence to act, and the enemy had the current advantage.

The CG answered his phone, "Major General Sturdevant."

Lightfoot said, "Sir, it's Beast."

Sturdevant replied, "Hey, Beast! How are you doing?"

"Not good. We're under attack on the northeast side of the flight line. I just saw a Harrier explode. We're launching the TIC section," informed Lightfoot.

Then Sturdevant heard a loud BOOM.

"Thank you," replied Sturdevant. He hung up and immediately directed the TACC floor to begin the required coordination for the ground QRF.

Sturdevant jumped up from his desk and ran down the hall to the TACC as he shared the building with them. The Senior Watch Officer ran towards him from the opposite direction, and at the same time, they both yelled, "We're under attack!"

"Let the squadrons know; go alert the flight lines!" ordered Sturdevant.

The senior watch officer took off to sound the alarm through the building. Calls started going out to different squadrons and their duty officers. From his headquarters, Sturdevant could see the fuel pits area burning.

•••

With pistol in hand, McDonald ran down the LSA stairway towards the one-story, followed by Ackerbauer and Martinez. The ground was gravel, and Martinez, who had just blown out his ACL, felt his knee go out. Thud! Like a sack of potatoes, he hit the ground, screaming in pain, "AAAHH!"

Ackerbauer, nearby, thought he got shot and tried to pick him up and do a fireman carry as Martinez cursed a stream, "Get the fuck off me. I'm fine. It was my knee. My knee!"

McDonald, nearing the one-story, soon saw rifles pointing out the entrances between the barricades.

"Stop!" a Marine screamed.

"Hey, it's Major McDonald."

Satisfied they knew him, McDonald came through the barricades, tiptoeing over sharp rocks all over the ground, still in PT attire.

An officer immediately approached and said, "We're getting the area locked down. We have security facing our forward, and CO Raible and Maj Chambless have jumped in a truck heading north towards the VMA flight line."

The bulk of the pilots were hunkered down in a blocked-off area. When they saw McDonald, a group of them walked over to inquire what was going on. Some of their buddies were in the HMLA-469 compound, where all the blasts and fire were coming from, so they were naturally anxious to do what they could and looked for guidance from McDonald.

•••

Lightfoot watched a fireball rise a hundred meters away as a Harrier jet exploded. He immediately thought they were being mortared by indirect fire, but soon realized the enemy was *inside the wire* among friendly positions. The Harrier flight line was north of his, where Cobras and Hueys lie, ready to be armed and deliver explosive firepower on enemy combatants.

HMLA-469 had large concrete bunkers that served as protection against shrapnel from mortars that could slice mercilessly through body parts. Lightfoot and other Marines ran to the bunkers, then systematically enacted a defensive position around the squadron.

•••

Tongan Security contractors had the tower job. So, what was happening—were they asleep on the job, as previous reports had indicated? Or were they just not there?

•••

"Nobody really told our side," Capt Adam Coker said about the battle.

Coker graduated from high school on a Wednesday in 1997 and entered Marine Corps boot camp on the following Sunday.

It was during training at Twentynine Palms in a combined arms exercise that Coker saw his future unfold. Cobra and Huey helicopters popped over the ridge a hundred feet over his head and shot rockets and guns right in front of their faces. It was love at first sight.

The AH-1W was the world's first dedicated attack helicopter. Both the AH-1W and UH-1N were legacy aircraft. From that moment on, Coker, who speaks with charming southern flair, said, "That's what I'm going to do."

He quickly advanced to aviator, flying off ships in low light level conditions, with no moon, which required supreme concentration.

CAMP PENDLETON, Calif. February 2020. (Former Capt) LtCol Adam Coker. (Photo by Jeanne McKinney)

To pilots like Coker, meeting the challenge successfully landed him in a small elite company. Over the ocean, it's extremely dark at night, even with NVDs. Coker soon discovered he couldn't tell the difference between the sky and the water. The stars shone off the water, so he couldn't distinguish whether the stars were reflections off the water or actually littering the sky. Learning to navigate in those conditions would hit him in the face when Afghanistan drew his name.

Coker was asked if he wanted to go to Weapons and Tactics Instructor (WTI) Course and deploy with HMLA-469 to the embattled country. Although he wanted to go to Afghanistan, he wanted more to stick with his current squadron 267. He answered, "No, I don't really want to do that."

The next day, 267's Executive Officer (XO) Jimmy Brown said

otherwise, "You're going to WTI and move over to 469 to get those guys ready for Bastion."

"Yessir," responded Coker.

During the hot summer days in Afghanistan, the burgeoning insurgency never let up. Up to September 14, the daily routine was repetitive. Aircraft teams worked two shifts, 1200 to 0000 (midnight) and 0000 to 1200. Each shift, Coker got a fair amount of TIC or Priority Immediate (PRI) calls. This took precedence over other jobs, including carrying passengers and cargo from place to place.

Coker worked out nearly every day. The HMLA makeshift gym had weights, elliptical machines, and treadmills so everyone could keep up their conditioning.

The chow hall food was good; Coker especially liked breakfast. Wi-Fi was available (although slow) at the Marines' living spaces. He

AFGHANISTAN. 2012. Capt Adam Coker flies over unnamed part of Afghanistan. Coker flew every mission with an American flag, a South Carolina state flag, and the University of South Carolina "Gamecocks" flag. (Photo courtesy of LtCol Adam Coker)

could email and talk to his wife and even watch some University of South Carolina football, his favorite.

The weather was hot, cresting 100 degrees by midday, and it was usually clear. Coker's sleeping patterns after a long twelve-hour shift would soon go from good to not so good. Most pilots love to fly. Coker was no different. His clear mind and steady hands offered ground troops the support they relied on. Sturdevant loved to fly with Coker. He'd joke around with Coker about the new heads-up display (HUD) attached to Coker's helmet, putting virtual controls in front of his eyes. A former CH-46 (Sea Knight) pilot himself, Sturdevant didn't have access to the same technology at Coker's fingertips. He was a checklist pilot and did just fine with that. One old school and one new school; Coker and Sturdevant had respect for each other that was unspoken.

HMLA-469 squadron was housed north of the fuel pits and south of the VMA-211 flight line and VMA headquarters, in between the two landmarks. The cryogenics lab was east of the access road to the south. At the HMLA flight line and operations center, a big plywood building stood parallel to an access road (that ran north/south) and had S shops (operations administration) and a ready room with a radio in it. The radio was the "Base" radio in which the operations duty officer (ODO) could talk to pilots in their aircraft.

The structure with the ready room was closest to the road. Another building the same size and parallel to the ready room building but closer to the flight line to the west had all the maintenance shops in it, including airframes, avionics, and quality assurance (Coker's shop at the time). Also, within the structure were flight line, maintenance control, and ordnance. Maj Robert "Troll" Weingart, Aviation Maintenance Officer, worked there along with airframes and avionics personnel.

HMLA-469 had an IDF bunker that could provide some protection during an attack. The Bremer Wall was made of twelve-foot-wide and eighteen-foot-high concrete T-wall barriers. The T-walls were sandwiched in between the ready room and maintenance spaces. A manned entry control point (established entry and exit point as part of layered security) stood at the access road.

Coker suspected the Taliban knew their crew changes schedule and would make their presence known. Frequently, they would get a troops in contact (TIC) call or PRI call exactly at shift change. It would be slow all day and get strangely busy as crews turned over.

That night, Coker, now a qualified Weapons and Tactics Instructor, saw an uptick in action working the 1200 to midnight shift. He and his crew had already gone out three times. Each mission required a minimum of two aircraft known as a section. Sometimes, the Huey would lead, and sometimes, the Cobra would lead, depending on who the section lead was on the day's ATO (flight schedule). Coker's Huey crew members were on call for the TIC section.

Around 2200, Coker, also a Quality Assurance Officer, was in the maintenance spaces doing a Sudoku puzzle. Sgt Rolfe, one of the Quality Assurance representatives, was with him. A deafening BANG startled them, and Coker and Rolfe stared at each other: "What the Fuck?"

The same sickening sounds were heard months earlier in Khost, Afghanistan.

• • •

The Washington Post ran a story about an insider attack only months before, on June 1st, 2012, when the Taliban used a truck bomb with 1,500 pounds of explosives in a brazen attempt to demolish Forward Operating Base Salerno, killing an American contractor and an American soldier and seriously wounding three dozen troops. Insurgents, including many individuals wearing suicide vests, had launched a coordinated assault that breached the perimeter of the American facility. The details of the attack were kept in the dark from the public.

"The Haqqanis have repeatedly tried to overrun the Salerno base in recent years, and it is a frequent target of rocket attacks. In August 2008, insurgents were beaten back during an assault on the camp's perimeter that lasted two days. Two years later, about three dozen Haqqani fighters were killed during a similar attack on Salerno and a nearby installation, Forward Operating Base Chapman," stated *Washington Post.*[38]

●●●

Yet, Capewell said that they had no reason to believe an attack on Camp Bastion could happen. Some people in high offices must have thought the same about the U.S. diplomatic compound in Benghazi, Libya, attacked three days prior on September 11, 2012. The military top chain of command back home in both Britain and the U.S. should've put the BLS Complex on hyperalert. Yet they were dealing with a lie concocted by the U.S. State Dept./Obama administration that an "anti-Islam video" caused the attack on the diplomatic consulate (killing four Americans). In fact, it was waves of organized, mobilized terrorists with ties to al-Qaeda. The reasons the U.S. waded deeply into a post-Gaddafi Libya in the first place are not clearly understood. Some speculated it was to build a front against al-Qaeda.

Business Insider reported in December 2012,[39] that heavy weapons were moving through Libya to jihadist Syrian rebels, countering Bashar al Assad's bombing campaign, indicating U.S. agents were already involved.

---

38 Partlow, Joshua, "Attack on U.S. outpost in Afghanistan worse than originally reported," *Washington Post*, June 16, 2012, https://www.washingtonpost.com/world/nationalsecurity/attack-on-us-outpost-in-afghanistan-worse-thanoriginally-reported/2012/06/16/gJQAIyaihV_story.html.

39 Ingersoll, Geoffrey, Kelley, Michael B., "The US Is Openly Sending Heavy Weapons From Libya To Syrian Rebels," *Business Insider*, December 9, 2012, https://www.businessinsider.com/obama-admin-admits-to-covertly-sending-heavy-weapons-to-syrian-rebels-2012-12.

ENEMIES INSIDE THE WIRE

What started with the CIA funding rebel fighters in Afghanistan led to a full-fledged war, involving tens of thousands of U.S. troops heading to a country plagued by conflict. By 2012, the war had marched on for eleven years, leaving a bloody trail. NATO allies and partner countries descended on the land after the multiple homeland terror attacks on 9/11 to "make sure that terrorists would not find safe haven in Afghanistan." The conflict grew as rebels who once fought together splintered; some turned on their U.S. benefactors. Yet Obama had a campaign promise to withdraw troops even though the indications did not spell out the cessation of fighting. Terrorists play the long game. They can wait until the moment to strike is best to serve their diabolical and murderous plans. They were done waiting on Bastion.

The vibe within and without Camp Bastion remained uncertain, coupled with a huge amount of pressure to get out of the country by September 30th. What would happen when they left? A little over a year prior, the Taliban and their al-Qaeda allies mourned the death of Osama bin Laden, who the U.S. finally tracked down and killed at his compound in Abbottabad, Pakistan, on May 2, 2011. Left still, were thousands of foreign troops who were deployed to Afghanistan in search of this ruthless terrorist and his allies who ran with this idol of death.

The insurgents hated the infidels that bin Laden had vowed to kill, and especially U.S. aircraft they had little defense for. Yet, in reality, many of the insurgents were foreigners themselves who came to occupy the land. Not welcome by the native Afghan people. The illegal opium deals were made as fast as they could harvest the poppies to fund the Islamic fatwa. Meetings took place in back alleys, private residences, and training camps. Insiders within official circles of government were collecting intelligence on the Americans, who must die for trying to stop them.

7
BATTLE READY

EARLIER IN THE DAY, ON September 14, Capt Kevin Smalley had been out flying, working on an AV-8B Harrier qualification with Raible, his instructor. Raible, a giant of a man, was not afraid to speak his mind. The flight was broken down into periods called a vulnerability (VUL) window. The plan later that night called for three VULs and two in-flight re-fuelings. Raible was known to be hard, but fair, on his pilots as they conducted their pre-flight briefs. Smalley was ready with a fifty-minute plan when Raible walked in and said, "Shut up. I don't want to hear your talk . . . I'm just going to tell you how I want you to sound the next time I come in here, 'cause I'm just tired of people talking to me right now."

"Roger that, sir," answered Smalley.

The Smalley family's military service goes back to the Civil War, Revolutionary War, and French and Indian Wars. Smalley's maternal great-grandfather was alleged to be the youngest American to participate in the Spanish-American War. His paternal grandparents both served in WWII, and his father served in the U.S. Marine Corps as a CH-53 pilot. Smalley carried out the family tradition and earned his wings in July 2008, then was selected to fly Harriers.

When Smalley deployed to Qatar to serve in the Combined Air Operations Center (CAOC) in 2010, the Battle for Marjah (Operation

CAMP BASTION, Afghanistan. 2012. Capt Kevin T. Smalley, VMA- 211, inspects an AV-8B Harrier before flight. (DVIDS photo by Sgt Keonaona Paulo)

Moshtarak) had kicked off. The Marines were fighting a heavily embedded and very violent insurgency. A massive air assault involving American, British, Canadian, Danish, and Estonian troops, and 15,000 Afghans, constituted the largest joint operation of the war, eliminating the last Taliban stronghold there.

Yet the Taliban didn't stay down for long—they just regrouped, recruited, and relocated . . . soon to be a deadly scourge in Sangin, Afghanistan, giving first the Brits and then U.S. Marines hell on earth each day.

•••

Smalley was amazed at how little he and Raible talked to each other during the mid-air fuel exchange, even though they flew together every couple of weeks. Smalley landed first and got ready for the debrief, when Raible cut the conversation short, "Great job, we didn't crash, debrief over. I'm going to get some chow, then talk to my wife for the first time in three weeks."

The Harrier squadron had recently moved from Kandahar to Bastion in July. Kandahar was a certain kind of paradise, where they had great internet, great service, and everything else was pretty cool for deployment living. They moved into brand-new buildings on Camp Bastion, minus Wi-Fi and many of the other amenities they had grown accustomed to in Kandahar. Everyone had to go to a different building to get on the internet or hop on the bus to get to the exchange.

Raible wanted his privacy. As CO, he rated that. Combat deployments were not geared to be comfort living, but efforts were made to provide a few basics for physical conditioning and mental refresh. The challenges were many. An opportunity arose two weeks prior, where the squadron could move their living spaces. They only relocated a hundred yards but had dedicated Wi-Fi in nine rooms. Smalley offered Raible his own Wi-Fi room.

After the debrief, Raible took off for the Chow Hall, leaving Smalley with Capt Pete Abramovs, the ODO. Abramovs, also a Harrier pilot, was one of the younger guys on the deployment. An ODO used three different computer networks to tell the aircrew what was going on in the area. Across those screens was the weather and incoming and outgoing info on the Army Battle Command System. Information was displayed reporting Marines in contact and when and where Marine Air was tasked to support ground troops. There were other messaging systems, like Internet Relay Chat (IRC), where air officers talked back and forth with the JTACs.

The drawdown led to lean manpower. They brought over a Marine from maintenance to answer phones in the VMA-211 command headquarters building housing administrative shops. There were also supposed to be three other Marines there—the intelligence clerk and two logistics guys, one of whom was the armorer.

Abramovs and Smalley left headquarters under the care of the other Marines as shift time was over. They grabbed keys for a crappy old black Toyota Hilux and started driving back to the LSA, a little more than a mile away. Abramovs complained about how badly he needed to go take a shit and bolted for the head as soon as they parked. Smalley heard the first explosion as he opened his car door.

What the hell is that? Smalley asked himself, remembering controlled detonations (dets) were done during the middle of the day—to the west. This sound came from the north, and it was close.

"That's weird. That shouldn't be going off," said Smalley to a nearby civilian contractor near a smoke pit.

"Yeah, that is weird. What's going on?" asked the civilian contractor.

Smalley had no good answer to give. Marines near the fuel pits area were asking themselves the same questions. Smalley hoped to grab Abramovs to tell him he was going back to VMA headquarters, but he was nowhere to be found. Smalley got back in the truck and started driving. He made a fast left, then right, and started driving up the hill to get out of the LSA area.

• • •

When troops entered a foreign country, they established forward bases to stage operations. That required a lot of logistical planning and supplies to make it ready for U.S. ground troops and aircraft. Someone managed all that.

Chief Warrant Officer Second Class (CW2) Timothy Killebrew always wanted to be a Marine. He grew up hearing stories about his grandfather, an Infantry Marine wounded on Iwo Jima, and his uncle, who served in the Navy during the Vietnam War. Killebrew was bound to carry that American flag forward.

He wanted to build airfields, and to whet his appetite, he deployed to Iraq in 2004 with Operation Iraqi Freedom. Killebrew and his Marines took over al-Taqaddum Air Base from the Army. They came in right after the surge, when President Bush invaded the country on the hunt for weapons of mass destruction, convinced Saddam Hussein was hiding them . . . or buying supplies to make them.

"I never thought about getting injured or killed. I had been in combat areas before and really believe that it's all random that some live and some don't, and there is no rhyme or reason, so nothing to worry about," said CWO2 Timothy Killebrew of battle.

Marine Wing Support Squadron 374 built Mudaysis, a military airfield located in Anbar Province, Iraq. The field was used by the Iraqi military, and, during the course of the Iraq War, it was used at various times by the United States military.

Saddam's Army hit the Marines' supplies, coming into al-Taqaddum for a while, causing a food shortage. A lot of rockets hit the base, and rifle rounds pierced aircraft on the flight lines. A couple of helos were lost. The airfield was mortared every day by multiple random assaults. The enemy didn't have artillery, just mortars, and they weren't very good at aiming. Thirty was the highest number of exploding bombs al-Taqaddum got in one day. Killebrew and his team would have to go out and fix the damage.

MARINE CORPS AIR STATION YUMA, AZ. March 31, 2015. Chief Warrant Officer 3 Timothy Killebrew measures the airfield soil subsurface with a dynamic cone penetrometer. (DVIDS photo LCpl Travis Jordan)

Killebrew built helo pads in Fallujah and was there during the first costly ground push into Fallujah, beginning spring 2004. U.S. Marines were indoctrinated quickly in heavy urban insurgent warfare and house-to-house combat, strengthened by the real meaning of being a Marine: protecting each other. There were 500-pound bombs all over the place, because of ordnance the Iraqi army never used was left on the airfields after the U.S. surge. MWSS-374's EOD unit had to find stray rockets and mortars that skipped everywhere, disarm, and blow them up so they could not harm anyone. They found both enemy and friendly ordnance buried around the airfield.

Insurgents tried to ambush convoys or kill Marines with roadside bombs almost daily. This was the dawn of the homemade improvised explosive device (IED) and its unconventional, atrocious power.

Insurgents called themselves the *New Mujahideen*, foreign fighters loyal to ousted Hussein and religious extremists. All claimed Fallujah as their new frontier for hardline Islamic rule, where religion and government were one.

A lot of CASEVACs were happening with heavy fighting in Fallujah and Ramadi, and al-Taqaddum was a casualty collection point.

It was eight months of improving al-Taqaddum and surrounding FOBs, repainting lines, relighting the airfield, and putting up signs. All under the daily mortar attacks. During one six-hour barrage, some of Killebrew's fellow Marines from MWSS-374 Heavy Equipment Platoon barely made it out alive when the ammunition dump was hit by enemy indirect fire. Some local Iraqis worked on the airfields and would get shot up, same as the Americans.

Killebrew discovered that fighting was completely different, depending on nationality and enemy tactics and weaponry. The Sunni and Shiite didn't like each other, which complicated visions of population control. The only thing they had in common was their hatred for Israel. Hussein had his Army and his dangerous ethnic cleansing ideas.

"The whole place was a big mess when we were there. It was kind of the Wild West," Killebrew would later remember.

He stayed away from the Iraqi nationals in the Iraqi Army—forces some called impotent. Iraqi tasks fell to infantry Marines. Killebrew never trusted anyone who wasn't in a U.S. military uniform.

As Killebrew advanced in rank, he became a master at setting up working airfields or re-purposing old ones to U.S. standards. Marines used AM-2 matting, described as big twelve-by-two-foot and six-by-two-foot aluminum planks that go together, to make an expeditionary military airfield.

Iraq looked modern compared to Afghanistan, the third-world country Killebrew would see next. The Afghans were the ground fighters with no formal army or uniform. Splintered tribal groups shared ingrained beliefs and handed down the resolve to hang on to their land.

In 2010, Killebrew was selected to be a warrant officer, expanding his job to include fire and emergency services as well as expeditionary airfields. His job was to provide aviation ground support for air bases, forward arming refueling points (FARPs), and combat outposts (COP). Aviation ground support increased the range of both fixed-wing (planes) and combat rotary-wing aircraft (helicopters), increasing their ability to support ground troops in kinetic areas embedded with hostile fighters. On Bastion, the lights, arresting gear, and emergency equipment were already in place. Killebrew was now in charge of support squadron MWSS-373, which augmented existing services.

His squadron was sent to the sprawling multi-national military complex to assist in the retrograde of Marine Corps aviation ground support equipment. Portions of Camp Bastion's airfield and parking area was built with AM-2 matting, as were many other airfields throughout the country. Killebrew and his team were tasked to prepare the remaining one million square feet for shipment out of the country in 2012.

The numbers of all officers and enlisted were reduced. Killebrew shouldered many official duties, including acting as Contracting Officer in charge of inspecting, negotiating, and assisting all contracts for airfield services that were in place without a full team. The mega-load of responsibility left hardly any time to breathe.

All these tasks still had to take place to run missions outside the wire, so ground forces were covered. Observing the tremendous workload performed, no one would have guessed a drawdown was in place. Everyone was shouldering the loads, counting on the British to do their jobs—including securing the airfield.

Unknown to the aviation combat element, their trust in British protection was built on sand as the Taliban made their way over open ground, fully confident they had the upper hand of surprise. Yet, once inside the wire, having made their presence known, they would charge head-on into a wall of no-bullshit Marines.

8

TOO LATE FOR "SEE SOMETHING, SAY SOMETHING"

STURDEVANT KNEW HIS PRIMARY focus was having qualified crews and aircraft projecting combat power. He couldn't have had a better group of Marines in place to accomplish that. It's a given Marines relied upon each other.

Everyone had a responsibility for force protection against terrorism following the "If You See Something, Say Something" Homeland Security directive used back in the States.[40]

Yet the window to warn had been closed to deaf British ears by their own tower guards, and the Taliban attackers were on base. The insurgents, dressed as Army soldiers, fumbled around, thinking they knew where they were going. The first group of five had an obvious advantage, able to see Harrier jets parked under their tents. Just a quick roll of the grenade was all it took before anyone was on to them. They could have traveled to just about any location, even the main side of the base, using the X-bus road, but didn't, and

---

40 "If you see something, say something," U.S. Department of Homeland Security, https://www.dhs.gov/see-something-say-something.

unfortunately for the Taliban, that road would be the thorn in their side once trying to cross over from east to west.

The X-bus access road ran north and south, located east of the flight lines. The X-bus base transit circled around the base to the main side. The road was key for transporting people located at the mid-point between the west and east sides. On the west side of the X-bus road lay the fuel pits and other fuels buildings within the compound used by Killebrew and his Marines. Aircraft didn't take off without their critical services, which were being handed over to third-party contractors due to the drawdown. The pilots didn't like outsiders having their aircrafts and lives in third-party hands.

At the resident housing units called *cans*, separated to the west from the fuels compound, Killebrew, in PT gear, was in a heated argument with his supply lieutenant who had run his mouth off to someone from the east coast unit, MWSS-273, scheduled to ship out the next day. The topic was AM-2 matting, something Killebrew was an expert on, contrasting the lieutenant's scant knowledge on the subject. Killebrew's Marines were in the process of providing relief in place with 273 Marines. There was a strange feeling in the air no one could put a finger on.

The argument ended, and they both went their separate ways. Killebrew walked down to talk to a leader counterpart, CW02 Hensley, a platoon commander with MWSS-273 ARFF. Hensley's unit was also staying in the cans, waiting to vacate that night; their job was done and Killebrew's was just beginning.

"Hey, look, my lieutenant talked out of line. This might come up with your colonel," said Killebrew, a no-nonsense guy.

Outside, both Killebrew and Hensley met up and talked to LtCol Ocloo, Commander, MWSS-373, and Hensley's squadron commander. Suddenly, they saw an explosion light up the ink-dark sky. Though a mile and a half away, they could not miss it. It was running distance from the British firehouse to the fuel pits. Killebrew saw several fireballs burst in the air over the fuel pits area. Both he and

Hensley grabbed weapons and flak jackets and jumped in a white truck, haulin' butt to the British checkpoint, west of the fuel pits.

They stopped abruptly at the checkpoint. The Brits aggressively pointed their loaded rifles out from every direction. Killebrew got out and walked over, defying a female Brit ready to shoot him.

"Whoa, same team," he told the Brits, "Hey, we're getting over to the fuel pits. Where is the enemy?"

"Everywhere," they said.

Killebrew replied, "That's a lot of places. Can you narrow it down?"

They replied determinedly, "No."

The Brits had no idea where the enemy was—at least, that's what Killebrew surmised.

The Brits repeated, "They are everywhere; they're dressed in cammies."

"Okay," acknowledged Killebrew, not keen to agitate them and just wanting to get through the checkpoint to the fuel pits. Killebrew and Hensley first drove to the British firehouse. The entire place was empty, with no movement or fire trucks in the area. Normally, some of Killebrew's men would be on post there. Four tactical British ambulances were lined up.

The Brit firefighting medical unit approached and asked Killebrew, "How do we get across the airfield?"

"We can get you across," replied Killebrew, impatience mounting.

Killebrew and Hensley jumped in one of the ambulances with some Brits and directed the vehicle convoy towards the explosions and small arms fire coming from the fuel pits. Once the ambulances arrived at the fuel ramp, Killebrew's ambulance driver asked, "Where next?"

"We don't know, and thanks for the ride," he replied and got out.

The driver departed immediately after, leaving one ambulance and one female British corpsman at their position. Killebrew and Hensley immediately took off to look for their Marines.

One trains and trains, and although many succeed to outthink an adversary, they can't always predict what tactics a determined enemy will employ. The Marines of 3rd MAW were finding out. Camp Bastion, a monolith base for combat planning and power projection—and an international hub hosting many nations' forces—should have been prepared by its British builders for a number of wartime contingencies.

There was nothing off limits to the Taliban. They were not afraid to bring their smaller numbers against much larger, better-equipped forces. Repeatedly, they demonstrated that raw boldness.

•••

In the House of Commons evidence session,[41] Lt. Gen. Capewell explained to the row of Defense Committee members with strained looks on their faces:

"The attack was significant in scale and ambition," Capewell said. "It was carefully planned and well executed by a group of determined and heavily armed insurgents on a moonless night. It is clear that they were prepared to die in the attack, regardless of any physical obstacles they may have faced."

One Committee member shook his head in disbelief at the lengths they were willing to go.

"Operations in Afghanistan are complex, dynamic and dangerous," Capewell rattled on. "The enemy has a vote. In such circumstances mistakes cannot be ruled out," he continued, with no blowback from Defense Committee members.

Later, under scrutiny, Gurganus would later use these same words, "The enemy has a vote," to be lambasted by his finger-pointers. He

---

41 House of Commons Defence Committee, "Afghanistan—Camp Bastion Attack," *The Stationery Office*, April 16, 2014, Ev. 3, https://publications.parliament.uk/pa/cm201314/cmselect/cmdfence/830/830vw.pdf.

was simply trying to convey that commanders aren't always able to control the time and place of battle. But they can be ready to meet the enemy, and that is what Gurganus and Sturdevant focused on throughout the Bastion mission, while forced into a squeezing framework of limitations put upon them by others.

Capewell's contradictions would stack up from his opening remarks at the lengthy inquisition. He would be insistent, claiming the British side did not bear any of the mistakes he would allude to, even though Gurganus had ninety-three Brits on his staff, and the British Task Force was commanded by a British brigadier general. There were plenty of decisions the British chain of command would have made to follow the 2011 MOU, outlining force and Bastion airfield protection . . . if the Brits had indeed followed it.

September 2012, Camp Bastion

After being briefed on perimeter security upon arrival to Bastion, the number one concern Gurganus articulated to his immediate boss, LTG Curtis Scaparrotti (IJC commander at the time), was the drawdown of TFBW from an Artillery Battalion to 180 Marines. A standard artillery battery has roughly six guns and up to 150 Marines; a battalion would include up to eighteen guns or three firing batteries. This substantial reduction severely limited the security patrols the U.S. forces could keep outside the wire.

ISAF commanders Allen and Bradshaw knew the Brits' responsibilities, that the poppy fields were untouched—that the Taliban had not changed their character or become benevolent. Everyone knew about the drawdown, especially the ruthless enemy.

And yet, why did the ISAF commanders and the ESG not see reduced manpower alone as an advantage to insurgents? The fighting was admittedly still heavy in the Helmand region and Bastion was an alluring target.

• • •

The RC(SW) mission was changing from counterinsurgency to security force assistance (SFA), with the Afghan National Army (ANA) in the lead. That alone was a daunting task, as described in the Dept. of the Army investigation.[42]

As LTG James Terry (IJC commander who replaced Scaparrotti) put it, "There was a constant balance between projecting forces and protecting the force during this period with priority to protecting the force that each RC commander determined."

LTG Terry understood both the challenges and sacrifices for American troops and their leaders in Afghanistan, as he assumed IJC command in June 2012, and embraced the mission now drawing down and transitioning after long years of heavy fighting, still ongoing.

"We left our comfortable homes and loved ones to become part of a team that will take the next steps in bringing lasting stability to Afghanistan," Terry said. "Our success also secures our own nations by denying Afghanistan as a safe haven for terrorists. We will make a difference, at home, in this region, and throughout the world."

Probing officials with an agenda would later twist higher-up's lack of cooperation and support for Gurganus to Gurganus thinking he was exempt from protecting the force.

Higher-up's narrative amounted to: *Here, drive the car they give you, but you're not getting the gas you need to get from point A to B. But don't think you're not expected to get there on fumes, and if you don't, it's your fault you didn't cry mission failure.* Gurganus was never going to own *mission failure* because higher-up failed him.

---

42 Garrett, William B., Murray, Thomas M., "Army Regulation (AR) 15-6 Report (Final)," Dept. of the Army Bastion Attack Investigation, August 19, 2013, Pg. 7, https://www.hqmc.marines.mil/Portals/142/USCENTCOM%20Bastion%20Attack%20Investigation%20Redacted%2015-6%20Report.pdf.

Higher-up, including friends of Gurganus, forgot the Marine he was and why he was put in top command. Those putting their heads in the sand never saw their own mistakes. Contrary to popular belief, ostriches do not bury their heads in the sand when sensing danger. When it can't run away, it will flop to the ground and remain still, attempting to blend in with the terrain. There was no blending in terrain with 3rd MAW leaders, nor no magician's ball. They attempted to achieve the impossible by doing everything possible.

Even Pentagon officials were aware of the vexing airfield vulnerabilities prior to September 14. Ignoring the devil may dare before their eyes.

U.S. CENTCOM Bastion Attack Summary:[43]

> "The Joint Staff Integrated Vulnerability Assessment (JSIVA) Program was managed by the Defense Threat Reduction Agency (DTRA) as the executive agent for the Chairman, Joint Chiefs of Staff. The JSIVA is a vulnerability-based assessment of military installations to determine susceptibility to a terrorist attack."

JSIVA recognized that a 3rd MAW flight line barrier plan request had been submitted on May 11, 2012, to emplace over 10,000 linear feet of HESCO barriers and 650 linear feet of T-Walls to protect the flight line. The request, submitted by 3rd MAW (Fwd), stated, "Without these improvements, the flight line equipment and personnel will remain vulnerable to enemy attack at multiple access points, including numerous high speed avenues of approach."

Sturdevant's staff identified these vulnerabilities one month prior to the JSIVA, submitted a request for improvements, and the ESG subsequently denied the request.

---

43 Garrett, William B., Murray, Thomas M., "USCENTCOM Bastion Attack Investigation Executive Summary," The United States Central Command (USCENTCOM), Accessed November 29, 2023, Pg. 6, https://www.hqmc.marines.mil/Portals/142/Docs/USCENTCOM%20Bastion%20Attack%20Investigation%20Executive%20Summary.pdf.

"The JSIVA Team provided an out-brief to the TFBW leaders and some of their UK counterparts at the conclusion of the JSIVA on 14 June 2012, and the team produced an official report, dated 7 August 2012. The JSIVA [subsequently] identified six vulnerabilities at the BLS Complex, including uncontrolled access to the airfield, which left personnel and equipment exposed. Commanders are not required to mitigate the force protection vulnerabilities and concerns identified by a JSIVA, nor does a JSIVA team have the responsibility to re-assess a base for compliance."

Even though JSIVA had a 3rd MAW flight line barrier plan in hand, the Dept. of the Army does not mention that.

JSIVA ignored the fact that Gurganus' RC(SW) command had gone to great lengths to mitigate security gaps in base access. That was their American side of things on a British-run base. That was 3rd MAW leaders doing their jobs.

On the British side, the U.K. 5 FP Wing had full operational control over 51st Squadron, RAF Regiment. The commanding officers of TFBW SECFOR and 5FP Wing coordinated a weekly patrolling plan, each forced to rely on the other camp to man the patrols. Yet, Capewell would hear the lie in his ear that the U.K. had no control over the tactical decisions on the ground. "There was no culpable failure on the part of U.K. forces at Camp Bastion," he would hammer home to U.K. Defense Committee members.

"Our job was not to guard the perimeter. That was the Brits' job. The folks that worked the flight line did exactly what they were supposed to do," Colonel Bew reminded future government hawks looking for prey. Bew understood 3rd MAW Marines to be as good or better than anyone.

It seemed ludicrous to put the safety of 3rd MAW Marines into another nation's hands.

•••

When local relationships push the protection of forces to a *complacent level,* then it's only a matter of time before the thinking enemy and their allies might plan a strike over tea.

A U.K. Ministry of Defense news story stated in April 2011 that the Brits were having tea, discussing civic-centered improvements with their Afghan neighbors, and leaving joint patrols of encroached perimeter settlements to the ANA and their Danish military mentors. How nice in a fighting season to give a hand to locals who would turn as soon as a Taliban threat came their way.

"With the expansion of the neighbouring military camps of Bastion (UK), Shorabak (Afghan), and Leatherneck (US), in Helmand province, a variety of small settlements have developed outside the Main Entry Point (MEP).

"Known locally as Shorab, this has, until recently, been a disorganized 'hotchpotch' of shacks and tents, offering basic services to the lorry (truck) drivers bringing supplies for the base. However, Shorab City, a new, more structured settlement, has been established slightly further to the north.

"Sergeants Ullah (ANA) and Muir (British RAF) were invited for chai (tea) by Mr Baryali and Mr Raim, two local shop owners. . . . They discussed a variety of topics including the expansion of the settlement. Mr. Baryali spoke of his plans which included the imminent opening of a petrol station, the building of a hotel (already part-constructed) with a recreation area containing snooker tables, and, for the longer term, a swimming pool."[44]

· · ·

---

44 Ministry of Defense, "RAF police support Afghan Army patrol," U.K. Government, April 27, 2011, https://www.gov.uk/government/news/raf-police-support-afghan-army-patrol.

September 2012, Camp Bastion

Gurganus' focus was not having tea parties with locals living too close, watching his combat operations, but pushing them away, creating observable, defensible space—just like you would need to prevent a wildfire from ripping through your home. Both Gurganus and Sturdevant's focus was keeping Marines safe and projecting firepower.

Neither did one of the Brits' own tower guards conducting daily surveillance approximately one mile from the future breach point focus on tea gatherings. The tower guard didn't give a shit about a snooker table either. When the tower guard tried to do his job, he was instead told to report any harassment towards the poppy farmers by ANDSF. The tower guards were instructed to radio the Guard Commander if any ANDSF entered the valley.

9
EVERYTHING'S ON FIRE

"THE NIGHT CAUGHT US by surprise. The majority of the squadron had not experienced ground side training since Marine Combat Training (MCT) or The Basic School. Every Marine on the line resorted back to their core training to defend the perimeter and squadron spaces," recollected Capt Brian Jordan.

From the age of three, Capt Brian "Catcher" Jordan had a dream to fly. His father flew a P-3 Orion in the Navy, an aircraft considered to be the ultimate airborne patrol aircraft, seeking out surface and sub-surface enemies of the deep.

Jordan learned how to tactically employ his Huey helicopter on the 15th MEU as part of the amphibious ready group (ARG). The MEU provides a quick-time response to hotspot crises that spring up across the globe. Jordan spread his flight wings during the takedown of the Magellan Star at sea—a 2010 counter-piracy operation that was the first USMC opposed boarding (meeting the resistance of the master and crew) of a pirated vessel. The Magellan Star's real captain and crew had locked themselves in what they called their *citadel*. Navy ship personnel and aviation Marines on the MEU worked to execute the takeover mission. All the Somali pirates who boarded the Magellan were detained, and every crew member was

CAMP BASTION, Afghanistan. June 2012. Capt Brian "Catcher" Jordan proudly displays American flag in front of UH—1Y Huey aircraft. (Photo courtesy of Maj Brian Jordan)

safe. Jordan would face his share of different enemies, from merciless pirates to violent insurgents, over the coming months.

In May 2012, Jordan deployed with HMLA-469 to Camp Bastion in Helmand Province, a notorious hotbed of insurgent activity in Afghanistan. This brought a different flying challenge, experiencing a daily barrage of fire from a ghost enemy who hid to fight. Only ground troops and the pilots and crews who protected them could describe the hardships of unconventional urban warfare and compound-to-compound engagements. They had to stay alive while juggling restrictive rules of engagement (ROE) created by those behind desks in Washington, not connected to those beating paths on dusty deserts riddled with explosives or rugged mountain terrain the locals knew all too well. The president, the State Department, and the foreign policy think tanks could not see or feel the unrelenting blows of Islamic jihadists recruited under the Taliban.

The plague of IEDs came down on foreign troops like the lightning of Thor's hammer. IEDs were planted all over the vast deserts, roads, wadis, compounds, fields, and even waterways.

On July 4, 2012, Jordan remembered fireworks, but not the kind seen in hometown America. Ground forces were taking it heavy. He had finished a mission and was transiting air space when he saw two Humvees strike IEDS and go about ten feet in the air.

He radioed down and was relieved to hear all personnel miraculously walked out of the vehicles uninjured. It wasn't their time to go.

Yet, the Taliban got their mobility kills, destroying the Humvees. No doubt they had more than that in mind. Jordan was driven to stop the carnage to his brothers-in-arms.

Marines are known for taking the fight to the enemy. Many of their missions had a benefit to the locals by eliminating Taliban brutality and rule.

Jordan became familiar with the ferocity of these turbaned warriors who had been fighting each other, the Russians, and any uninvited colonizer. They made targets of government officials and local security forces. Jordan and his squadron, nicknamed "Righteous Vengeance," were set smack dab in the middle of a religious blood feud—as well as a fight for supremacy in the opium drug trade.

Close air support aircraft laid down fire near ground troops danger close to the enemy. The geometry of fires had to line up to avoid blue-on-blue (friendly fire) incidents. One of Jordan's mentors once told him, "Nothing needs to happen fast, and anything that does happen fast, can happen smooth."

Then again, sometimes things need to happen fast. On June 21, 2012, it was a routine mission near Gereshk, Afghanistan. A British Grenadier Guardsman platoon had orders to block the Taliban from moving west, while a large deployment of the ANA pushed west to clear the area of insurgents. The small platoon came under fire, tracking an enemy sniper along the Helmand River, and Jordan's section engaged the enemy to cover the ground combat element (GCE) until the enemy stopped firing. The Brits made it through a wadi to a compound—to their objective.

Jordan and his crew were in the air, about five minutes from bingo and their last reconnaissance pass prior to returning to Bastion. On board was pilot Jordan, co-pilot Capt "Ozzy" Miller, GySgt Andrew Bond, SSgt Steven Seay, and Cpl Joshua Martinez when everything unfolded.

The unplanned broke loose. One of the Guardsmen struck an IED.

A British JTAC screamed over the radio, "Man down, man down, request immediate MEDEVAC!"

A Guardsman had lost both his legs and was going into shock. Another Guardsman was wounded in the abdomen. The urgency of a dying man left nothing to speculation and little to protocol.

A lot was going through Jordan's head. They were told not to conduct a CASEVAC during their in-brief. Normally, British CASEVAC birds were dispatched to pick up the British wounded; they had a very capable MEDEVAC platform. Everything boiled down to Jordan and the air crew being the best close option and providing the least amount of time to get the at-risk-of-dying British Grenadiers out to better medical care. Jordan checked with his section leader, LtCol Lightfoot, and all agreed Jordan would go in and retrieve the critically wounded.

Two years later, for heroic actions that saved those two Guardsmen's lives as well as the rest of the platoon, Jordan was awarded the British Flying Cross from the Queen of England. He was one of three Americans ever to receive the award and the second Marine since World War II to do so.

Jordan admonished, "I am only the face of the crew," and "we were simply taking care of our ground troops."

Three months later into the deployment, Jordan and his squadron would answer a shocking call that the Taliban were inside the wire. His fellow Marines and wing commander would have to muster all the savvy and strength within at a moment's notice.

CAMP BASTION, Afghanistan. July 26, 2012. Post flying missions with MajGen Sturdevant on board. (Left to right) MajGen Gregg Sturdevant, Sgt Fitzgerald, GySgt Andrew Bond, Capt Brian Jordan. (Photo courtesy of Maj Brian Jordan)

• • •

"The very nature of war makes certainty impossible; all actions in war will be based on incomplete, inaccurate, or even contradictory information," from the USMC *Warfighting Manual*.

Leaders need to let their Marines be Marines who are trained to adapt to the crises before them.

Lightfoot, "the Beast," who grew up in Azusa, California, compared the sound of a TIC horn to a tornado horn in small-town

America. It set off the squadron's choreography to get aircraft airborne within minutes. Maintenance Marines sprinted to the aircraft, started it up and armed it, then launched them on their way to troops in contact. This highly-rehearsed chain of events had been polished to a T over the previous four months of combat support in Afghanistan.

Lightfoot's HMLA-469 squadron did it day after day—regardless of extreme 120-degree heat or freezing cold temperatures. They were on a 24/7 tether. Lightfoot was first up to praise his Marines, not missing a beat of their hard work and selfless service.

"It's mission first, people always," said Lightfoot, who made sure his Marines had all the tools they need to train successfully, because every Marine is more than their job. They were warriors, thrust into Afghanistan's gauntlets of danger.

"Every Marine is a rifleman," is how the saying went. Leadership was aware things could go very badly without warning, forcing every Marine to rely on their training . . . and each other.

Regret, guilt, and failure were not on the flight checklist. They were unworkable human conditions that had no place in the mission. Not that day, not ever.

Earlier in the day, HMLA-469 aircraft operations were buzzing. Those in the garage stayed busy helping to launch Hueys and Cobras and their crews on shift. Maintenance Marines banged wrenches, did pre-flight checks, went over safety equipment, and added ordnance to the rails. Maintenance workers trained laser focus on safety—and were considered a pilot's best friend.

When explosions rattled the ground at 2200, Lightfoot thought it was an odd time to hear a controlled det. When Marines confiscated enemy ordnance, they would find and roll it up in C-4 and destroy it. Sometimes, dets took place out in the objective operating areas, near the Helmand River. Sometimes, controlled dets were near the base. Yet—they always heard about them taking place first, usually during the day.

•••

The USMC Bastion Attack Narrative Summary report, dated September 14, 2012, was an impressive collection of synchronized actions that unfolded, stating:

> "In the [HMLA] squadron headquarters building, the first explosion sounded louder than a normal controlled detonation, followed by a second more powerful explosion within ten seconds. Marines from within the building quickly ran outside to determine what was happening and immediately saw the flames and smoke billowing on the VMA-211 flight line 100 meters to the north of the HMLA 469 flight line. Near simultaneously, Marines called out, 'IDF, IDF, get to the bunkers!'"[45]

Nearing VMA-211 headquarters, Raible stopped his vehicle just south of the squadron spaces as Harriers exploded into flames, and machine gun fire cracked around them. He led Chambless and Warren, while clearing a southern hangar. He rushed to the VMA-211 hangar (outside workspaces), where he knew Marines were, not knowing the buildings were already riddled with bullets and that the insurgents had already attacked through one of the hangars. A shout went out to identify his three-man group, "Friendlies!"

Raible, Chambless, and Warren entered the maintenance spaces where the majority of his night crew had established defensive positions.

•••

45 "OEF Enemy Attack on Camp Bastion, 14 September 2012, NARRATIVE SUMMARY, HMLA 469" (Private source)

As he started to crest the hill, Smalley's eyes did not lie. "Well, shit!" he yelled. Everything was on fire at VMA! Not fully grasping the situation but understanding something was terribly wrong, Smalley grabbed his 9mm out of his holster and racked a round for the first time. Although he'd racked a round for every flight, he went Condition 1 as he drove, meaning having a round chambered, a full magazine in place, the hammer cocked, and safety on. He saw the X-bus transport on the side of the road, not sure of its condition. What he didn't see were Taliban bullet holes in the side.

Focused on the flight line, Smalley raced ahead in the Toyota. He approached an S-curve before reaching the maintenance building. On the far side of the S-curve was a twelve-foot ditch. The truck was in terrible driving condition, and he was going over sixty MPH. Smalley took the turn way too fast and almost went into the ditch, scaring the crap out of himself. He collected himself up, cursing, and sped precariously on.

10

FROM FUELERS TO WARFIGHTERS

INITIAL MARINES' RESPONSE AT the fuel pits and surrounding area went from chaos to calculated.

As the Harrier blasts were kicking off, MWSS-373 Marines were doing regular business. SSgts O'Connor, Thomas, and Nicolae, and Sgts Mautz, Monroe, and Rihn were at the west fuel farm when the first rockets struck twenty feet from their position. SSgt O'Connor assisted in moving Marines to the east face of the fuels compound to set up forward defensive positions near the Fleet Readiness Building, a.k.a. fuels building. SSgt Thomas alerted all Marines an attack was occurring and organized security for fifteen TCN civilians and three contractors who worked at the fuels compound. Enemy contact kept repeating from the east. Thomas ensured the Fuels Marines were gathering weapons and donning flak jackets and Kevlar at the fuels building before sending them to defensive positions on the eastern side of the fuels compound.

Rifle fire snapped around SSgt Nicolae as he headed to the east side of the fuels compound, eliminating any doubt that an attack was in motion. Nicolae and O'Connor began to organize defensive positions with the Fuels Marines in their area to repel the rapid-repeating small arms while trying to identify its source. While under enemy fire, Nicolae continued to place Marines in key positions around the east side of the fuels compound. Marines began to open fire on the hidden Taliban plaguing them.

Lance Corporal Bustos was on the west side of the fuels compound when it was hit by small arms fire and RPGs. He saw the fuel bags catch on fire. He was ordered to take up a position defending civilian workers that SSgt Thomas was vigorously trying to keep alive.

Thomas's thoughts were racing. Only the buildings near the fuel pits had T-walls and concertina wire on top. The rest was open space in front of the fuels building (facing east where the enemy fire seemed to be originating from). The fuel bags in the fuel pits had dirt berms surrounding them, so they sat at a lower elevation. An enemy with rockets positioned east at a higher elevation across the X-bus road, had a direct line of sight to shoot into the fuel bags, or the buildings closest to the road, or the fuels compound south of the Clamshell. The Clamshell was an open hangar serving as a holding area for shipping boxes and other stuff. Thomas told the TCNS and contractors to go to the back of the fuels building and stay behind the protective HESCO barriers located there. HESCOs are military fortifications made of a collapsible wire mesh container and heavy-duty fabric liner that are filled with sand or dirt and used as a blast wall against explosions or small arms. The gears of battle were clicking in motion across the fuel farm.

This was far from the typical call for Fuels Marines, whose job was to support aircraft on the airfield and all things associated with that. While mobilizing defensive positions around the fuels building, the Marines continued to be targeted by enemy small arms fire. It was hard to see people in the darkness. Except for tracer fire, Fuels Marines didn't know the enemy numbers they were up against. It could have been one or two or a hundred and two, as they fired back in the direction the bullets were coming from.

East of the X-bus road at the bulk fuel installation, a hose ran underground from a staggering three million gallons of massive fuel storage to pop out at the fueling ramp on the west side of the fuel farm. Also parked near there were the 970 trucks used to move fuel out to the aircraft lined up to take off. If the Taliban knew about the BFI and planned to hit it, Camp Bastion would suffer a magnitude crippling blow.

•••

Killebrew and Hensley immediately hooked up with both West and East Coast Marines who were beginning to shelter at the fuels building. Killebrew ran inside and gained initial accountability of MWSS-373 Marines. Not all had gathered yet. The only comfort was that Killebrew knew fuelers were more than people who kept aircraft flying in daily operations; they were capable warfighters.

He could not find that same comfort about the unarmed TCNs mixed in with the Fuels Marines, or private contractors recruited to do basic airfield jobs that freed Marines to focus on training, readiness, and fighting.

Private contractor DynCorp was hired for this deployment. Yet if a pilot was asked, he'd say he preferred their own Marines to fuel their aircraft. These men were more vested in the outcome of air operations. DynCorp trained TCNs to do one job—to run the 970 fuel trucks out and fuel aircraft. It was just a hodgepodge of people working there. Killebrew thought most of them came from Africa. TCNs weren't vetted by the USMC or the government, who trusted DynCorp to send in the right people, who would not amount to any threat.

Then, all that mattered was keeping everyone alive. Killebrew saw TCNs his Marines had brought to the safety of the fuels building, sitting together crying. That is not something a trained warrior with years of experience in battle zones is used to.

A wounded Brit approached the fuels building. He had an injured shoulder but was still lucid and walking, able to talk. Killebrew wasn't sure where he got hit. Someone yelled, "Medic!"

"You take care of this guy. I'll walk the medic out here," Killebrew said to a Marine.

Killebrew walked the Brit Corpsman that had come with him in the ambulance to the wounded Brit.

"Hey, we need to get him outta here," he told the Brit corpsman, wondering when the bullets would hit them.

"Do you want to go to the hospital?" he asked the wounded Brit.

"Yeah," the Brit answered with surety.

Killebrew picked up one side, and the Brit corpsman picked up the other, assisted by Sgt Rihn, the only female sergeant in Killebrew's unit, who ran out to help move the guy. Rihn had flown the American flag at the fuels building earlier that day. The team had to carry the wounded Brit close to the fuel bag on fire to reach the ambulance the Brits left. They loaded the wounded soldier, and the ambulance took off.

Another Brit was lying on the ground, his hands over his face, and Killebrew thought the worst. He asked a British soldier standing nearby, "Is he dead?"

"I don't know," the British soldier replied.

"Are you alright?" Killebrew asked of the Brit on the ground. He pushed him to see if there was a response.

"I'm fine," said the Brit.

"Whatta you doin'?" asked Killebrew. The Brit didn't have a weapon.

"I don't know," he said as if in a daze, not in charge of himself.

"How 'bout you get up and you move over here," said Killebrew impatiently, pointing to some HESCO barriers near the fuels building. The Brit did not move.

"Now," Killebrew shouted, getting the Brit to move out. They were sitting ducks in the open, taking fire from who knew how many attackers.

Something eerie and hair-raising was also happening at the Harrier flight line, but Killebrew and Hensley did not know what. They saw big, fiery explosions, thinking they were coming from

HMLA-469, LtCol Lightfoot's squadron, only about a half-mile away from their position. The sound of an M-240 pierced their ears. It was hard to tell exactly, but Killebrew thought, *It came from HMLA's T-walls.*

Though no stranger to indirect fire and mortars in Iraq, Killebrew had not experienced direct fire from combatants up close. *Remain calm* was Killebrew's thought process. *Do your job.* He knew if he were calm, his Marines would be calm. If he were erratic, his Marines wouldn't trust him. He could trust them to do the right thing as hell broke loose without having to babysit.

• • •

Fuels Marine Sgt Klapperich, Cpl Turk, and Cpl Hidgeons were walking back from the entrance of the BFI Motor Pool when they saw RPGs and small arms fire directed at the fuels compound. They started to run towards it, Klapperich taking up a defensive position at the front. He saw Taliban RPG strikes on the fuel pits, starting a fire. Once the 50,000-gallon fuel bags were hit, the fire soon became uncontrollable, forcing anyone in the vicinity to move.

Corporal Byrnes and a civilian worker were headed towards the motor pool on the east side of the X-bus road also saw and heard it, then turned and ran back to the west side of the fuels compound and put the contractor in a protective HESCO bunker at the fuels building. Then, doubling back to the east, he stood to defend, seeing two insurgents running toward them. Byrnes fired in their direction. A stirred ant hill described the chaos as Marines came in and converged at the fuels building to get in position to strike back with strength in numbers.

The searing hot flames of jet fuel erupted into the sky, like a dormant volcano waking up. No one on the ground west of the X-bus road knew what Marines were doing east of the X-bus road as the enemy fired bullets and rockets in all directions.

Corporal Stillman was working inside the fuels testing lab, located north of the fuels building and west of the X-bus road, near the fuel pits. While recirculating fuel in a 50,000-gallon bag, Stillman felt the shock of rocket explosions and repeating rifle fire reverberating loudly, breaking the silence of the night. LCpls King and Wallace were also there testing fuel, along with civilians, who looked to him for an explanation.

All he really knew was that anyone in the fuel testing lab was at risk of burning up or getting shot. King and Wallace immediately left. King headed to the west side of the fuels compound to take a position protecting civilian workers. Wallace took up a position on the east while bullets zipped around them all.

Stillman saw a civilian worker in the open at the fuel pump and began to run towards him, when an RPG landed twenty meters from them, throwing both he and the civilian into a concrete T-wall. Sgt Rihn, who saw what happened, gave medical aid to Stillman, who miraculously did not sustain any major injuries. Stillman followed orders from SSgt Thomas to go and watch over the civilian workers at the fuels building.

The far left fuel bag arched up in hundred-foot flames, and fire engulfed some of the large fire extinguisher bottles that held HALON and PKP and were on wheels. Halon, a liquefied, compressed gas, stops the spread of fire by chemically disrupting combustion. Potassium bicarbonate (PKP) is a dry chemical principally used as a fire-fighting agent for flammable liquid fires. PKP extinguishes the flame by breaking the combustion chain. Because of its excellent firefighting effectiveness, PKP was widely used where the fire risk is high.

The Fuels Marines who were so scattered had formed a human shield around the civilians and contractors, and established firing positions while under enemy fire. No one had to ask twice. The Taliban bullets and rockets kept coming, seemingly unstoppable.

● ● ●

A group of five heavily armed Taliban fighters wearing stolen U.S. Army uniforms had planned for a lot of fighting, having a rich supply of RPGs and ammunition. They thought they could distract 3rd MAW Marines by setting the airfield on fire to kill Marines they encountered. The blood-thirsty marauders had already hit the Harriers with force, but seeing Marines fall under their fire was the real coup. Why stop at Harriers? The CH-53s and MV-22 Ospreys sat on flight lines a little further south. Unfortunately for them, HMLA-469 helicopters stood between the Harriers and their next aircraft targets. That was no small barrier.

The Taliban, in their rudimentary training in the months preceding the attack, miscalculated not only the airfield structures and geography of their battlefield, but also their range of movement, as well the fact that the Marines would be waiting, armed, and ready once the reality of the insider attack clicked in.

11

COMING FACE–TO–FACE WITH TERROR

SERGEANT MIKE DOMAN, SGT Jammie Hawkins, Sgt Shanks, and Sgt Gonzales heard the Harrier explosions when they were eating at a makeshift tented gym located directly west behind the fuels building. The explosions startled Hawkins and Doman, and like others who heard it across the airfield, thought it was a controlled det. Unsure, they immediately headed to the fuels building and the T-walls. Although dressed in PT gear, both Doman and Hawkins had their M-4 rifles with them.

Doman took a position on the east side of the fuels building (between two rows of T-walls) covering a vital flank, with Hawkins several feet south of him. West of Doman and Hawkins behind the last T-wall, Gonzales joined Nicolae, already at the front of the fuels compound fending off enemy small arms and RPG fires. Gonzales saw IDF hit the fuels testing lab, and it exploded into flames. Marines, TCNs, and civilian contractors already gathered at the fuels building (south of the lab) felt the energy and the heat. They prepared to evacuate even further away from the encroaching enemy and jet fuel fire inferno.

Shanks left his forward defensive position to assess damage from RPG IDF impacts on fuels equipment. Seeing a fire break out, he sprinted to get the Twin-Agent Unit (TAU) to extinguish it. The TAU combined dry chemicals for rapid flame knockout with aqueous film-forming foam that secured the fire area. When enemy small arms fire hit the TAU fully-contained unit, he ran back to his east defensive position. He would be no good to fight fires dead. The Fuels Marines were taking charge to help ARFF Marines extinguish the fires, yet they had not reached that moment yet because the enemy was effectively suppressing the movement. Then, moving to a defensive position further south of the fuels compound, Shanks saw two insurgents in the open but was unable to engage due to friendly forces moving towards the enemy position.

•••

Doman and Hawkins stiffened suddenly upon seeing five uniden-tifiable individuals about fifteen feet in front of them. They could see they had beards, wore white tennis shoes, and one had an RPG launcher. The Taliban invaders were pretty quiet; no one was talking. Their position at the T-walls was about fifty yards from the fuel pit holding 300,000 gallons of aircraft fuel. The not-so-stealth enemy group had crossed the X-bus road traveling from east to west and were standing unafraid in the open. They obviously knew where the fuel bags were—heading in that direction to create major chaos, shooting anyone that stood in their way.

"Identify yourselves!" yelled Doman, with Hawkins ready to fire next to him.

The insurgents did not answer. As the two Marines struggled to see in the pitch black, three of the insurgents came into view, and Doman could see they were wearing Army fatigues. The imposters in their midst sent a chill through the two sergeants.

When an RPG flew over the T-wall and hit one of six 50,000-gallon fuel bags set down in a pit, the direct hit caused it to burst into flames. This threatened the Marines, TCNs, and contractors gathering at the fuels building for protection. Doman warned Hawkins to hold back his rifle, "Wait, the X-bus is coming."

He had eyes on the X-bus, an enclosed transport van with windows, driving from north to south, making its normal scheduled rounds, seemingly oblivious to the danger. Any wrong move from them could hurt whoever was driving that bus. The insurgents suddenly directed rifle fire towards the bus, wounding the Macedonian driver in the arm. The X-bus limped along about a hundred yards before coming to a stop. The window was shot out of the back, bullet holes peppered the cab, the tires were blown out, and fluids were leaking. The VMM-161 Osprey squadron was alerted by this attack.

Sgt Doman and Sgt Hawkins fire on Taliban attackers approaching the fuel pits and fuels compound. (Combat art by Sean Sullivan)

Both Doman and Hawkins fired on the insurgents. Hawkins went ballistic, vigorously unloading his M4 on the attackers. Sgt Mautz, also near, fired on them. Hawkins hit two, and they fell to the ground, lifeless, and were presumed dead. SSgt O'Connor witnessed the Fuels Marines engaging the Taliban, but could not follow in the darkness, where the other three insurgents moved to, one wounded. As they ran out of view to scatter, the enemy insurgents returned fire.

The area around the fuel pits began to catch fire, taking out a second fuel bag and gym tent, which stored a lot of gear the Marines used when they worked out. The threats of Marines getting injured or killed remained high in the billowing smoke from the fires.

Hawkins told the rest of the Marines that the enemy was inside the Bastion defenses and they should engage them as soon as they had positive identification, noting he saw them in U.S. Army digital uniforms and that they were well-armed. No one really knew who knew what the night would bring, but they were taking charge. The lethal situation was changing rapidly. What was threatening one moment could move and change the next. Word-of-mouth communications floated around on all parts of the fuels compound—everyone striving to keep each other alive.

One hundred feet west of Hawkins's position, firefighting equipment between the fuels building and the fuel berms began to burn out of control. Multiple explosions kicked off like fireworks as the fuel pumps and hoses were consumed in the inferno. The fire threatened the fuel ramp, between the fuel pits and the VMM-161 flight line.

Sgt Bradley Atwell, part of the Intermediate Maintenance Activity (IMA) with Marine Aviation Logistics Squadron-16 (Forward), known as MALS-16, had just finished a quick recon outside of his shop and ran back to alert other avionics personnel that the base was under attack.

"Get your weapons and go to condition one," Atwell yelled to the Marines around him.

He grabbed his helmet and flak jacket and started running north to the sounds of gunfire when he was killed by a piece of shrapnel from an RPG as he passed by the V-22 flight line. MALS and VMM-161 Marines were now in the mix, and the MALS building would soon become the next "bastion" for defense.

Shortly after RPGs hit the fuel bags and began to spread, Killebrew's ARFF Marines, Sgt Bently, Cpl Yeomans, and LCpls Budgen, Phelps, Williams, and Coca responded to the fire at the fuel ramp and began to receive rifle fire from the south through the actual smoke and

YUMA, Arizona. September, 2012. Sgt Bradley Atwell. (DVIDS photo by Cpl Sean Dennison)

fire. The LCpls immediately took up defensive positions around the firefighting vehicles, positioning themselves to return fire. It was doubly dangerous as they could not get a positive identification of the enemy veiled by flames and smoke. A lot of scattered chess pieces were on the board and moving.

Williams provided security for both fellow Marines and British firefighters trying to tame the hungry fire as they were exposed as targets, like in a carnival shooting gallery, for the Taliban to pick off. But the Taliban weren't good shooters.

Bentley dropped his firefighting gear and picked up a rifle, moving towards the Clamshell. He oriented security to the east with both Budgen and Coca, who'd migrated there with him. Bentley saw two RPGs fly from the east over his head.

Yeomans and Phelps saw a British soldier get wounded in the arm and heard the call for a medic by a British soldier south of their position. They remained in position covering their sector of fire.

•••

Looking for his ARFF Marines, Killebrew saw both American and British firefighters pinned down, hesitant to move. The counter response had to quickly evolve from scattered to consolidated. Before the response could fully congeal, Marines were taking care of business as best they could.

Fuels and ARFF Marines fighting at the fuel pits could not pinpoint every possible Taliban location. Comms with the CJOC did not exist at this point. Comms were not yet up with anyone, even beyond the fuelers' fighting positions. Killebrew was unaware that Hawkins and Doman had seen the first group of Taliban and engaged. The Marines' gunfight stopped the Taliban group of five from advancing unrestricted and culled their numbers by two at least. Doman and Hawkins were able to ascertain from which general direction the Taliban group had come.

CAMP BASTION, Afghanistan. September 14, 2012. Aircraft Rescue and Firefighting Marines fight the fuel pit fires during the insurgent attack on Camp Bastion flight line. (DVIDS photo)

Killebrew's eyes zoned in on his Marines' hasty defense and yelled at them to get away from their firefighting vehicles.

Killebrew told Hensley, "We need a Marine Corps officer with the British to do the firefighting. I'm going to stay with Fuels."

He switched his pistol with Hensley's rifle. Killebrew had given out his own M-16 magazines, because guys during the Relief in Place (RIP) had only the initial set of rounds. Ammo was lean. Killebrew asked MSgt Parker, MWSS-273 Fuels Senior Non-Commissioned Officer in Charge (SNCOIC), "What's the chance of this blowin' up? What's the chance?"

"Probably won't blow up," replied Parker.

Probably, that's not good enough, Killebrew argued in his head, *This bag went up, that bag went up. Bag number three started to go up. That's 150,000 gallons of fuel.*

•••

A Brit Killebrew thought was with a QRF was talking on a radio and wouldn't get out of his way as he began to form a defensive circle on the fuel ramp. Some Brits thought they were in charge, and that irritated him. These Marines were Killebrew's responsibility, and he knew their specific training dictated their actions. Beyond that, individual critical thinking, gut sense, and courage, as well as knowing how to use a rifle, would empower them.

Killebrew pulled his firefighters into an elongated 360-degree position. Sporadic fire still came in from an undetermined direction, but it was nonetheless deadly if it made contact. Killebrew and Hensley went through the Clamshell and gathered up the remaining ARFF, including Bentley, Budgen, and Coca, and placed them in the 360-degree circle. Killebrew reminded his Marines of the ROEs. They had to acquire positive identification (PID).

"Don't fire, because nobody knows where anyone is . . . we're worried about shooting our own people," ordered Killebrew, in charge.

Killebrew and his Marines could not see much ahead. East Coast ARFF personnel showed up at the fuel ramp. MSgt Craft, who worked for Hensley and GySgt Stone (a Senior NCO), who worked for Killebrew, drove up in a white vehicle. Killebrew rapidly processed what to do with the blinding fuel fire roaring, spiking, and spewing toxic smoke before his eyes. They couldn't get to it because they were pinned down by the attacking Taliban.

An argument erupted with a Brit who wasn't being calm. Everyone was amped and didn't need a reason to do something knee-jerk, like shoot a friendly. Killebrew reasoned with the Brit about how your actions affect people around you in high-octane combative situations.

"Hey, be calm. Look at what you're shooting. Look at what's behind your target, because people are running all over the place," said Killebrew to the ARFF Marines.

Personnel from 3rd MAW were in undisclosed locations all over the base. The enemy could be everywhere, too. There was no Predator drone view they could access, no control other than what Killebrew was trying to establish on the ground in the mayhem. He reiterated, "Make sure you know what you're shooting at before you fire."

Communications were starting to flow from the flight lines to command headquarters, but Killebrew's Marines were still isolated. ARFF usually had comms with the airfield tower when they were working on the airfield, but he didn't know if anyone was in the tower at the time.

It was very hot. The fire created its own climate, and the wind pushed the smoke in different directions. A decision on what to do next had to be made.

Marines were exposed on the fuel ramp to enemy fire and a hot inferno thirty-five to forty feet north of them at the fuel pits—the sound deafening as the fire gulped in delicious jet fuel. There was nothing to hide behind.

The British sent a runner to call the firefighters back to the firehouse with the intent to keep them there until the enemy was destroyed at the fuels compound. The Brits believed battling the jet fuel fire was unobtainable. Killebrew, Hensley, and Craft argued otherwise. Although the Brits were good firefighters, they were not trained or required to be proficient with a rifle. British higher-ups were worried about the manpower needed to fight other, more containable fires, like the Harriers.

Killebrew told his ARFF guys to follow the Brits, too, because they had to unify their efforts in firefighting. Killebrew knew they couldn't stay there and still have all the firefighting assets to do what they needed to do on the entire airfield.

Hensley and both Brit and Marine ARFF firefighters reluctantly fell back with their P19 firetrucks and gear. Killebrew's ARFF Marines promised to break off from the British and "come back to fight the fires." That's where they wanted to be more than ever.

All Killebrew's Marines felt like, "It's ownership. That's our real estate . . . and we're not going to get knocked off our place." The truth was they were comfortable being Marines in a very dangerous situation. The fight came naturally, despite its surprise nature. The fuel bags continued to burn.

Killebrew and Nicolae moved towards a British QRF in front of the fuels building close to the X-bus road. They quickly gave the Brits a status report on the fuel pits fire to their rear. Then, they returned to the group gathered at the fuels building, growing more and more at risk. Two hours had passed, and now Killebrew sat on top of a fuel keg with a handful of Fuels Marines and the group of frightened TCNs, holed up. He was formulating a plan on the go to get them to safety.

• • •

It was critical the men kept their heads about them and worked together. MWSS-373 Marines were determined to hold the front of the fuels compound, telling Killebrew in unity, "No, we're not going to let this thing go."

The avowed attackers didn't care what or who they hit—they just wanted to annihilate.

•••

The insurgent hate had been evolving since the first U.S. boot touched ground in Afghanistan. Retaliation goes both ways. The U.S. had a lot of 9/11 retaliation to do. The last thing on the Taliban attackers' minds were the families of 3rd MAW Marines back at home, unknowing of what their loved ones were experiencing. Those Marines still in the country faced an even greater threat of being killed or injured due to the massive drawdown. Relying on local Afghan forces to do the same counterinsurgency, antiterrorism jobs the Marines did with every ounce of their will and might was a political pipe dream. A dream that turned into a nightmare; you cannot replicate Marines.

By 2010, then-President Barack Obama had built up U.S. military presence to 100,000 in Afghanistan. In 2011, he announced his plan to withdraw troops with scant regard for Afghanistan's security—an opposite turn of his former 2008 promise to beat the Taliban.

Foreign Policy reported in March 2016, that while on the campaign trail in 2008, Obama said, "As president, I will make the fight against al-Qaeda and the Taliban the top priority that it should be. This is a war that we have to win."[46]

---

46 Miller, Paul D., "Setting the Record Straight on Obama's Afghanistan Promises," *Foreign Policy*, March 26, 2016, https://foreignpolicy.com/2016/03/29/setting-the-record-straight-on-obamas-afghanistan-promises/.

In that Foreign Policy report, Paul D. Miller, former Whitehouse staffer and academic under presidents George W. Bush and Barack Obama, said:

"Obama did not enter office bent on getting out of Afghanistan. He entered office bent on winning in Afghanistan. Those are different things. You can get out of a war anytime you like, so long as you don't care what happens afterwards and are not fighting for anything terribly important. But Obama clearly and repeatedly said he cared, and said he believed that war was vitally important, which is why he wanted to *win* it, not *end* it."

Yet, removing deterrence creates a power vacuum that a determined enemy will fill. In a June 22, 2011, drawdown speech from the White House, Obama drastically changed his former plans, now saying that Afghanistan was no longer a "terrorist threat to the United States," and declaring, "The tide of war is receding."

Even though the greater war in Afghanistan had not been won, no one had spelled out specifically what winning looked like. Obama or at least his advisors must have known the Afghan National Security Forces (ANSF), made up of the Afghan National Army (ANA), Afghan National Police (ANP), Afghan Air Force (AAF), and Afghan Specialty Security Forces (ASSF), were not ready to take on the Taliban and al-Qaeda allies themselves. The lack of readiness was, in part, an Afghan government problem due to a lack of support for their troops, and some top U.S. military leaders serving in Afghanistan knew this.

In that same drawdown speech in 2011, Obama announced that 10,000 troops would be withdrawn by the end of 2011 and an additional 23,000 troops will leave the country by the summer of 2012. He said the drawdown would continue at a steady pace until the United States handed over security to the Afghan authorities in 2014. "We are starting this drawdown from a position of strength. Al-Qaeda is under more pressure than at any time since 9/11."

In 2011, Obama stated that by 2014, "The Afghan people will be responsible for their own security."[47] Ready or not. Without pressure from U.S. involvement—al Qaeda and the Taliban would only strengthen. Seven months after Obama's announcement, *Reuters* reported on February 2, 2012, ". . . excerpts of a classified U.S. report [said] that the Taliban, backed by Pakistan, remained confident of regaining control in Afghanistan despite a decade of NATO efforts."[48]

Later, in 2017, a top military leader still serving in Afghanistan laid out the nature of the enemy we were still fighting. General John W. Nicholson Jr, former commander of Resolute Support and U.S. Forces in Afghanistan, said in a Dept. of Defense press briefing Nov 28, 2017, "First, the Taliban is not a popular insurgency. The Afghan people outright reject them. Up to 90 percent believe that a return to Taliban rule would be bad for the country.

"And notice that I didn't use the word 'govern.' The Taliban do not govern, they rule through force. They impose their rule on the people. And, increasingly, they are primarily interested in making money. And they are making more money than they need to operate.

"So we believe that the Taliban, in some ways, have evolved into a criminal or narco-insurgency. They are fighting to defend their revenue streams. They have increasingly lost whatever ideological anchor they once had. They fight to preserve and expand their sources of revenue. This includes narcotics trafficking, illegal mining, taxing people throughout Afghanistan, kidnapping and murder-for-hire: all criminal endeavors."[49]

47 Office of the Press Secretary, "Remarks by the President on the Way Forward in Afghanistan," The White House, June 22, 2011, https://obamawhitehouse.archives.gov/the-press-office/2011/06/22/remarks-president-way-forward-Afghanistan.

48 Alexander, David, Brunnstrom, David, "U.S. tries to ease confusion over Afghan plans," *Reuters*, February 2, 2012, https://www.reuters.com/article/us-afghanistan/talibanvows-to-retake-afghanistan-reportidUSTRE8100E520120201.

49 General Nicholson, John W. Jr., "Department of Defense Press Briefing by General Nicholson via teleconference from Kabul, Afghanistan," U.S. Department of Defense, Nov. 28, 2017, https://www.defense.gov/News/Transcripts/Transcript/Article/1382901/department-of-defense-press-briefing-by-general-nicholson-via-teleconference-fr/.

What had taken eleven years to build and achieve in terms of security presence, deterrence, and counterterrorism training for local Afghan military and police forces was quickly dissolving in 2012. Insurgent fighters who had survived U.S. counterstrikes were in for as long as it took to fill the power vacuum when the U.S. withdrew their forces.

Killing Marines could exalt insurgent status to martyrdom and paradise. Martyrdom jumped up the morale of fighters left behind. Dying, to them, didn't mean much, at least on the surface.

12

SAVING GRACE AND BASTION

SMALL ARMS FIRE AND RPGs kept Fuels Marines on the move. Killebrew had to imagine what the VMA and HMLA side of the airfield was experiencing based on what he could make out in the darkness or hear. He ordered Nicolae to go to MALS and give the status report to MWSS-273 Air Ground Special Operations Command (AGSOC), located further west of the towering inferno. Killebrew needed to know the enemy engagement status.

His Marines took charge of security without him, continuing to migrate south with the civilians, away from the fuel fire, to a T-walled MALS building at the VMM-161 compound to set up defensive positions as the surrounding area remained under fire. Another Taliban group of five positioned east near the cryo lab was likely trying to cross the X-bus road and made no haste to add to the lethal melee going on in the fuels compound. SSgt O'Connor moved through the fuels compound area to make sure all Marines were accounted for and no one was left behind. It was not easy to tell in the dark of night, filled with smoke and particles of burning fuels equipment.

•••

An American contractor informed Sgt Gonzales that another contractor named Grace was still at the fuels building area they had just abandoned. Gonzales and Sgt Hanky (from MWSS-273) and a few others volunteered to go back to find her. They moved under fire, Gonzales covering.

On the way, they saw Grace lying next to a modular international shipping container (ISO). Gonzales picked Grace up off the ground and sandwiched her between them, using their bodies as shields until they returned the contractor to the safety of T-walls at the MALS building.

Grace reported the possibility of TCN casualties at the fuel farm. Sgt Starleigh and Sgt Camacho (ARFF-273) and Klapperich and Wallace (Fuels-373) volunteered to advance back to the fuels compound to search for them. En route, they received enemy fire while clearing ISO shipping containers, searching for wounded TCNs, just south of the Clamshell.

A Taliban attacker was hiding behind two aluminum boxes, about fifteen feet away. The attacker pointed his weapon at the four Marines who fired their M4s at him. The attacker returned fire and then ducked behind the aluminum boxes, the enemy's rounds impacting within one foot of their positions.

The Marines fell back while continuing to fire into the aluminum boxes, killing the insurgent in the process of throwing a grenade. They saw the explosion behind the aluminum boxes and then returned to the MALS T-walls to discover the TCNs had been diligently recovered intact. Yet, if they had not had the balls to reconnoiter in search of the TCNs, there would still be one more insurgent trying to take them down. Instead, he lay in pieces, tricked by the lies some paradise awaited for those who murder in the name of a twisted religious dogma.

∙∙∙

Killebrew walked from place to place throughout the fuels compound, calming and clarifying the situation with his men as they mobilized defenses and found himself starkly alone. He had to move past the shipping containers, not certain of all actions taking place. Although he couldn't get to everyone to get a report, he was doing his best to be a messenger. He was carrying Hensley's rifle, because his was at the armory. The fuel bags on fire poisoned the air at the shipping containers. Breathing sucked.

He moved cautiously through the boxes, row by row. Body parts of the attacker who had blown himself up were everywhere, making him cringe. Sights and smells were surreal, but he had no time to dwell on it.

•••

The quickly moving fuel fire threatened everyone and everything in the vicinity. MSgt Parker ordered Hawkins to move all Marines, TCNs, and contractors to the MALS building, located 150 feet to the south (directly adjacent to the fuel ramp). It didn't matter if you were East Coast or West Coast Marines who had responded to the attack in progress, a whole new defense of that building was quickly set in motion. Doman and Nicolae remained behind despite the danger of massive fuel explosions in order to provide covering fire while they transited.

CAMP BASTION, Afghanistan. 2012. Sgt Michael Doman. (Photo courtesy of Sgt Michael Doman)

Killebrew's Marines could then join forces with MALS Marines setting up defensive positions to protect each other as well as the MV-22 and CH-53 squadron flight lines. There was no shortage of bravery, of duty, of intensity to stop the enemy in their tracks. This was a moment in time like no other where the Marine inside each person would dictate the outcome of a shocking assault they were turning to their advantage.

Doman and Hawkins took up a defensive position east of the MALS building—where the enemy would be most likely to approach from.

Seeing no other activity in the shipping boxes, Killebrew investigated the fuel ramp to check for any remaining Marines, then headed to the MALS building to connect with his Fuels Marines once again. The vibe there was tense; people were in disarray. MSgt Parker was there trying to pull it all together, managing Marines, TCNs, and civilians. With everyone now relocated to a safer area—could they take a breath? Not a chance.

•••

At the House of Commons evidence session,[50] Capewell held the floor of the Defense Committee, determined from his opening statements to vilify his U.S. allies, painting a picture that exonerated himself:

> "This operation is a coalition operation. It has a coalition chain of command, the ISAF chain of command. Those two American generals were commanders of RC Southwest, and commanders in RC Southwest at the time. The whole footprint of Bastion, therefore, in those terms, was their responsibility," states Capewell, veering away from documented truth, spelled out clearly in the 2011 MOU. "I absolutely accept that there were British officers

---

50 House of Commons Defence Committee, "Afghanistan—Camp Bastion Attack," *The Stationery Office*, April 16, 2014, Ev. 4, https://publications.parliament.uk/pa/cm201314/cmselect/cmdfence/830/830vw.pdf.

in that chain of command but none of those British officers were the direct commanders in the ISAF chain of command."

Capewell was wrong. The Brit commander in charge of logistics and Bastion Security did not report to U.S. MajGen Gurganus. Lt. Gen. Adrian Bradshaw (a Brit) was deputy commander to ISAF commander U.S. Gen John Allen. As he stood in the snare of a lie, Capewell did not flinch or twist nervously. The sound of Taliban rifles and RPGs inside the wire of a base that "had never been attacked" was in that evidence room, just not heard. The enemy threat was not written on Capewell's list—yet it was written in blood. That blood had his name on it for lying about the Brits not being responsible for the protection of all those using airfield.

• • •

September 2012, Camp Bastion

This was not the standard Taliban they were fighting. They were all equally outfitted. They had command and control, recounted Sturdevant after a long, exhausting night. Their advantage of surprise had been strengthened for months by the British lenient policies towards their next-door neighbors and trusting the local governors to do their own policing, akin to trusting a criminal to investigate his own crime. The Taliban were inside, and it didn't take long for Marines on all sides of the airfield to realize that. It was immediately evident to the brazen attackers that these Marines were not complacent warfighters—and, once ramped up, they were going to kill them. Leadership under fire was not to be underestimated as the night unfolded.

• • •

A sharp order brought about cohesion, dispelling doubt or confusion on what to do. One thing was clear: Marines dropped their wrenches and went for their rifles.

"What the fuck?" mumbled Smalley as he walked over to maintenance control in the back left corner of the VMA-211 maintenance building, and all the Marines were gathered.

"Hey guys, you do know the jets are on fire out there?" yelled Smalley.

"Yeah, but we need a—" popped off one of the Marines.

"Get some fucking tugs (tow tractors) and get them out there and save the good jets, so we can meet the fucking flight schedule. We've gotta go out there and do some firefighting," ordered Smalley.

"They're firing at us," said SSgt Calime.

"Yeah, I just said that—the jets are on fire."

"No! We are under ATTACK. The Taliban is on the flight line."

Smalley looked at his 9mm, thoughts spiraling. He went from shop to shop in the maintenance building, opened doors, and asked, "Hey, you got an extra rifle?"

In every shop, Marines were laid out on the floor, weapons pointed at the door. No one was giving up a rifle. He went back to maintenance control and found a civilian contractor, Dan Day, on the phone.

"Oh man! That's not good. Okay, hold on . . . here's Capt Smalley," said Day and handed the phone to him.

An anxious female intel clerk was on the other end of the line at VMA-211 headquarters about a hundred meters north: "I'm all by myself over here; someone just pulled on the door. I don't know what's going on. I'm really scared. I need somebody to come over here," she pleaded.

"Okay, I'm on my way," assured Smalley.

Both VMA headquarters and the maintenance shops were less than a hundred meters from the Harrier jets ablaze due to Taliban arsonists rolling grenades like a bocce ball under them. Each thirty million-dollar aircraft was melting down into twisted metal heaps.

Lance Corporals Jenkins and Weekly heard the distress in the intel clerk's voice. As Smalley hung up the phone, he exchanged looks with the two Marines, "We're going with you," they said.

"Okay, we need two more," added Smalley.

Smalley went back to the Avionics shop and opened the door.

"I need two of you," said Smalley, pointing to Cpls Wang and Smith. "You guys are coming with me."

They went outside the building and headed to where Smalley had parked the truck, away from the flight line.

"Alright, here's the deal, guys. We have an isolated Marine over there, pointing to headquarters."

"We need to move from here to there, and we don't know where the Taliban is. So, we're going to bound from ditch to ditch to get close to that building," and in the same breath, adds, "We're going to get up behind that twenty-foot container. We'll go in pairs as we do this."

Smalley's orders were easily understood. In fact, they were standard infantry tactics taught to all Marines.

"Roger that, sir," they responded.

The five of them started running from ditches that ran north/south along the flight line. Smalley got close enough to the enemy to hear Afghan music blasting from some portable device. Smoke was everywhere. They finally reached the twenty-foot container close to the headquarters building.

Smith peered around a corner cautiously, "Hey, I think I see one of them over there."

The plan was not to be seen. They had to maintain the element of surprise.

"Next time he pops his head out, shoot him," ordered Smalley.

Bam! Bam! Smith fired at the Taliban attacker right away. They thought they had solved the problem. Then they heard enemy rounds impacting the steel container, but they stopped after Smith put a couple more of his rounds toward the attacker. Unbeknownst to the Marines in contact was that the Taliban insurgent was still alive, though badly wounded.

They ran up to headquarters, Smalley clutching his 9mm. Two of the Marines with rifles stepped up to go first, rounding a corner, and saw nothing there.

The headquarters building had three doors. The main hallway was like an upside down backwards F. At the top of the F, two doors faced the flight line, and one faced north. One of those top doors was a double, and assuredly the fastest way to the ready room. Nobody ever used the door at the middle part of the F, but Smalley knew the combo being the logistics officer and had recently changed the combination. The far north door was the CO's entrance.

There was no clear avenue of fire to the middle door. Smalley dashed to it, slung it open, and shouted, "Marines, coming in!"

Down the hallway, he could see the intel clerk and two armory Marines who were supposed to be at the ready room. He repeated loudly, "Hey, we're coming in!"

He confronted the armory guys, "Where the fuck were you?"

"Well, we were out playing basketball—we're throwing it in the chute, and we saw some guys in camouflage and didn't know what was going on. Then they started shooting—like fuck! Then we ran away."

"Yeah, probably a good idea," answered Smalley,

Simultaneously, he assessed there were eight of them in the building. His fire team comprised of Smith, Wang, Jenkins, and Weekly. He didn't have any intel on how many of the enemy were out there setting fires and shooting the flight line, but calculated the situation. Seemingly, all his jets were on fire, so he assumed the Taliban were more than just a squad. He ordered the Marines to barricade headquarters doors. Smalley had them set up lanes of fire so they could cover all the entrances and exits, just in case.

He picked up the phone and called Tom McKay at the maintenance building, "I'm here. We've got everything secure. I'm going to start calling 'higher.'"

Smalley got on the line with SSgt Andrew Calime at maintenance control, who reported, "Oh, yeah, LtCol Raible and Maj Chambless have arrived, and they're engaging with the Marines right now."

•••

Prior to Raible's arrival:

A maintenance bay/hangar shack stood in the back corner of the VMA-211 Harrier flight line. Normally, during daily airfield operations, a couple of jets would be there for maintenance work or testing. The rest were parked on the flight line, ready to go. On the night of September 14, the Maintenance Marines were getting ready for a large flight sortie in the morning. They had a bunch of Joint Direct Attack Munitions (JDAMs) ready. The JDAM was a guidance kit that converted unguided bombs into all-weather precision-guidance munitions.

The Marines were finishing up with two Harrier jets. Around 2230, they were done with their checks. They were never done before midnight; it always took forever. There was always more stuff to do on the aircraft—to oil them, get the fluids right, etc. That night, it seemed like everything was in harmony, nearly perfect, so they went back into the hangar shack.

Once inside, the Maintenance Marines in the hangar shack heard TAT, TAT, TAT, and then dings like bullets hitting the building. They thought, *What the heck is going on?* Then they heard a very loud explosion. LCpl Asiatic Ealey was closest to the door, and he looked out. They all started to barricade the doors.

Mobilization happened quickly—everyone grabbed all the ammunition they could find. Sgt Jon Cudo, Cpl Matthew Eason and Ealey were positioned at the front; everyone had rifles pointing towards the door. A few minutes passed, and that seemed like an eternity.

13
CHARGING INTO THE FRAY

RAIBLE PUSHED INTO THE maintenance building. Somebody fired off a shot, and Raible yelled, "It's me, it's me."

Raible sought out his men to do an accountability check. *The Maintenance Marines were all fricking, fucking air-wingers*, thought Cudo. They were fondly referred to as personnel other than grunts (POGs). Cudo was pumped up by their commander, telling them to pick up their rifles and follow him, as flames from exploding jets licked the dark night sky.

"D'ya want to be Marines?" Raible thundered.

"Yessir!" the Marines responded.

"Well, get your fucking gun, and let's get the fuck outside," ordered their leader, a superhero in their eyes. Most importantly, he was someone they trusted and wanted to serve with their heart, might, and minds, no matter the uncertainty.

Raible assembled ten Marines with rifles to exit the maintenance building and move further towards the northernmost VMA-211 headquarters building, where it was possible one or more Marines had been isolated. They exited the maintenance building in two groups, Raible leading one group immediately north and Chambless leading the other group west to establish forward defensive positions. As soon as they stepped off, gunfire erupted.

None of the Maintenance Marines had any body armor. Ammo was in short supply because Marines normally carried only twenty-five rounds each, per USMC protocol.

Cudo was behind a little QuadCon (storage container) with Chambless' group, ready to fire. The Taliban were approximately twenty-five feet in front of them behind a concrete barrier. Raible, to the right of Cudo, was heard ordering his Marines in the counter-attack over the noise of six burning aircraft exploding and enemy small arms fire. SSgt Jesse Colburn stood next to Maj Chambless, who pointed and gave an okay sign, indicating he was firing in a specific direction. Colburn would fire the other way as they changed their fields of fire.

Maintenance Marines didn't train for this—while they had rifle skills, everything proceeded forward fluidly as if they had trained for it. Chambless continued to motion using hand signals, no yelling. An eerie calm permeated the chaos as if in the eye of a Category 5 hurricane. Cudo and Colburn covered Chambless' back.

• • •

Smalley next called 3rd MAW headquarters from VMA headquarters to talk to the fixed-wing tasker at the TACC, located on the other end of the 3rd MAW headquarters building that housed Sturdevant.

"Hey, what's going on, man," asked the fixed-wing tasker, a guy Smalley knew.

"We're under attack. I need some fucking help," blurted out Smalley. "Just send the QRF over here. Okay?"

"Oh, OH, okay, yeah."

One of Smalley's best friends, Capt Dave Caribardi, worked at the TACC on the day shift. Smalley had visited him there and knew the building and what they had going on. It was a miniature CAOC, located on the Bastion side of the sprawling complex, pretty far to the west. Smalley spent a lot of time talking to Dave, watching how he worked. The TACC had access to unmanned aerial systems (UAS) feeds for the area. Smalley wondered how he, firstly, got the feeds up and, secondly, was able to watch them from the TAAC.

Caribardi told him about a website offering links for each platform on the station throughout the area of operations or whatever he wanted to look at and keep watch. Smalley got on the networks from his position at VMA-211 headquarters. He brought up the Battle Command Display that was showing a stack of aircraft over the top of Camp Bastion.

Smalley called back to the TACC, "Hey, what's the UAS that's overhead right now? And what channel is it on? What MIRC chatroom is the base defense on?"

The fixed-wing tasker sent the link and the call sign of the MQ09 Reaper above. A UAS video downlink popped up on the screen, showing the Reaper feed over the airfield. From this, Smalley could identify positions and try to ascertain where the bad guys were located.

• • •

Raible headed back to the maintenance building to get more Marines and more ammo to continue to press the fight. He was going in the north door of the north wall when the enemy fired off a series of RPGs. Raible got hit with the brunt of that barrage. Cudo was struck with part of it, but he was shielded more than Raible. The shrapnel hit Raible in the neck, killing him instantly. There was blood everywhere. Shrapnel hit Cudo all alongside the back of his

Sgt Jon Cudo. (Photo courtesy of Sgt Jon Cudo)

skull area, and some on the face. Chambless dragged Cudo inside the building. Everything was in a haze as SSgt Calime quickly wrapped up Cudo's head.

Cudo was carried out to a vehicle to CASEVAC him to the hospital on the Leatherneck side, as Taliban fired on the vehicle and explosions pounded the eardrums in the smoke-filled air.

Raible's body was brought into the maintenance building and covered with a drape. Chambless took over, not knowing that Raible's next in line of command was fighting through the Taliban to get to them.

Chambless picked up when Smalley called back over to the maintenance building, "Hey, Six is dead."

"Who the hell is Six? What guy are you talking about?" asked Smalley.

"The CO man, he's dead!"

Smalley was gut-punched, stunned. He had just been on the phone with wing headquarters, asking where the QRF was. The wing reported, "They'd be here in five minutes," and Smalley relayed that to Chambless.

"We're going to pull our guys in, because we don't want any blue-on-blue," said Smalley.

"Okay," answered Chambless.

"Alright, the QRF's about to be here, so just hang out," said Smalley to the Marines following his lead.

The Marines at the VMA compound were pulled in no later than approximately 2300. The rationale was that the VMA-211 Marines did not have positive communication with the QRF, and the QRF would have been firing directly at the Marines as they advanced west to east across the airfield.

No one in the room had any idea what was immediately next. They couldn't risk fratricide if the QRF was on its way—yet the Taliban were out there moving. Time was not their friend; seconds, minutes counted. Smalley still had his pistol. How many Marines were still out there, no one knew. He had to trust they'd come in to mobilize, seeking out who was in charge.

Smalley was doing his best to contact whoever was in charge of TFBW security—that vague divided task assigned by the 2011 MOU. The British were not on site, although he knew there was a QRF for the base. What he didn't know was there was no QRF specifically assigned to the airfield. And he didn't know who knew how much danger they were in. He was only sure of what was happening in his sphere of battle, and that was plenty to deal with under hellish fire and explosions. The QRF did not show up, and Six was dead. The Marines at VMA-211 headquarters and the maintenance buildings were all alone, trying to process the grief of losing their CO, while anticipating the attackers' next move.

• • •

Months before the breach, a Taliban fighter stood in front of a camera and said, "Islam is not terrorism. Islam teaches the lesson of the brotherhood to us. We are not terrorists."

History said otherwise. On September 09, 2001, Ahmad Shah Massoud, commander of the Northern Alliance, an anti-Taliban coalition, was assassinated by al-Qaeda.

TOLO News reported, "Two suicide bombers posing as journalists set off an explosion in Khajwa Bahawuddin district of Takhar."[51]

Al Jazeera published a story in 2014 about the legendary Afghan freedom fighter, who was known as the Lion of the Panshir, a master of guerilla warfare. Of Tajik descent, he led the Mujahideen's fight against the Soviet occupation of Afghanistan, capturing Kabul in 1992. Ethnic and tribal fault lines divided the Mujahideen, and

---

51 Daryosh, Mohammad Farshad, "21st Anniversary Of Ahmad Shah Massoud's Assassination," *TOLO News*, September 9, 2022, https://tolonews.com/afghanistan-179776.

a civil war erupted. The children of Afghan refugees were trained in Pakistani *religious* schools and mushroomed into a force to be reckoned with and called themselves the Taliban. They were a "conglomerate of disenfranchised Pashtun tribal fighters who dreaded the fact that a non-Pashtun had taken control of the capital [Kabul]."

The newly formed Taliban became "the Trojan Horse of Pashtun nationalism, but in the name of Islam," and managed to capture most of Afghanistan "with the support of Pakistan, Saudi Arabia, and U.S. petroleum companies."[52]

Massoud's death dealt a heavy blow to the anti-Taliban resistance. The Taliban were complicit in bin Laden's protection while President Bush's justice for grievous attacks on American soil knocked on their door. There was a heavy cost to the Taliban alliance with al-Qaeda.

●●●

LtCol Raible and Sgt Bradley Atwell, once full of life and vigor, lay lifeless in the darkness, their futures snuffed out. These Taliban did not know these men. But it was a war zone, and the Taliban spared no one who opposed or tried to stop them. The Marines had remained in Afghanistan at the invitation of the Afghan government, which could not reign in the rebellious, unlawful insurgent violence by themselves. American troops were there following orders from their government to get out of Afghanistan, which would happen before the upcoming presidential election. For Obama, it was a re-election. Yet, there was still heavy fighting in the province, and ground troops needed air support.

The Taliban fighters videotaped a drawing on a whiteboard of the layout of the airfield as best they could. They also filmed the recruits cutting a fence wire. They got things wrong in their layout.

---

52 Moslih, Hashmat, "Afghanistan in the shadow of Ahmad Shah Massoud," *Aljazeera*, September 9, 2014, https://www.aljazeera.com/opinions/2014/9/9/afghanistan-in-the-shadow-of-ahmad-shah-massoud.

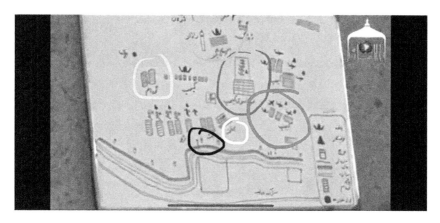

Insurgent Orientation. Taliban hand-drawn map of Camp Bastion airfield used in planning insider attack. (HMLA/VMA Camp Bastion Attack Presentation 2015)

That meant anything could happen once they were inside the wire, and the Marines were wide awake.

Fighting had been bred into tribal genes over centuries, and modern-day Middle East was still very tribal—especially in Afghanistan, bridging the Middle East and Central and South Asia.

Even Alexander the Great underestimated the people in what is now Afghanistan. He had conquered most of the world known to him in the fourth century BC. In 327 BC, he invaded Afghanistan and found a steel wall of resistance.

"May God keep you away from the venom of the cobra, the teeth of the tiger, and the revenge of the Afghans," Alexander the Great is quoted as saying.

In times when conquerors like Alexander the Great traveled through Bactria and Ariana (ancient Afghanistan), the native inhabitants of the land planted seeds of resistance that grew over millennia. Tribal warriors would go to any length, including sacrificing their lives, to expel them. The earliest mention of the term "Afghanistan" appeared in the thirteenth century. In the twenty-first century, Afghanistan would become a country known worldwide as one of the most violent places on earth.

●●●

McDonald, who had borrowed a flight suit and boots too small for him, could see the fuel fires, hear cook-offs from RPGs, and knew the night crew was working at VMA-211. There was a good possibility some people were wounded, and early response meant saving lives.

He asked a Marine nearby, "Where's Doc Winegar?"

"Oh, he's here," answered the Marine.

Casualty protocol surged through McDonald's thoughts. He assumed *there was no medical personnel at the explosion site.*

"I'm going up there," he told Maj Traylor, VMA-211's Material Maintenance Control officer. "I'm going to run for it and I think I can make it. You're the senior member of our squadron—you're in charge down here."

Assigning Traylor as acting CO of the Marines in place freed McDonald to check on the others up north.

"I'm going with you," said CWO Joe Ball, a good friend of McDonald, who replied, "Okay."

As they were leaving, ODO Abramovs (who Smalley had dropped off at the LSAs before the first explosion and later could not find him) said he wanted to accompany the group.

"Okay, but that's it. We've gotta move fast," cinched McDonald.

14

THE HUNTED BECOME THE HUNTERS

A USMC BASTION ATTACK Narrative Summary report on the battle continued:[53]

"Because of the twenty-four-hour contingency support required of the HMLA-469 squadron during Operation Enduring Freedom, multiple shifts were necessary in order to cover 24-hour flight operations. As a result, over half of the squadron's personnel were either still asleep or were finishing dinner in the chow hall when the Taliban made their first strikes. Many Marines in the LSA were awakened by the concussive blast of the first IDF impacts detonating to their north, but like many, believed them to be an unusually scheduled controlled detonation. When the explosions continued in frequency, and increased in intensity, most knew something was wrong. The first series of small arms fire occurred as the Marines, now fully awake, began milling outside of their LSA rooms, trying to determine the source and reason of the explosions.

---

53 "OEF Enemy Attack on Camp Bastion, 14 September 2012, NARRATIVE SUMMARY, HMLA 469" (Private source).

"Immediately, Marines rushed back into their rooms and began donning flak jackets and Kevlars, while simultaneously arming themselves with their personal weapons. Officers and SNCOs began directing their Marines to proceed to the IDF bunkers to the west and east of the LSA; posting four points of security at each bunker."

This was a variety of aviation Marines, none of them infantry, although some may have flown in combat zones.

"There was no information available, due to the lack of communication with any of the squadrons along the flight line, so everyone was preparing themselves for anything, and assuming the worst.

"What those at the LSA did know, was that an attack was in progress, and the fuel farm in the vicinity of the Rotary Wing Arrival/Departure Air Control Group (A/DACG) had been hit and was now engulfed in flames. Small arms could be heard snapping overhead, and it appeared all fires were originating from north of the LSA. With this small amount of available information, Maj Vasilios Pappas, HMLA 469's Executive Officer (XO), took command as the senior member at the LSA. Maj Pappas began assigning officers as compound commanders, while Maj Seth Wolcott, the Assistant Aviation Maintenance Officer (AAMO), began tasking groups of Marines to push out to establish security positions in the vicinity of the LSA-13 gymnasium located closest to the eastern fence line.

"Major Wolcott then ordered Capt William Oren, an experienced infantry officer, to take charge of post at the gym. Oren immediately identified an old HESCO position 150 meters north of the gym and led a team northward to establish a listening post/observation post (LP/OP). Oren was accompanied by Capt Andrew Berkeley (Director of Safety and Standardization

(DOSS), Capt Anthony Casey Flight Line Acting Official in Charge (AOIC), Sgt Richard Black, Cpl Andrew Noguez, Cpl Anthony Ro, LCpl David Gerencher, LCpl Cory Williams, and LCpl Brandon Thompson, who all volunteered to move north to the LP/OP. Oren, with the assistance of Berkeley and Casey, began assigning sectors of fire towards the most likely avenues of approach."

The LSA Marines' synchronization from sleep to security was eerily transformative. The warfighter within a variety of individuals raised its gnarly head to defend its ground—quickly rising to the occasion. The unlucky devils surrounded by pissed-off Marines would have no time to redeem themselves. They were going down.

• • •

Staying out of sight was at the forefront of McDonald's mind. Simply, the more people in tow, the more chance of discovery. The three had left the LSA and crossed over to the west side of the X-bus road to move north. Initially, they were met with guns pointed at them by guys attached to MALS.

"Get down! Who are you? What are you doing there?" screamed the MALS Marines.

McDonald put his hands in the air, yelling his identity, but all the confusion and background noise drowned him out. He realized moving fast enough to get to his guys put them at risk for friendly fire.

The MALS Marines let McDonald through, and he, Ball, and Abramovs ran up the line toward the northern flight lines. Danger hung like a shroud as they crossed open ground and jumped from squadron to squadron.

• • •

Lightfoot, a man of detail, linked up with HMLA-469's Operations Officer (OPSO), Maj Nathan Marvel, who had just checked out his M-4 from the armory. A quick discussion ensued about weapons issues and security on the airfield perimeter. The extent, direction, or full intent of the enemy breach or how many attackers were on their base was unknown.

Marvel had already begun directing Marines to the perimeter and worked with SgtMaj Keith Massi, to hone and execute the plan to defend the airfield.

Lightfoot asked MSgt Bobby Sparkman, Maintenance Control Chief, how many aircraft were ready to launch. Sparkman said two AH-1Ws (Cobras) and one UH-1Y (Huey) backup aircraft were good to go. Lightfoot grabbed Capt Paul Eckert, the airframe officer in charge (OIC), and ordered him to man up a Cobra as his copilot.

Anything on the flight line was at risk once the battle had begun. The Harriers spit and spewed fire and flames, and Lightfoot didn't want that happening to his helo squadron. An undetected bullet hole in an important working spot could lead to a crash. Getting the aircraft up meant keeping them air-worthy and not finding out the hard way that they were not.

In the air and with forward-looking infrared (FLIR) and night vision devices, they would have a better advantage over the Taliban below. He kept worry at bay and focused on the blaring task.

Marines working on the HMLA-469 flight line had seen a single rocket fly across the VMA-211 flight line. They thought it was a negligent rocket discharge from an AV-8B until they heard subsequent explosions louder than they'd ever heard before, rattling the whole building. A second loud explosion went off. They could feel the concussion inside.

They ran to the door facing the Harriers and a third thunderous clap blasted their ears.

"Get in the bunkers, get in the bunkers," Capt Coker yelled to everyone within earshot.

Coker had recently returned from a training flight. SSgt Robert Wise, UH-1Y's crew chief, was in his shop conducting a debrief with Cpl Benjamin Hebert, the left gunner who operated the GAU-21, a .50 caliber (12.7 × 99mm) machine gun. Wise manned the right gun in flight, the GAU-17 7.62mm mini-gun. LCpl Seamus Clarke was on the flight as well, learning training codes from Wise.

Was it a det? Wise wondered, confused at the timing. It was the repeated reaction of the night, as controlled dets were a regular occurrence in a fighting season. It was always fighting season in Helmand Province, a piece of earth scorched by the blood of many who had trod the ground since 9/11, when terror became a household word.

Wise immediately coordinated with SSgt Michael Meusz in maintenance control to clear all personnel off of the flight line and direct them to the squadron compound. The scope of the threat was still unknown, but protocol drove him like a cattle prod.

The IDF bunkers were the *go-to* shield position when taking fire. As Marines and PKL civilians (aviation readiness defense contractors) converged on the bunkers, Coker tried to get accountability as best he could. There had been no procedure for IDF, other than to *get in the bunkers*. And that depended on where the bunkers were on base. Marines quickly scrambled to don flak jackets and Kevlar.

He surmised they were taking indirect fire, mortars, and rockets from outside the base. *What else would it be?* Coker asked himself. In the past, while deployed to another firebase, a rocket landed ten meters away from him as he was sprinting to his aircraft to launch. The rocket came from outside the base, not an uncommon occurrence wherever U.S. forces were housed. There was never any welcome sign from the insurgents, who were entrenched and hidden everywhere.

Small arms fire began to snap around the northern and eastern perimeter from their location.

Assessments pressed his mind at Mach speed. *What are the Harrier guys doing?* Coker thought, believing the small arms fire were Marines shooting from the VMA 211 flight line to the east.

He climbed on top of the IDF bunker to witness huge flames coming from the other side. He couldn't see much else due to the dark sky, heavy-laden with smoke from the Harriers' burning metal and fuel. The air was rank, making it hard to breathe. Green enemy tracers flew over his head as he returned to the bunkers.

Tracers are specialized bullets built with a small pyrotechnic charge used to mark targets. When the round leaves the muzzle, an illuminating chemical in its base produces a bright light and burns for about a hundred yards. Barium salts cause Russian or Chinese-made ammunition tracers to generate green. A mixture of strontium compounds causes NATO ammunition tracers (including the U.S.) to yield a bright red light.

Pilots are normally armed only with M9 pistols, which could be no match for automatic assault rifles and RPGs. Wise and Coker ran from the bunker to the maintenance building. They drew rifles from the racks and handed them out to everyone in the bunker. The rounds were already in the magazine on the buttstocks of the rifles.

Coker directed fellow Marines into defensive positions, then went towards the Harrier flight line. Some type of hasty defense had to be built to prevent the attackers from entering the HMLA "Righteous" compound.

Staff Sergeants Timothy Clouatre, Joseph Moran, Juan Arce, and Lance Gray gathered their Marines and issued orders to disperse across the squadron compound. UH1-Y crew-served M240 machine guns were retrieved, and egress kits were installed to utilize them in a ground defense.

The Marines with M240s were broken into fire team-sized elements (four Marines per team) and posted at strategic locations along the Righteous T-walls and barriers. Officers and SNCOICs assigned each element a sector of fire and ordered them to engage, only if PID on the enemy fighters could be obtained.

Coker grabbed someone's uniform by the back of the neck and told him to follow him. He ran over to a T-wall and said, "Lay down!" Coker pointed to the area he wanted the Marine to set his fire.

"You've got from here to here," he instructed while pointing.

Then Coker grabbed another Marine and led him down towards the road a small distance.

"You've got it from here to here. So, you have it?"

"Yeah, yeah," answered the Marine.

"Alright, I'm going in. Cover me!" ordered Coker, thinking *he sounded like a character in some movie*. He wanted to make sure he was covered, moving over open ground.

As Marines maneuvered into position to close the gaps in the hasty defense, they heard 7.62 rounds narrowly passing by. Coker ran towards the HMLA hangar and a small gym. A concrete slab over a foot thick dropped off on the east side, running along the end of the hangar towards the road.

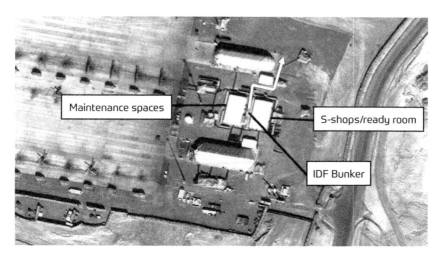

Capt Coker's low crawl to gain situational awareness during attacks on the VMA flight line and to shoot any attackers if identified.

Coker did a low crawl next to the slab, all the way up to the Harrier flight line. Once at that location, the Marine covering him could not see him anymore. Only concertina wire separated HMLA-469 from the Harriers.

Coker trusted his own ability to shoot. After all, he grew up in South Carolina, where guns and pro-Second Amendment people lived. He thought if he could possibly identify an armed enemy, then he knew he could take care of the threat. He positioned himself in a corner at the end of the concrete slab, not knowing the status of the Harrier jets or any Marines in the area. Nothing was in front of him.

He looked through his advanced combat optical gunsight. All he could see was fire. He could feel the heat radiating from the closest Harrier several hundred meters away.

It quickly dawned on him that being in the open wasn't very smart. He could potentially take a round and wouldn't be good to anybody injured or dead. He started crawling back to where he came from. When he got to a corner close to the maintenance building, he stood up and ran.

•••

Lightfoot was worried that the aircraft would get blown up. Without aircraft, there's no one to protect Infantry Marines on the ground. The next day, when there's a TIC call, no pilots and crews would be running to their birds. Lightfoot directed ODO Capt James Gianelloni to sound the TIC horn. Gianelloni was Coker's co-pilot.

Two sets of aircrew equipped with AH-1W and UH-1Y helicopters were ordered to launch in order to locate, close with, and destroy the enemy forces.

Lightfoot knew getting aircraft in the air minimized aircraft targets sitting on flight lines for the Taliban to engage.

Marines from maintenance shops sprinted to the TIC aircraft as small arms fire snapped in and around the flight line. The air support choreography began as they began removing tie-downs, pillows, and covers, while others provided 360-degree security to prevent the attackers from getting close enough to engage the aircraft or kill Marines.

In a fast sprint to the HMLA ready room, Coker saw Lightfoot come out, and they practically collided. Lightfoot had a rifle and was wearing a flight helmet and a flak jacket.

"Part, we gotta get aircraft in the air," he said. "Part" was Coker's call sign.

"Sir, do you want me to launch now?" asked Coker.

"Affirm," Lightfoot replied decisively.

"Aye, Aye, Sir!" answered Coker.

Per Lightfoot's orders, Gianelloni called the TACC Senior Watch Officer and informed him of the attack in progress on the northeast side of the airfield, near the VMA and HMLA flight lines. Information was starting flow back and forth, which helped everyone get factual situational awareness.

•••

Coker checked his rifle. It was on safety. He had on his flight suit, a flight helmet, and an aircrew vest (that had Kevlar and SAPI plates). As he ran to his helicopter on the HMLA-469 flight line, he handed the rifle to someone he identified as a Marine.

"Here, take this!" said Coker.

Hebert and Clarke came up behind Coker. More green tracers whizzed overhead as they ran.

During a TIC, everything is already on the aircraft, including flak jackets, Kevlar helmets, gloves, and the crew's rifles. Ordnance Marines waited in front of the Huey for the pilots and crew to gear up and get on. Coker and Hebert boarded the Huey, followed by Wise and Clarke, who jumped on board. Wise took his seat behind the GAU-17.

Gianelloni showed up a few minutes later to co-pilot.

It was a stroke of luck as the five-man crew were the actual Marines scheduled to fly. Maj Robert Weingart who piloted a Cobra, and Capt Jeremy Elliot (weapons operator) were the only other ones on duty.

Coker cranked the engine up, handed the checklist to Gianelloni, nicknamed "Geno," and said, "You take over the start."

The right-seat pilot did the start, and the left seat got all the systems ready and prepared the aircraft to launch.

Coker was ready to arm up. "Hey, you ready to go?"

"Yeah, yeah ready," Geno answered.

Coker looked over, and half of the checklist wasn't done, so he finished it off.

Coker saw tracers going overhead and yelled at the Ordnance Marines on the flight line, at parade rest waiting to arm the aircraft. It was amazingly true that training kicked in, and they were just doing their job even though exposed to grave danger.

"Get behind the HESCO barriers!" Coker yelled out to them.

Rounds continued overhead as they ran behind the barriers, big cans that looked like giant Lego blocks filled with sand on the inside. Although the Taliban were using the flight line for a shooting gallery, the roles were about to reverse when those helos launched. By leaving a trail of American blood, the attackers asked for what was coming—they asked for the big guns to hunt them down. Helicopter pilots are not common; attack helicopters are slower, more low-flying than fighter jets, and susceptible to hidden enemies below them. Yet they make up for it with the flexible mount GAU-17 Gatling gun on board that can humble the fiercest as it shreds a body on impact.

Coker called the Ordnance Marines back to arm the Huey. He couldn't wait to get that bird up to track down the enemy positions.

At the same time, Maj Weingart, the lead in the Cobra, called up and said, "Part, you ready?"

"Yessir, right here!"

"Okay, Roger."

It was almost perfect—the pilots and crews of the Righteous 54 (RS 54) (Weingart and Elliot) and Righteous 55 (RS 55) (Coker, Gianelloni, Hebert, Wise, and Clarke) aircraft section of two were ready to go at the same time. They had spent countless hours in the air together, and that night would define *taking the fight to the enemy* in a new way as the next tick on the HMLA-469 battle board unfolded with ferocious reality.

Although not scheduled to fly that night, Lightfoot's section of three (two Cobras) was also readying to launch, with a third aircraft (one Huey) to join them later. Lightfoot gave out call signs to his section as Righteous 56 (RS 56) and to the Huey Righteous 57 (RS 57).

CAMP BASTION, Afghanistan. 2012. HMLA Marines in front of "Battle Boards." Strikes are printed with black and red lightning bolts. MEDEVAC painted with red crosses. The boards served as a constant reminder of the importance of the mission and tracked progress. (Left to right) SSgt Robert Wise, LCpl Seamus Clarke, Cpl Benjamin Hebert, Capt James Gianelloni, Capt Adam Coker, Maj Robert Weingart, Capt Jeremy Elliot. (Photo courtesy of LtCol Adam Coker)

Weingart called the tower, run by the British, and gave the standard protocol every time they were ready to lift off, "Tower, this is Righteous-54, 55 flight of two," relayed Weingart. "Lead Cobra and Dash 2 Huey on the Righteous flight line ready for take-off to the north."

"Roger, the airfield's yours," said the tower in a British accent.

Normal flight operations direct helos to taxi up the runway and lift off. But Weingart took off from where his bird was parked on the HMLA flight line, and Coker followed. He stayed right behind him and headed north. They flew low, getting airspeed, passing by a bunch of Harriers, some on fire and burnt to the ground. The ordnance was cooking off, and Coker saw really bright white flashes. The air temperature was much hotter than the usual desert hot.

Lightfoot and co-pilot Capt Eckert took off despite a malfunction in Lightfoot's Cobra number-one engine. When Lightfoot started that engine (after starting the number-two engine first), it went into an overspeed mode, which forced him to manually take control of

CAMP BASTION, Afghanistan. September 15, 2012. Aerial view from UH-1Y Huey over VMA-211 flight line with six AV-8B Harriers and sunshades destroyed by insurgent attack Sept 14, 2012. (Photo by Cpl Benjamin Hebert, courtesy LtCol Adam Coker)

the engine and reduce the overspeed. That was an emergency procedure that would normally preclude flight. However, due to the dire circumstances, Lightfoot chose to fly the aircraft anyway to provide air support to the flight line.

Lightfoot's division flew high to provide overall support as well as monitor the challenge of five aircraft flying in the same congested airspace. The potential for collision was exacerbated by the attackers below in undetermined positions of fire while also flying through huge billowing clouds of smoke.

Weingart's section flew low, trying to attract small arms fire so they could locate where the enemy was and engage them. Jordan's Huey joined them, flying low with an improvised crew.

•••

Earlier, Jordan, in his Huey, called his squadron commander on the radio, "Sir, I'm in the aircraft. I'm ready to take off. I don't have a co-pilot, but I have a crew chief in the front seat." The crew chief was the only person he could find.

"Do you want me to take off?" he asked Lightfoot.

"Yeah, yeah, get airborne," said Lightfoot.

•••

Coker came over the 469 base radio to Jordan, "Make sure you're just flying. That's your job, flying. Don't worry about the sensor."

It was very dark, with smoke filling the air. Coker wanted Jordan to just focus on safely flying his aircraft and not try to use the FLIR sensor. On the Huey, the FLIR was the Britestar Block II, advertised by Teledyne (its maker) as the "world's sixth sense." FLIR offered superpower vision.

The FLIR system uses a thermographic camera. The sensor installed in FLIR cameras detects infrared radiation, typically emitted from a heat source (thermal radiation), to create an image assembled for video output. FLIRs are used to help pilots fly their aircraft at night and in fog or to detect warm objects against a cooler background.

Although he didn't say it to Jordan, Coker didn't want him to fly and monitor the sensor and have something bad happen. Coker had no idea how much difficulty Jordan would have with a crew chief acting as his co-pilot. Yet one improvises with so many lives on the line.

"Roger, roger," said Jordan.

15
DON'T SHOOT THE FRIENDLIES

Camp Bastion: A Few Months Earlier

NUMEROUS HOURS OF COMBAT flying welded crews together. They worked on strong crew resource management in the cockpit, focused on interpersonal communication, leadership, and decision-making. Just over halfway through the deployment, Jordan had a solid rhythm with his combat crews at Bastion. Getting shot at in flight occurred regularly and had started to feel normal. The tempo of operations was high, which helped keep the deployment pace going fast. Pilots and crews didn't have much downtime. They wouldn't want it anyway; they deployed to provide combat support. The utmost care and skill is employed to make sure attack aircraft don't hit friendly forces and produce as little collateral damage as possible. With modern technology and a skilled crew, they can pinpoint strikes to an exact match to target.

Bastion: Initial Explosions, September 14

After hearing the first blasts of Harriers blowing up, Jordan led his Marines to the south HMLA- 469 bunker, between the main building and his office. Maj Marvel, call sign "MOG," approached and asked Jordan to run to the entry control point and grab the Marines who were standing guard. Jordan sprinted across an open area full of rocks and made it to the Marines, who were confused like everyone else and unaware of how dangerously close they were to a heavily armed enemy. Jordan ordered them to follow him back to the HMLA bunker.

On the way back, an RPG was fired toward them from the Harrier flight line, landing about twenty-five feet away. It hit the concertina wire and tumbled, preventing it from detonating. The RPG fin contacted the wire and caused the flight path to impact at an odd angle rather than on point, sparing the Marines in its path.

Jordan's adrenaline ramped up. It was clear to him and others this was not a mortar attack, and an enemy had made it through the airfield perimeter. Back at the bunker, a few Marines yelled out that the squadron CO was asking for another Huey pilot to get airborne. Jordan was all over that to help get aircraft in the sky to build their situational awareness to find and destroy the enemy. As he ran to his Huey parked at the end of the flight line, tracers flew over the T-walls. There was a lot of smoke in the ink-black sky.

Jordan expected to see his co-pilot, Capt Ken "Bronco" Hampshire, assuming he would have heard the call for pilots. Jordan didn't know that Hampshire had gone out to the perimeter to see what was going on. It was a dangerous move.

Since Hampshire was not immediately around, Jordan had to look for a co-pilot, but could not find one due to most of the Marines manning positions along the outer perimeter. He ran into Cpl Jeffery Allen and directed him to be one of his crew chiefs. When he got to his Huey, Jordan told a Maintenance Marine to go find a co-pilot and another crew chief to man a crew-served weapon.

Cpls Lorena Castillo and Roberto Guerrero (both UH-1Y crew chiefs) ran up to Jordan, reporting they couldn't find any pilots. Jordan told Guerrero to get in and man the GAU-17. He told Castillo to jump in the front left seat and be his co-pilot. Jordan counted on her having some familiarization with the systems as a crew chief. When it came to operating the FLIR, Jordan would do most of the work.

Jordan knew a crew chief acting as a co-pilot during the extreme low light with other aircraft in a very small piece of sky was far from an ideal situation. Yet, he could not delay the take-off any longer, and Castillo was his best candidate.

•••

One of the most difficult tasks was to identify friendly forces and communicate that to QRF and other airborne aircraft trying to sort surface-to-surface small arms fire below. Along with the Taliban, pilots had to consider the blue-on-blue threat. At one point in flight, Lightfoot saw movement across the HMLA flight lines. He notified his division, "Hey, we've got some people crossing over."

Tactical patience cannot be underestimated in a confusing battlespace such as the cards they were dealt that night. There was no winner here—only the victor and the vanquished. With FLIR optics, the airborne helo pilots could identify them as friendlies. They saw Maj McDonald moving Marines up north to safety at the HMLA-469 compound. Lightfoot was correct to assume they were on their way to get situational awareness of the Harrier flight line. McDonald had seen combat and was a hell of a fighter pilot. Chasing your dream to fly combat missions in both Iraq and Afghanistan changed a man to become a force to reckon with. McDonald had run the war on terror gauntlet, and Lightfoot knew that he knew the fight was far from over, or otherwise, they wouldn't be there.

Being directly on top of the movement, Lightfoot could determine the uniform, hair, how many, and even how they were walking. The Army cammies the Taliban had on did not trick Lightfoot as Marines did not have beards.

There was no place in the aircraft stack that night for trigger-happy pilots. The response could not play out worse than the threat. The figures Lightfoot saw walking across the lines were not shooting, and that factored into identifying the good guys from bad guys.

•••

McDonald had run over a mile up the airfield and, along the way, was engaged with active enemy fire. He had no intent to kill the attackers using only a pistol. Nonetheless, he had no intention of getting killed. He'd do whatever it took to take down the bastards.

He thought it best to establish a solid defensive line and engage the Taliban from there. He would have to organize, gather the men, give orders, and disperse weapons needed for enemy encroachment. Not a moment was wasted, even though he had to guess what the whole battle space entailed. He dealt with what was in front of him.

Moving across an open area, the fuel pits fire raged to his west. He saw vehicles approaching, including a big armored vehicle and a Humvee-type. Who was driving, he could not make out, but assumed they were British QRF.

The dark was lit up by explosions still cooking off and bad guys running around undeterred, and that was maddening. He saw a chance to up their game and move faster. He told Ball and Abramovs to hide behind a dirt pile, then stepped into the middle of the track the vehicles were headed on. He held up his hands, and the vehicles stopped, lights blinding. McDonald walked, still with hands up, to the passenger side of the lead QRF vehicle, where an officer was sitting. An assumptive, but bold move, perhaps? Then again, a Taliban-driven vehicle would have already run him down, not stopping for questions.

"Me and my guys are moving north. We're only halfway to the Harrier line, where all the fighting is going on. Will you give us a ride?" asked McDonald.

As he tried to hitch a ride, no one knew of the fight happening in the fuels compound other than huge flames licking the skies. That alone produced some ugly scenarios, and the comms were sketchy at best. The west side of the airfield was on fire. The north didn't know what the south side was doing. Marines were putting it all together everywhere, best they could based on what they knew and what they could see and hear. Protecting lives was a number one priority.

Southeast Marines observing West Side Marines firing east:

LSA Marines manning sectors of fire at an elevated LP/OP were observing tracer fire directed at the cryogenics lab, ready to go at the call.

Sergeants Diana Barnes and Carolina Alvarado volunteered to help MALS-16 conduct a search of approximately one hundred TCN civilian contractors moved from the LSAs to the MALS-16 hangar across from the LSA. Captain Anthony Casey led a security team as the MALS Marines escorted the TCNs to the more defended location. Others, trained as combat lifesavers, grabbed medical kits and manned the casualty collection point established by the squadron's XO. These actions were later documented in the USMC Bastion Attack Narrative Summary report.

Heading north situation:

"Nope, sorry mate. Not going that way," said the British QRF officer to McDonald, as if the group was hitching a ride on the streets of London.

McDonald stepped in front of the second British QRF vehicle and made the same request to get to the Harrier flight line and his guys.

"Move out of the way; we're not going up there," said the Brits in the second vehicle before driving off.

McDonald thought it too incredulous to argue in the emergent situation, but the Brits' disrespect and making light of a critical request from an American officer would grate at him. So, McDonald turned back to the men who would gladly give aid, volunteering for the fight. He summoned his Marines from behind the dirt pile, "Follow me," he ordered.

They came from the south across an open area, heading towards the HMLA-469 flight line. HMLA Marines had positioned themselves behind some HESCO barriers. The squadron had seen it fortify their buildings and aircraft.

The Marines were lined up facing north and a tad east in the direction of the flames and explosions on the Harrier flight line. McDonald saw them peeking over the makeshift barricade they had constructed, their weapons trained ninety degrees away from him. He started screaming and yelling about a hundred yards out, but

CAMP BASTION, Afghanistan, 2012. Hesco barriers at HMLA-469 flight line fortify defenses. (Photo courtesy of LtCol Adam Coker)

they couldn't hear him because of the ruckus from the Harriers on fire.

McDonald, Ball, and Abramovs approached carefully until they were nearly upon the Marines behind the barricade. Rifles were aimed at all three, still unidentified. McDonald ordered his buddies to hide again in a dirt berm, away from him, in case he got shot.

Hands in the air, he continued forward, closer and closer. One of the Marines saw McDonald and did a double-take, eyes as big as dinner plates. He turned his weapon on McDonald and screamed something unintelligible.

McDonald froze, hands still in the air, as the others turned rifles on him. One jockeyed an M240G machine gun, the ground version of the original M240, designed as a coaxial/pintle-mounted machine gun for tanks and light armored vehicles. The M240G was modified for infantry ground use by installing a kit comprised of a flash suppressor, front sight, carrying handle for the barrel, a butt-stock, an infantry-length pistol grip, bipod, and rear sight assembly. Adaptation for all types of warfare was not an accident and was proving its worth.

McDonald, locked in the M240G's crosshairs, screamed, "Don't shoot, don't shoot. I'm American, VMA-211 . . . Major McDonald . . . Marine Corps!"

The Marines squinted, trying to identify McDonald in the shadows.

"Hell yeah, yeah. C'mon sir," they shouted urgently.

"I've got to get through," retorted McDonald with an edge of *do or die*.

A couple of Marines put down their weapons and leaned over the barricade. They grabbed his wrists to pull him up and over. Next, they hoisted Ball and Abramovs over.

An HMLA Chief Warrant Officer asked the obvious, "What are you doing?"

"We're going to the Harriers," McDonald replied, letting him figure out why.

McDonald and his men jumped the barricade to move forward, catching a sudden, shocking view of the Harrier flight line. All the jets were on fire except one or two.

•••

Positioned to defend the front/north side of the T-walled MALS building, Hawkins, Doman, and Gonzales identified an armed Taliban attacker coming towards them from a covered position on the east side of the MALS building. It was dark and hard to pinpoint the target. All three sergeants simultaneously fired. The Taliban, visibly wounded, moved towards cover in rows of shipping boxes directly north of the MALS building. Doman saw the attacker popping his head up from the boxes. The three continued to fire until he fell to the ground. Positioned on the north side of the T-walled MALS building, Cpl Byrnes saw the Taliban on the ground moving towards what he believed to be a weapon and engaged the enemy until he stopped moving.

Stalwart in their defensive positions, Fuels Marines were danger close, receiving small arms fire within feet of their positions and RPGS close behind. Two enemy combatants were killed at the shipping boxes—one inside in the rows and one outside the shipping boxes on open ground. Two Taliban lay dead near the X-bus road. One combatant believed to be injured was still missing.

More attacks were coming from the east, or so they assessed. They saw a British vehicle pull into position down the road from the fuels compound closer to the road that led to the air terminal. The vehicle was hit by an enemy RPG. Injuries were unknown at the time, as so much was happening simultaneously from multiple enemy positions.

16

TAKING COMMAND OVER BLOOD- STAINED GROUND

MCDONALD, BALL, AND ABRAMOVS, nearing the VMA flight line, saw the jet hides (big tents) over the burning Harriers as the apocalypse descended on his home base. The hideous site invoked rising anger for the loss of the multi-million-dollar aircraft he knew so well. Attack aircraft helped win the distributed ground wars throughout Afghanistan that added up to the greater war. Anger threatened to cloud his actions, but McDonald fought it, knowing with every fiber of his being that clear thinking would be the better weapon to find and destroy the enemy he knew so well.

"Slow down," barked McDonald to Ball and Abramovs, who were moving too fast towards the VMA flight line, pumped up by the hostile environment. It was time to do a quick recon.

The men squatted down to get a lay of the land and locate where the attackers might be. McDonald clutched his pistol. Ball leaned on his shoulder, as if it were a regular day, and said, "Well. It looks like we're not making the flight schedule tomorrow."

Marines learn to maintain composure when facing deadly situations others would call terrifying. Still, it hit McDonald as a strange reminder at that point in time. Without air support the next day, ground troops are uncomfortably vulnerable. That could not happen.

McDonald couldn't see enemy movement, but things were blowing up everywhere.

● ● ●

McDonald and his crew hustled over to the northernmost VMA-211 hangar, where all the maintenance spaces and shops were. This was holy ground where missions began and ended.

He could see windows had been shot out of the hangar. Bullet holes all over the side stung deeply, erupting in grave concern for his Marines. A couple of holes were so large they could only mean an RPG had rammed through the siding.

Hearing no movement from inside, McDonald went to one of the doors and stuck his left hand up in the window, protecting his trigger hand from injury. He waved his hand, pulled it back down, and started yelling as loud as he could, "I'm going to show my face," he shouted into the hangar. McDonald could not be stopped from strategically making his way to VMA headquarters. The biggest risk of all was doing nothing and letting the attackers have the advantage to overrun Marines pinned down in a building.

No sounds came from inside as he lifted his face up to the window—seeing two large rooms separated by a narrow hallway. His steely gaze locked on the southernmost room, the size of a gymnasium. Clustered in the entrance of the hallway were as many rifles as you could fit pointed at the window and his face. Screams pierced his ears as he ducked and fell away from the door, yelling his name.

"It's Major McDonald!" hollered one of the Marines from inside. "Come-on, get in here, sir."

McDonald thanked God that no one had shot him. He jumped up, opened the door, and ran in. A couple of Marines ran up to him but didn't really say anything. The blank stares on their faces spelled pain. Chambless walked up to him, pale yet wide-eyed on the edge, and lamented, "Six is dead."

Six is the communications brevity code used for a commanding officer.

"Show me his body," ordered McDonald, who now was the next in line to command.

Chambless walked with McDonald towards the flight equipment office, a place where pilots get dressed, and repairs are made to harnesses and flight equipment.

"We've got several wounded," added Chambless as they walked. "There's some other people that have been taken out. Not sure how many."

"God, man," said McDonald, the nightmare unfolding. "Take me to Otis."

Chambless led McDonald into the flight equipment office. Raible was lying on his back in a sprawled position. He was covered with a piece of desert camouflage canvas—the same as Marine uniforms.

McDonald pulled the canvas back from his friend and now-fallen commander's eyes that were open, staring straight ahead. He was pale white in the darkened room. The sight crushed McDonald, yet he now had to wear the mantle of leadership Raible wore. Raible, a Marine whom others followed into battle, gave in the tense hours of his final fight—the last full measure of his devotion. McDonald put his hand on Raible's carotid artery, yearning to find a pulse. He felt the sickening hole in his neck, and McDonald knew his squadron commander bled out from there, from either a bullet or shrapnel. He stuck his finger in the hole to retrieve what looked like a piece of metal.

McDonald confirmed Raible was dead from his wounds.

His jaw clenched, holding back a dam of emotion; McDonald grabbed Raible's wallet out of his flight suit and put it in his pocket. He crossed his legs and crossed his arms over his waist, and he and the Marines wrapped him to hold his limbs in place. He went outside the flight equipment office and addressed the Maintenance Marines.

"I'm taking command," stated McDonald. "We're going to get out of here."

The hangar walls were very thin corrugated tin, not able to slow down the Taliban bullets. Fifty VMA Marines sat, backs against the wall, in the narrow hallway totally dejected that their CO was dead and some of their buddies wounded.

Explosions and weapons firing outside blasted the ears. McDonald knew they had to move out of the hangar fast. Not knowing how many Taliban attackers were out there, McDonald was not going to allow the Taliban to rip them all apart at any time.

He stood in front of the fifty VMA-211 Marines, "Hey, does anyone know how to fire a pistol," asked McDonald. "I need to trade weapons."

He knew one of the lance corporals well—a solid guy. He showed his pistol. "Know how to fire an M9?" asked McDonald.

McDonald's pistol was a Beretta 92FS. The lance corporal affirmed he knew how to shoot it, and McDonald traded the M9 for a rifle. He checked the magazines and the chambered round and ordered Ball and a pilot to go out the back door with him.

His plan was to get everyone to the VMA-211 headquarters about a hundred yards away, a building fortified with thirty-foot concrete T-wall barriers.

McDonald wasn't going to run the Marines out in the open. It had to be a route they could feasibly do with minimal exposure. He posted two guys at the hangar's back door—telling them to squat and watch his back.

He ran from the maintenance hangar and ducked down behind some air-conditioning vents to have a good look around. Then, he sprinted across a short open area, through a ditch, over another area, through another ditch, and then up to the back of VMA-211 headquarters.

Having been briefed, McDonald knew there was a captain inside and four other enlisted Marines. Wary of being shot, he opted out of running up and opening the door. Yet, he had to communicate and coordinate with them somehow.

As far as McDonald was concerned, whether there were one, fifty, or one hundred Taliban fighters, the job was the same. He must not abandon caution and be mistaken for the enemy.

Back home, his wife, baby and children knew nothing of the peril he was in. The home phones didn't ring until foreign battles were officially over, having personnel accounted for and damage assessed. Combat is an ever-changing beast that can go from chaos to control back to chaos in a flash.

After clearing a route, McDonald ran back to the VMA maintenance hangar, unseen, confident with his plan. He told the fifty VMA Marines awaiting his orders.

"We're going to move. Groups of six and as fast as we can. Get about ten feet apart and move fast and low. Try to look inconspicuous." He pulled out a couple of Marines. "You and you—put the CO on a stretcher and take his body with us."

While they were getting the first stick of six ready to move, a Marine named Cattrall got on a direct phone line to VMA headquarters, reaching Smalley: "Tell Smalley that we are coming. That it will be us charging through the hole in the concrete barriers," McDonald ordered, with an indomitable will to succeed.

• • •

The HMLA-469 compound was surrounded by fires, and the VMA-211 flight line, only a hundred meters to the north, had six AV-8B jets on fire. The cryogenics lab, 400 meters to the southeast, was an unknown, on-the-horizon firebomb. Then, 300 meters to the south, the fuel pits' fires emanated greater than a hundred-foot flames, creating black billowing smoke that reduced visibility considerably.

A moonless night combined with a moderate wind from the south created conditions either intensely bright or extremely dark. There was enough dust in the air to obscure the horizon, reducing visibility to less than one statute mile and no visibility with the ground at higher than 500 feet altitude above ground level (AGL) when flying across the desert.

Coker flew his Huey past the Harriers towards the east, because they thought the Harrier flight line was still taking direct fire from all the booms they were hearing. They started searching for the point of origin (POO) of the attack, at first searching for mortar teams outside the fence line. Both Coker's Huey and Weingart's Cobra (with Elliot operating the weapons system in the front seat) continued to operate at 300 feet in order to identify friendly and enemy positions. British and American JTACs operating from the base defense operations center (BDOC) were unsure of the friendly positions and were passing friendly positions as enemy ones, based on visuals they observed via the UAS feeds streaming into the BDOC. Weingart deconflicted numerous fires and clarified erroneous information on many occasions.

The heat from all the fires did not affect the flight of the helos, but ordnance cooking off was another matter and a valid threat. They flew danger close to the raging infernos.

Considerably reduced visibility forced Coker and Weingart to descend again. Already flying low, they dropped to 200 feet over the raging fuel pit. The fire was so bright, looking through the NVDs, that it bloomed everything out. Nothing could be seen on the ground or otherwise.

Coker's focus was on keeping sight of Weingart, which was made difficult by the conditions and having to fly the aircraft. Wise was glued to his post by the GAU-17 on the right of the helo. Hebert manned the GAU-21 on the left. The GAU-21 .50 caliber single barrel rapid-fire machine gun could deliver defensive firepower ranging out to nearly 2,000 meters. Clarke sat in the middle.

CAMP BASTION, Afghanistan. September 14, 2012. Aerial view from UH-1Y Huey over the fuel farm. Taliban set 50,000 gallon fuel bags on fire with RPGs. (Photo by Cpl Benjamin Hebert, courtesy LtCol Adam Coker)

"Clarke, your only job is to keep sight of Lead," commanded Coker. "At all times, let me know where he is."

When a pilot is flying, sometimes the companion aircraft flies out of view, but trained eyes can search the skies and find them. In Bastion's heavy fire and smoke, an eagle would have had trouble following the lead. Clarke kept the Cobra in sight like a hawk on prey. Flight radio frequencies were lit up, ready for battle chatter, including intel, ground, and air reports.

The Huey had three radios, and the Cobra had two. Radio one was the base defense frequency. Radio two was interflight—the frequency Coker could talk to Weingart on. Radio three was HMLA-469 base frequency, with OPSO Marvel at the communications helm. Coker scanned and monitored two radio frequencies typically. More than three got a little busy.

In addition to processing multiple frequencies, Coker had to respond effectively to the battle unfolding, a feverish task at best. The aircraft sections overhead were dogged to gain the upper hand over the surprise attackers moving in the darkness.

During a TIC, it was standard procedure for pilots to receive an influx of information about who to support, call signs, friendly and enemy locations, and frequencies from either base Direct Air Support Center (DASC) or MIRC. The Brits had not previously briefed Coker on who to talk to at Base Defense.

The prevailing thought, according to Lt. Gen. Capewell, was, *Why worry about an insider attack on Bastion?* No intel suggested they should be concerned, and no precedent of an insider attack at Bastion had been set, according to him wearing a blindfold. Who needs protocol for base defense comms during a crisis with his mindset? Capewell lied there, too, for Capewell's complacent tact towards insider threats did not fly in Taliban planning dens, illustrated by previous insider incursions not that far back.

•••

Army Specialist Mabry Anders grew "increasingly worried he might not come home from Afghanistan," his father relayed after he was killed by an Afghan Army soldier on August 27, 2012, eighteen days before the attack on Camp Bastion.[54] The insider attack also took the life of Sgt Christopher Birdwell. Interviews in Afghanistan and the U.S. uncovered details that revealed that the Afghan soldier was prepared for the killings by the Taliban.

"'After the shooting incident a group of Taliban came to my house and said that Welayat Khan was their man,' said Nazar Khan, the brother of the Afghan soldier who was killed by U.S. forces after he opened fire on the Americans.

---

54 Stewart, Phil, Shalizi, Hamid, "Insight—In U.S. soldier's death, a window into Afghan insider killings," *Reuters*, September 27, 2012, https://www.reuters.com/article/uk-usa-afghanistaninsider-attacks/insight-in-u-s-soldiers-death-a-windowinto-afghan-insider-killings-idUKBRE88P1TG20120926.

""We have trained him for this mission and you must be proud of his martyrdom,"' Khan quoted a local Taliban commander as saying."

17

THE BASTION ANTI-TERRORISM PLAN THAT BLEW UP

MANY OF THE GREEN-ON-BLUE attacks committed by the Afghan forces were due to the real threats their families received if they failed to comply. Everyone was well aware of the incidents of green-on-blue when an Afghan soldier attacked U.S. troops.

Everyone at Bastion needed only to remember March 14, 2012, and the "burning man" incident. MajGen Gurganus was waiting with British General Skeates, SgtMaj Tanksley, 1st Sgt Driver, his personal security officer (PSO), and Aide de Camp Capt Bryan Yerger for Secretary of Defense Leon Panetta's plane to land. All the vehicles to pick up Panetta's entourage were lined up on the side of the road staged directly across from the crash crew/fire station. They could see his plane in the distance.

The sound of an engine revving aroused attention. Although it wasn't an unusual sound, as crash crew vehicles make a lot of noise, it still didn't feel right. All of a sudden, a car driven by an Afghan employee who worked for the Brits sped by close to Gurganus and his welcome team. The intruder drove about a hundred meters onto the tarmac and stopped. This was happening as Defense Secretary

Panetta's plane was landing and being directed to the far end of the runway. Top U.S. and U.K. military leaders on the flight line wondered if the crazed intruder's car had a bomb inside or if the driver would jump out wearing a suicide vest or begin shooting a rifle.

Personnel were beginning to respond when they saw smoke coming from the vehicle. The driver had a gas can and set himself on fire. It was pretty confusing, but when he got out of the vehicle, they could see what he had done. He left the vehicle in gear, and it continued to roll toward the runway as he ran around the tarmac screaming. A Royal MP drove on to the tarmac to assist, but the man jumped on the running board of the MP's vehicle and attempted to grab the steering wheel. The MP was able to force him off the vehicle, and the man, still on fire, fell to the ground. The MP used a fire extinguisher to put out the fire. They medevaced the

CAMP BASTION, Afghanistan. March 14, 2012. Secretary of Defense Leon E. Panetta (right) and U.S. Marine Corps MajGen Mark Gurganus, commanding general NATO RC(SW) walk from a V-22 Osprey tiltrotor aircraft. (DVIDS photo by Petty Officer 1st Class Chad McNeeley)

badly-burned intruder to the Bastion Role 3 hospital, but he later died. As Gurganus met the Secretary when he deplaned, he said to Gurganus, "Heard you had a little excitement this morning."

Both U.S. forces and U.K. forces took this incident seriously.

The CENTCOM Bastion Attack Summary described how this startling "burning man" incursion prompted the creation of OP CONGO:[55] "an RC(SW)-approved US/UK crisis action and consequence management plan to be coordinated out of the CJOC for major incidents that occurred within the BLS Complex or AOBW." According to OP CONGO, the command structure for a response to an incident inside the BLS Complex or outside the wire of AOBW was delegated to the supported commander and supporting commander trading lines of authority between U.S. Camp Leatherneck and U.K. Camp Bastion (including the U.K. Bastion airfield).

When Gurganus learned of USCENTCOM and U.K. Permanent Joint Headquarters (PJHQ) same C2 split arrangements in the 2011 MOU created prior to his arrival, he got a sense the two camps were separate sovereign territories, though not clearly demarcated. Gurganus identified and red-flagged this unconventional split of authority that violated USMC unity of command doctrine, came up with the solutions, and was ignored.

After the March 14, 2012 airfield incursion, Gurganus directed his Chief of Staff to draft a new MOU "which unifed command . . ." The Chief of Staff stated his effort to clarify the C2 met with "friction." Neither IJC nor ISAF supported combining the two camps, and Gurganus was told to continue with the supporting/supported command arrangement.

Gurganus' 3rd MAW ACE was supporting ground fighting every day in areas of responsibility near the BLS complex. No command

---

55 Garrett, William B., Murray, Thomas M., "USCENTCOM Bastion Attack Investigation Executive Summary," The United States Central Command (USCENTCOM), Accessed November 29, 2023, Pg. 6, https://www.hqmc.marines.mil/Portals/142/Docs/USCENT COM%20Bastion%20Attack%20Investigation%20Executive%20Summary.pdf.

confusion should dictate the outcome of any attack or situation, nor lax or different attitudes towards security.

Forced by those who did not understand the complexities of the split command that risked being disjointed when a battle demanded command unity, Gurganus focused on strengthening the unity of effort, resulting in OP CONGO better integrating the CJOC into the anti-terrorism force protection.

Although he got lemons, Gurganus set out to make lemonade. Yet this turndown would be a kick in the teeth for the ESG, IJC, and ISAF, who were not there when the Taliban cut that wire and started to blow up Harrier jets. Marines were forced to face confusion and a lack of unified response and took matters into their own hands. They discovered the split command structure was built on sand. The Brits (CO Bastion) were supposed to be the "supported commander" (or lead) a counter-terror response if an attack occurred on Bastion airfield, according to OP CONGO. In addition, the U.K. defensive plan for Camp Bastion, as well as the OP CONGO crisis response plan, did not integrate 3rd MAW into them.[56] So, why in the world would the Brits take the lead of U.S. Marines when their own commanders were the men qualified for the job?

•••

Capt Bryan Yerger was asked to be Aide de Camp to Gen Gurganus by Gurganus himself. He'd already deployed to Helmand Province once before in 2010, based in Garmsir with 3rd Battalion, 1st Marines, serving as a communications officer. In 2010, Taliban fighters, trained in Pakistan, were coming in droves to Afghanistan. Some were of Pakistani origin. History shows years of training and recruitment of the Taliban that followed in the tactical footsteps of their friends and allies, al-Qaeda.

---

56 "CENTCOM Bastion Attack Investigation Executive Summary," Pg. 5.

Combatting Terrorism Center at West Point, February 2013:[57]

Maulvi Nazir, a senior Taliban commander, was the leader of one of four militant groups in Pakistan's Federally Administered Tribal Areas (FATA) and ". . . closely aligned with Afghan Taliban, the Haqqani network, and the Hafiz Gul Bahadur Taliban faction." By 2006-2007, his network spanned parts of Afghanistan, including Helmand. Nazir was impressed with the modern guerilla techniques used by al-Qaeda fighters as he worked to improve the skills of his own fighters. In an interview, Nazir said that al-Qaeda and ". . . the Taliban are one and the same. At an operational level, we might have different strategies, but at the policy level, we are one and the same."

"In 2009 and 2010, Nazir reportedly helped deploy hundreds of well-trained 'Punjabi' Taliban militants of Pakistani origin inside Afghan territory to pressure U.S. and coalition forces ahead of their withdrawal."

Whether or not Mohammed Nazeer, leading fourteen Taliban fighters onto the Bastion airfield, came out of the Maulvi Nazir ranks is unknown. But it is not out of the question. Though from different tribes, regions, and with their own plans—insurgents all sort of blend together in one massive terror threat.

•••

Yerger was Gurganus's "gatekeeper," focusing on his schedule, getting him where he needed to be at the appropriate time, complete with talking points. He also scheduled travel itineraries. On an

---

57 Rehman, Zia Ur, "The Significance of Maulvi Nazir's Death in Pakistan," Combating Terrorism Center, February 2013, Volume 6, Issue 2, https://ctc.westpoint.edu/the-significance-of-maulvi-nazirs-death-in-pakistan/.

AFGHANISTAN 2012. Capt Bryan Yerger (Left) with MajGen Gurganus' personal security officer (POS). (Photo courtesy Capt Bryan Yerger)

average of three to four days a week, he and Gurganus were traveling to the different bases in RC(SW). Not content to sit back at headquarters and wait for a second-hand report, Gurganus wanted to talk directly to Marines on the ground to get their perspective. That sometimes involved the general getting into a tactical vehicle and going out on a patrol. Gurganus believed his Marines' greatest weapon was they didn't want to die, and they were more than happy to kill the enemy trying to kill them. He believed the only thing that earned him the rank of a general was his Marines. He thought about them first every day.

•••

General Allen and USMC Commandant James Amos both knew and understood the insider threat as well. Short of completely disengaging with their Afghan partners, this was a risk everyone assumed. Forces under Gurganus' command doubled security efforts when green-on-blue incidents started, but Gurganus observed the most effective deterrent was Major General Sayed Malouk, commanding general of the Afghan National Army's 215th Corps. Sturdevant provided the aircraft so Gurganus could fly with Malouk to visit with every single battalion in his Corps. General Malouk visited Gurganus after each incident and would cry as he apologized for the death and damage inflicted by one of his Aghan soldiers.

•••

There was a rash of green-on-blue attacks in August and September, Gurganus recalled. The Brits suffered a large part of these incidents as RC(SW) had begun turning the lead for combat operations over to Malouk's forces. This was by design due to the mandated drawdown of USMC forces. Ninety-six hundred Marines had to be out of the country by September 30th, forcing remaining USMC personnel to change the way they operated.

It was primarily the 1st MarDiv and Brit forces who were partnered with the Afghan forces. Green-on-blue expedited when U.S. forces transitioned into an advise/assist role rather than accompanying Afghan forces during operations. However, 3rd MAW was still heavily involved with advising and providing intel, air support, and medevac. Yet looming for 3rd MAW and out of their control were the simple, unchanging facts of how and where Bastion was built and how it was guarded.

•••

Coker called the tower and asked if there was a base defense radio frequency.

"Yes, it is x, y, z," came from the tower, who gave out the classified info Coker needed.

He switched over to the base defense frequency and first talked to a Marine. Then a Brit with the call sign "Rugger" came on. Rugger knew about the attack because Lightfoot had alerted Sturdevant at higher command on the west side of the base.

•••

Sturdevant knew there was a lot going on and had few details. He had felt the urgency in Lightfoot's voice and could easily surmise Beast was on the move. Lightfoot was a more than capable commander of HMLA-469 and was confident he could identify the enemy who had breached the eastern perimeter where Lightfoot and his men operated. After all, Lightfoot had flown a U.S. president around.

Sturdevant trusted his top officers on the ground. The last thing he wanted to do was get in the way of whatever fighting was taking place.

Due to the confusion of split command (forcing Gurganus and Sturdevant to rely on the Brits taking responsibility for the airfield seriously), Sturdevant didn't have enough armored vehicles at his disposal, nor good comms with the quick reaction forces. There were two QRFs in place for the airfield: one was British that fell under British command and one was U.S. Infantry Command. The wing had no QRF of its own.

Sturdevant had not seen an established TFBW anti-terrorism plan that was later said to exist by the Department of the Army, which investigated post-attack. The documents, once classified as "SECRET," were "APPROVED FOR RELEASE" on August 19, 2013.

The Dept. of the Army Bastion Attack Investigation said that "a determined terrorist force may be successful in breaching the security perimeter of the Base and executing an attack."[58]

"However, RC(SW) and TFBW assessed the primary threats against the BLS complex to be a vehicle-borne improvised explosive device (VBIED) attack against an ECP [entry control point], an insider threat attack, and indirect fire (IDF)."

An "insider threat attack" can mean different things—specifically a secret enemy who has base access or one who breaches the perimeter to get in. There are a lot of details and logistics to bring together when troops deploy to a combat region on a base owned by another country. Standards aren't mirrored, nor is military protocol. What is critical, though, is a *coming together* of protecting forces on their home turf. It was strident, not optional, to brief all officers (especially the two in charge) on an existing TFBW anti-terrorism plan for Camp Bastion. In other words, having proper defensible space inside and outside in the hinterlands where the Taliban and their allies roamed.

Or was it instead Sturdevant's job as CO of 3rd MAW to run USMC airfield operations, keeping his Marines properly supported out in the fighting fields? Reassurance was not given to Sturdevant upon 3rd MAW's arrival to Bastion that security on, and surrounding the airfield, was well in hand (as stated in the 2011 MOU). All one had to do was open their eyes. Yet they were forced to trust their host who saw security differently . . . or didn't look at all at what was before them. If the British didn't anticipate an inside threat attack, despite multiple warning signs and preferred to have tea with unvetted neighbors, how could the Brits promise an effective response?

---

58 Garrett, William B., Murray, Thomas M., "Army Regulation (AR) 15-6 Report (Final)," Dept. of the Army Bastion Attack Investigation, August 19, 2013 Pgs. 3-4, https://www.hqmc.marines.mil/Portals/142/USCENTCOM%20Bastion%20Attack%20Investigation%20Redacted%2015-6%20Report.pdf.

Conversely, Sturdevant's pilots, crews, maintainers, fuels and ARFF personnel, employed civilians on the airfield, and all USMC support set down in a precarious and very vulnerable environment. All lived and worked daily under the building peril of a secret Taliban attack in the making.

Dept. of the Army Bastion Attack Investigation:

> The planning, according to one Taliban survivor, began in 2011 and was scheduled to occur in July 2012. A postponement to September occurred to recruit a new assault force when several fighters were killed by an IED.[59]

In January 2013, *TOLO News* reported that someone in the higher chain of Taliban command was responsible for providing weapons of destruction.[60] Other suspects were apprehended and captured post-attack—people known for coordinating attacks in southern Helmand Province against Coalition forces. Nothing happened randomly with this enemy.

Sturdevant believed that the area outside the wire provided cover and concealment for an enemy approaching from the east.

Gurganus knew there was always an insider threat due to the large number of TCNs and Afghan workers employed by contractors. The wing conducted daily security searches and placed diligent guards at entry points to check IDs and badges.

It was lawyers who advised Gen Allen that U.S. forces could not be involved in poppy eradication. Gurganus wanted to use the tanks to clear the fields, especially the ones near Bastion/Leatherneck. Lawyers from above said no.

---

59 "Army Regulation (AR) 15-6 Report (Final)," Pg. 4.
60 TOLOnews, "3 Local Taliban Leaders Captured in Afghan Offensive," *TOLO News*, January 28, 2013, https://tolonews.com/afghanistan/3-local-taliban-leaders-captured-afghan-offensive.

Yet, Gurganus remained adamant about clearing the poppy out so the air wing could have clear fields of view/fields of fire. It was logical to maintain a defensible space. Lawyers prevented his astute requests from being approved. After all, on that eastern perimeter in September 2012, the lives of over 1,900 who made up the ACE were at stake, along with over five billion dollars in aircraft, not to mention other U.S. personnel and assets on the base itself.

18

SOMEONE'S ABOUT TO HAVE A BAD NIGHT

COKER PASSED THE BASE defense frequency to Weingart, and he made contact. Coker switched his third radio to HMLA-469 base frequency. He and Weingart relayed and received information in an exchange between those on the ground and those diligently monitoring.

Top commanding officers at headquarters had the sense to turn it over to officers in charge of the squadrons facing the threat. They knew the USMC chain of leadership; if one fell away, the next in rank would take charge. Coker was not aware of any response to the attackers from the British.

Weingart took control of the aircraft stack over the airfield. He told supporting aircraft where to hold and gave them tasking. Another AH-1W had launched to assist Lightfoot's division. Dash 3 was piloted by Maj Patrick Weinert and co-piloted 1stLt Frank Jablonski. Weinert and Jablonski had joined the stack about fifteen minutes after Coker and Lightfoot's launches, forced to run through an obstacle course of fire and concertina wire to get to the HMLA-469 squadron from the LSA barracks.

British Apaches were returning to BLS from a mission and found themselves in the air with U.S. helicopters in attack mode. Too many aircraft in a small air space spelled danger to those flying. It made sense to separate American and British aircraft by the runway. The Apaches were asked by the Marines in the air to stand off.

Weingart became the Forward Air Controller (Airborne) FAC (A) and told the Apaches to stay west of the runway. Rugger, at base defense, maintained control over the Apaches. No one knew if there would be attacks deeper into Camp Bastion.

The Marines on the ground set up a defense around HMLA-469's entire flight line using available HESCO barriers. Mechanics and aviation personnel mobilized individually, with some taking defensive action and some sheltering in the HMLA hangar. Coker was not able to directly communicate with HMLA Marines on the ground.

Capt Smalley took the initiative to set up a makeshift operations center and comms. This was air to breathe for those depending on accurate battlefield situations.

An AC-130 (called in from Kandahar) dropped flares for illumination. Air Force F-15E tactical fighter jets flew overhead. The F-15E Strike Eagle is a dual-role fighter and can fly at low altitudes, day or night, and in all weather.

At one point, F-18s flew in. The Super Hornet is a rapid-response, dependable tactical fighter used by the United States Navy and Marines. But the helicopter pilots couldn't safely coordinate with the fast, multi-system jets, not knowing where friendlies and enemies were. Weingart told them to hold. Word of the attack had spread. Yet, all needed the appropriate response tools for the job at hand.

The Combined Forces Air Component Commander (CFACC) pushed a Predator drone to Bastion. That video feed was the most useful information for the pilots and for Generals Gurganus and Sturdevant.

Coker got his SA on the ground by talking to HMLA-469 base. He felt an icy fear hearing a drone report saying, "Enemy entering the building where the skids were, second one from the road." The same building Coker had just come from. His heart dropped, thinking, *Those are all my Marines*. He was momentarily seized by a wild thought of an attacker spraying an AK-47 at his Marine brothers. A concerned voice on the radio brought him back to the present.

Marvel on HMLA base frequency adamantly repeated, "Negative, negative, those are friendlies, those are friendlies."

Coker wasn't sure how Marvel knew that. Normally, Coker talked to a JTAC on the ground to get a visual on the enemy location. But that wasn't possible until McDonald arrived on the scene.

"We're going to look for the POO to the east," said Coker to Marvel.

• • •

Two hours had passed, and now Killebrew sat on top of a fuel keg while a handful of Fuels Marines and the group of frightened TCNs were holed up in the MALS building. He was formulating plans on the go to get out of there.

The decision to move the Marines, TCNs, and DynCorp contractors further south to the MALS VMM-161 (Tiltrotor Osprey) compound and flight line was a prudent one. There, they had a sufficient stand-off from the fuel fire.

Killebrew flashed back on a distressed Major, who wanted to stay at the fuel farm, reporting he had two missing Marines in the cryo lab bunker. Killebrew, who saw enemy fire coming from the cryo makeshift bunker, told the Major, "That's unattainable." Killebrew didn't want to allow the Major to go back into a nest of Taliban without knowing more. Already that night, dangerous reconnoiters had occurred, turning up with no missing persons.

The Taliban had the advantage of some cover, and they didn't. On the ground, they couldn't see well through the haze. The bunker offered the attackers a solid fighting position with good fields of fire.

Killebrew was ticked off; he had no comms to tell anyone what they were doing. They had tried to kick a building door in to get to a phone and couldn't. If people were in there, they could have barricaded the door and be ready with rifles. He told his Staff Sergeants and NCOS to continue to surround the TCNs. His big fear was the TCNs would get shot. They don't look like Marines. Everyone's freaking out in the controlled chaos.

A Huey came up overhead.

"Someone's about to have a bad day," said Killebrew, as a chill ran through his body, while silently cheering the sight of a USMC gunship that could deliver.

• • •

It was hard to see. Tracers were still coming. The smoke was very thick. Marvel told Coker there were Taliban at the cryo facility, directly across and south from the HMLA 469's flight line.

19

DEADLY SHOOTOUT AT THE CRYO LAB

MULTIPLE STRINGS OF GREEN tracers were directed towards the HMLA compound from a single POO near the southern boundary of the MALS-16 (FWD) cryogenics compound. Marines would not be shooting at their own flight line. In response to the incoming fire, the Marines at HMLA responded with M-240 machine guns positioned along HMLA's T-walls. Manning the guns were SSgt Clouatre, Cpl Anderson, and LCpls Belles, Cleaves, Frisan, and Sierra.

They witnessed the Taliban firing upon the British QRF vehicles, positioned fifty meters west of the cryogenics compound on a ridge line. The Brits had skylined themselves on the ridge, allowing their presence to be visible, and it didn't go so well. An RPG round hit the column of British Mastiff Protected Patrol Vehicles (PPVs). Marines fired east using M16s, M4s, and M240s to suppress enemy fires long enough to allow the QRF team to direct a response toward the cryogenics lab, where five of the Taliban were fighting for their lives.

Unknown to Coker and Weingart above was that MWSS-373 Marines on the fuels side had stopped the movement of a second group of five Taliban. Due to the Fuels Marines' actions, the Taliban could not move to the west across the X-bus road to get to the skids (that had a HESCO wall around it). It was the place where Cobra and Huey helicopters launched.

Unknown to MWSS-373 Marines was the counterattack coming from HMLA Marines firing east at the cryo lab. The Taliban were stuck, prevented from moving forward or back. They holed up in the lab, a literal powder keg, where Marines made and stored liquid oxygen. The Taliban fired in both east and west directions at Marines in both locations. The cryo lab was the only place where east-side and west-side personnel connected in response to the attackers who'd capitalized on cutting a hole in a fence without being seen.

Cryogenics is the technology and art behind producing cool temperatures. In cryogenics, there is liquid oxygen, primarily used as an aviator's breathing oxygen, and liquid nitrogen, used to service the emergency power unit, the immediate source of electrical and hydraulic power in the event the onboard generators or engine fails on fighter jets. Helicopters do not use cryo.

USMC News states, "The pure oxygen allows pilots to breathe, ensuring they can support ground Marines effectively.

"'When pilots are flying over [certain altitudes], the smallest amount of Argon, Helium or any impure gases can cause a black out,' said Sgt. Micheal Bell, a work center supervisor with the Marine Aviation Logistics Squadron 11. 'Because so little oxygen is in the atmosphere when a pilot is flying, any bad air we might think is miniscule here, is a big problem that can cause the brain to shut itself down up there.'"[61]

The cryogenics lab produced pure oxygen and nitrogen, stored it, and used it to service aircraft. If things went wrong in the cryogenics lab, it's not only a close call, but serious injuries or death could occur. Unchecked deterioration on hoses (made of braided metal

---

61 "Cryogenics Marines Keepin' It Cool," *Marine Corps Air Station Miramar-EMS*, Accessed December 23, 2023. https://www.miramar-ems.marines.mil/News/News-Article-Display/Article/557734/cryogenics-marines-keepin-it-cool/.

and aluminum and wrapped together to form a tight seal) could result in an explosion. Shrapnel would disperse everywhere if that happened. Since liquid oxygen is combustible, and liquid nitrogen displaces oxygen, asphyxiation was a risk no one wants to take.

"If foreign materials, such as grease and fuel, mix with either the nitrogen or oxygen it could result in a chemical explosion."[62]

The lab, now occupied by the second group of Taliban in a make-shift bunker, was a ticking time bomb.

From their perspective, Coker and Weingart saw the threat, which amped their frustration of having no PID. They knew all their friendlies were on the ground with undetermined enemy numbers.

They turned on their searchlights to draw fire. *At least if the enemy was shooting at the helicopters, they weren't shooting at guys on the ground,* thought Coker. The searchlights helped them see each other's aircraft.

They put their sensors on the ground below without much success. They couldn't pick out the friendlies. Weingart told Rugger to see if any friendlies knew where the enemy was.

An RPG came up on Coker's aircraft from the cryo lab. The crew chiefs called Coker and Weingart to break, missing it. They came around as Coker talked on base defense frequency, repeating, "If any of our guys get PID and can get rounds on them, we'll be able to engage."

They quickly came back around towards the cryo lab when Wise yelled, "Our ECP is fucking lighting up!"

While most of the suppressive fires provided by the Marines of Righteous were fired from the ECP, SSgt Seay, Sgt Rodriguez, and LCpls Conner, Mulrenin, and Cleaves had pushed into a berm to the east of the ECP and set up their M240s. From this position, they

---

62 Lance Cpl. Quesada, Elyssa, "Cryogenics Keeping Fightertown Cool," Marine Corps Air Station Beaufort, October 31, 2008, https://www.beaufort.marines.mil/CommStrat/News/News-View/Article/524064/cryogenics-keeping-fightertown-cool/.

CAMP BASTION, Afghanistan. September 15, 2012. Brass left on the ground from the position SSgt Steven Seay and others had across from the cryo lab. Tracers from Seay's rifle helped pilots above determine from what position the Taliban enemies were firing from and what direction friendlies were returning fire. (Photo courtesy of LtCol Adam Coker)

were able to pick out the Taliban moving through the cryogenics lab and were accurately able to identify the enemy's positions. Seay fired several long bursts from his rifle, realizing that his tracers would provide the aircraft with an adequate mark for Coker to gain tally and engage the Taliban.

•••

Down south at the LSAs, another mobilization was in full swing. USMC Bastion Attack Narrative Summary report:[63]

> During the initial LSA Marines' mobilization, "Capt Christopher Scheele (Flight Equipment OIC), GySgt Richard Ley, Sgt Daniel Fitzgerald and Sgt Wright, Cpl Paul Garcia, and LCpl Mario Fabian established a listening post/observation post (LP/OP) on the dirt berm surrounding the LSA, 150 meters west of Capt Oren's HESCO position. Scheele and Ley had assigned sectors of fire at the northern LP/OP. From these elevated positions the Marines were able to observe tracer fire, directed at the cryogenics Lab."

•••

Coker looked down and could see rifle fire emanating from Gunny Clouatre, positioned near the HMLA-469 ECP and shooting southeast toward the cryo lab. From directly west across the X-bus road, Coker could also see SSgt Seay's M240 tracers going towards a cryo bunker on the east side. From two separate points, red (USMC/NATO) tracers were aimed at the same target—the cryo lab. Yeah, Coker was sure—the enemy was in there.

Any gunner in the military would have told you that firing specific weapons without tracers is not easy. A tracer's light showed the trajectory of the bullets, allowing a gunner to *walk* his fire to the intended target. This was an enhancement for a minigun, as most machine guns are difficult to aim, some with awful sights.

Add the wind that can vary a lot over a hundred yards. Lighted rounds mapped the trajectory of lethal bullets, because tracer and standard rounds are nearly identical ballistically.

---

63 "OEF Enemy Attack on Camp Bastion, 14 September 2012, NARRATIVE SUMMARY, HMLA 469" (Private source)

Coker, behind Weingart, saw Seay's tracers and sorted the good guys from the bad. Weingart radioed base defense, confident they gained eyes on the enemy position.

"We're tally, visual in," reported Weingart.

"Roger, cleared hot," replied Rugger 14.

Weingart told Coker, "Part trail, left pull."

"Trail, left pull," acknowledged Coker, knowing exactly what to do.

It was approximately 0115 when the order, "Trail left pull," told Coker the spacing and which way to turn after powerfully delivering the ordnance below. Coker's number two aircraft was behind Weingart's lead Cobra. Once Weingart was in position to deliver ordnance targeting Taliban positions at the cryogenics lab below, he would pull off target, allowing for sequential fires from Coker's Huey.

It was the best choice in that situation, one that needed immediate accuracy. It's a gun dance; no missteps allowed.

Weingart's Cobra carried a 20mm cannon and Hellfire missiles. In a normal flight operation, Coker's Huey would lase for the Cobra's Hellfire—meaning the Huey put the laser where the missile needed to go, and then the Cobra shoots and tracks the laser.

Because of the risk of collateral damage, no lase or Hellfire could engage. Weingart started shooting the 20mm, having to adjust to make target. Earlier in the day, he'd had some bore sight issues, so he told his co-pilot Elliot to shoot a little long and walk the rounds onto the target, a tactical technique to fire a weapon and observe its impact point. Then, the gunner adjusts his aim to get the next rounds closer to the target. Elliot walked his fire perfectly. The cannon shot semi-armor piercing high-explosive incendiaries (SAPHEI) rounds—basically like little grenades.

Weingart delivered about a hundred rounds at danger close distances, then pulled off, saying, "I'm off left."

Coker started, "Left gun open fire."

Coker, as pilot, could fire Advanced Precision Kill Weapon System (APKWS) laser-guided rockets. He also had flechette rockets (M149 Mod 0), which have 1179 60-grain flechettes or nails. Not knowing exactly where friendlies or the attackers were—the rockets were not a good weapons-to-target match. Coker had to decide fast what to use to strike. The job fell to Hebert and Wise on crew-served weapons, the GAU 21 .50 caliber on the left and the GAU-17 Gatling rotating minigun on the right.

Hebert fired the GAU-21 first directly on the cryo bunker with a combination of ball, tracer, armor-piercing, and armor-piercing incendiary .50 caliber rounds. The left gun ceased fire. As Coker pulled off the target, he said to Wise, "Right gun, open fire."

Wise engaged the GAU-17 at the cryo facility. Six spinning barrels shot 3,000 rounds per minute, forming a continuous stream of red-orange that was seen by friendly forces across the flight line.

Capt Coker's Huey gunners Cpl Hebert and SSgt Wise fire on Taliban attackers bunkered in cryo lab. (Combat art by Sean Sullivan)

"Right gun cease fire."

After Weingart and Coker finished shooting, a Brit PPV gunner directed fire at the cryo lab bunker with an automatic grenade launcher. Coker pulled off left and flew over their left shoulder between 200 and 300 feet. He did not see any more problems from the cryo area. Yet after the hellfire reign of enemy fire ceased, another fire began to grow, threatening hazardous waste.

20

DOING WHAT NEEDED TO BE DONE

OVER AT THE BRITISH firehouse, SSgt Matthew Wilson was in charge of ARFF-373 at the ready. Wilson was called by British fire-fighters to perform direct offensive fire operations at the cryogenics compound that was now on fire. Wilson assigned Sgt Morales, ARFF-373 crew leader, to lead a three-man team including himself, Harvilla, and Phelps (assigned to overwatch). A senior British leader advised that attackers had been spotted near the cryo lab and that their status was unknown. He also warned that explosive armaments and hazardous materials were stored inside containers at the cryo compound. Specifics of the situation were not available.

Despite the inherent dangers, SSgt Wilson and his crew left for the cryo compound. Sgt Morales led his Marines to extinguish a fire inside the cryo lab bunker, where they found five dead Taliban still holding AK-47s and RPGs.

Along with the enemy attackers, there was a clear and distinct blue-on-blue threat to consider since every position inside the wire was a friendly position.

• • •

Immediately following the RS 54 and RS 55 attack on the cryo lab, a report came in of a group of roughly fifteen to twenty individuals moving from the VMA-211 flight line to the HMLA-469 compound (from north to south). Capt Eckert, in Lightfoot's section, found them with the sensor and determined they were friendly, but could not identify them or what they were doing in the big scheme of the battle. Still, no one knew how many attackers were roaming on base.

The crews from RS 54, RS 55, RS 56, and RS 57 were nearing the end of their time on station because they were running low on fuel. Bastion, due to the current situation, was unable to provide fuel. Therefore, RS 54, Coker's flight of two, planned to cycle off the station to obtain fuel and return to the overhead at the Bastion airfield. RS 56 and 57, Lightfoot's flight of three, proceeded to Combat Outpost (COP) Shukvani, while RS 54 and RS 55 were sent to FOB Price to refuel.

There was a limit to the number of hours a pilot could fly in one day, unless approved to go over. Coker's crew day was already at twelve hours. There was no one to approve over the limit, and the attack was still ongoing.

Coker and Weingart's aircraft headed east to FOB Price, another British base. It was very dark, making the flight more difficult. They tried to get someone on the radio at Price, but no one answered. They couldn't see a landing strip at first, but as they got closer, a square helo pad popped into view.

Weingart asked Coker, "Your .50 cal's NATO?"

"Yeah," replied Coker.

"See if you can get some ordnance from these guys."

At FOB Price, Coker's flight was finally contacted and told to go to COP Shukvani. They first got some fuel at Price, then headed out. Shukvani was a base the U.S. took over from the Georgians, located even further east. Three flags flew over the remote spartan outpost—American, Afghanistan, and Georgian. Memories of Marines and Georgian soldiers in another fight lived on in the namesake of the outpost.

Second Line of Defense stated in 2011:[64] "It was September 5, 2010. 'In the hot, dry [treacherous] hills northwest of Sangin,' writes the [Marine Corps] Gazette, '1Lt Mukhran Shukvani was pushing a small team of Georgian soldiers forward from their dismount position in search of a future patrol base. As 1Lt Shukvani and his team crested one ridge line, they came under small arms fire from well concealed enemy positions. As the company commander rose to determine exactly where the enemy was located, a well-aimed round caught him just above his body armor.'" COP Shukvani was staked out later that day by U.S. Marines and Georgian soldiers.

Shukvani housed an HMLA-469 maintenance detachment that could troubleshoot the malfunctioning engine fuel system and sensor in Lightfoot's Cobra. The TAAC decided that RS 56 would remain there and stand by for further tasking. Lightfoot decided RS 57, Jordan's flight, would remain at Shukvani regardless, due to Jordan flying single-piloted.

Coker and Weingart landed at Shukvani, and as soon as they got inside, they were told, "Go again. They want you back on station."

Weingart asked Coker, "Are your guys good to go?"

Everyone had an overflow of adrenaline running through them. There was no call to end air operations over Bastion airfield, so the enemy was still out there. It was more than caution that sent them back. It was the drive to totally annihilate any possible hidden or obvious threat.

Coker talked to his crew chiefs about returning to the fight but already knew their answer, "Yeah, absolutely," he relayed to Weingart.

●●●

64 Smith, David, "These Guys are in the Fight," *Second Line of Defense*, September 28, 2011, https://sldinfo.com/2011/09/these-guys-are-in-the-fight/.

It seemed like an eternity, but only a half hour had passed by when Smalley got a call from Chambless at the VMA-211 maintenance hangar.

"Hey, Robb T.'s here. He wants to move everybody over to VMA headquarters. Be ready to receive them. They're also gonna bring over LtCol Raible's body."

The headquarters building was surrounded by six-foot-tall concrete barriers, making it a safer and more defensible position.

"Okay," responded Smalley.

•••

McDonald led the first group of six (of fifty VMA Marines) out of the bullet-ridden hangar, and they ran behind him. Approaching the concrete barriers surrounding VMA-211 headquarters, he could see four entrances or gaps one could enter through. McDonald posted the first six on security at one of the gaps. He ran back and got the next six. He posted them to the left of flight line security.

As he led more Marines there, he posted security at the remaining entrances, rifles pointed outboard. He brought the rest of the Marines inside headquarters. The Marines brought Raible over on a stretcher, his body covered. Rather than peel back that cover to see him, Smalley put him in the briefing room he and Raible had used only a few hours before. Shaken by his death, he sadly closed the door.

After leading fifty VMA Marines to headquarters, McDonald took one Marine and doubled back once more to the maintenance hangar. He ran through it one more time to make sure no one was knocked out on the floor or dead. The hangar appeared empty.

He searched the open flight line to see if anyone hid under an aircraft. Yeah, he could have been shot being out in the open, but he couldn't live with leaving a Marine behind. Yet he wasn't impervious to bullets. What would his admiral grandfather do? Was he guiding and protecting his grandson? Maybe, but then again, it was most likely the ingrained response of a Marine, driven by a code of honor to account for his own.

McDonald came into the makeshift operations center Smalley had set up at headquarters.

McDonald thought Smalley was a very smart guy and effective in his duties. He could see that Smalley had already tapped into the UAS, by hacking its feed on a computer and plugging it into a TV.

"What the fuck have you been doing?" he asked Smalley, surprised to see the Reaper feed.

"What? This is not normal. This is what we always do," answered Smalley, who proceeded to explain.

Unfortunately, the UAS completely ignored the Harrier flight line, where so much was happening. So far, the attacks had stopped short of neighbor HMLA-469's flight line.

McDonald and Smalley watched the UAS feed to the south of the Harrier flight line. It appeared the enemy had moved on. "Smalls," as McDonald nicknamed him, called several higher echelons of command to apprise them of the battle and search on the airfield's eastern side.

Smalley shared with higher headquarters what he could from his limited point of view. He was inside this little walled compound, going off what the computer and the maintenance personnel were calling over and telling him. There were three separate areas of the airfield engaged and no consistent comms. Sights, sounds, and smells gave the broader picture, but could not begin to tell all the details on the ground.

Thoughts swirled through various Marines' asking, *Are reinforcements coming in a second assault while Marines were responding to the first one, including any casualties?* That was a typical Taliban tactic. *Were they planting bombs in the dark as they traveled?* Bombs were made of anything they could find—using old, discarded batteries left behind as trash. *Were the attackers wearing hidden suicide vests loaded with C4 to cause even greater destruction than by their hands alone?*

Marines deployed to Sangin in 2010 were instructed not to leave batteries lying around. For combat Engineer Sgt David Noblit, assigned to Ronin 3 Platoon, 3rd Battalion Fifth Marines (3/5 Darkhorse), picking up a discarded battery cost him both his legs. The Taliban had planted an IED next to the battery they knew Marines would pick up. There is no end to their trickery and sabotage. The Taliban strive, without end, to make us remember them, and that part of their character didn't change on the night of September 14, 2012.

•••

From the time McDonald left the LSAs to get to the VMA aircraft maintenance hangar, he'd estimated it took about twenty minutes (going as fast as he could over the death-defying mile). It took another fifteen to twenty minutes to go from the hangar to the headquarters building. In all the explosions and confusion—and dark of night—it was hard to estimate time. It felt both painfully slow, yet really fast to McDonald.

Once his Marines were consolidated, McDonald's first concern had been accountability. When he encountered Chambless and saw Raible had been killed, he also found out several Marines had been wounded. An attempt was made to retrieve people with a truck from HMLA-469 but the truck was shot at on the way out, so that idea was abandoned. McDonald did not know how many people were missing.

•••

McDonald spoke to several non-commissioned officers (NCOs) at VMA-211 headquarters, "You're the Sergeant of the Guard. Go outside where I have security posted and make sure everyone's aware. Keep moving from post to post and make sure everything is tight. Rotate guys in and out as they get tired," he ordered the first NCO.

To the others, he ordered, "You guys go through the building and go around to the post-op side. Count everybody and get a solid headcount. Go opposite directions, and don't confer with each other on your headcount. Report your separate head counts to CWO Ball. He's going to be standing up here."

Ball knew all the Marines who worked for him in maintenance. To Smalley, at the makeshift operations center, he said, "Try to get a roster of all the people in our squadron. Find out who's on the night crew, including the night crew on shift. Figure out where everyone is."

While orders were executed, McDonald ran around mobilizing and overseeing. Phones were ringing off the hook. A couple of guys that had just left the country were trying to reach them to see what was going on. Somehow, they knew, while the rest of the world didn't. VMA-211's Marine Aviation Detachment (MAD) commander in Yuma called in. The secret phone line hadn't been secured. MajGen Gurganus was at the Leatherneck command post processing information coming in about the fight on the airfield, and what was happening with his troops, and getting that up to higher-up, Army LTG James Terry, Gurganus' boss.

The command post was about one to one-half miles for direct line of sight, but more distance separated by ground. A mile on a base as big as Bastion is a decent amount of geography. Aide de camp Yerger made sure the right personnel were there, including LtCol Jeff Tuggle, who was the G3, and LtCol John Walker, who was the G2. They wanted intel on casualties, damage to aircraft, and damage to buildings. Yerger observed that Gurganus took the loss of any Marine very personally and saw as information on Marine casualties came in, it hit Gurganus hard.

21

TURNING DESTRUCTION INTO DOMINATION

BACK AT THE FIREHOUSE where both U.K. and U.S. firefighters had been pulled back, Hensley was tired of waiting and doing nothing. He told the ARFF Marines, "Oh, this is crap. I'm gonna send the P-19s back over. We're gonna fight these fires."

At that moment, it was ARFF Marines from both coasts creating their own follow-on mission. There was no regular chain of command because of the sudden, brazen attack. Command headquarters for MWSS-273 was over a mile away in Camp Leatherneck. Killebrew, nor Hensley, had any way to communicate. They had situational awareness before them, and demands were emergent. A drone feed over the fuels compound would have been a godsend.

Hensley split up the available assets despite the British saying the fires could not be extinguished. Hensley, Stone, and other firefighters that had pulled back with the British were eager to return to the catastrophic demon devouring precious fuel and threatening life. They knew the P-19s only held 1,000 gallons of water. The assets and manpower had to be divided to fight all the fires on base, including the Harriers.

Hensley told the Brits they were leaving to attack the fuel fires. "We're going to go," confirmed Hensley with steely intent. They left, headed for the fuel pits.

Stone, senior non-commissioned officer in charge, started foaming the top of the fire with the P-19s. LCpl Phelps manned the turret, a high-powered master stream of water and foam. The blanket of foam is what extinguished a fire by separating fuel from oxygen.

No British firefighter was on site. Killebrew figured the Brits were worried about Prince Harry, who was reportedly on Camp Bastion at some undisclosed location. He had to mentally remind himself, *The British are firefighters first, and that he and his men are Marines first, firefighters and fuelers, second.* In his head, he surmised, *British firefighters don't go in and make an incident larger by losing their trucks or themselves, not armed or able to defend one another.* Killebrew's ARFF guys went into the chaos with the skill to use a rifle and didn't look back.

Killebrew worried about 1.2 million gallons of bulk fuel storage and was compelled to cut the feed from BFI to the fuel pits. He ordered MSgt Parker to grab a couple of Marines. They got in one of the smaller Mine Resistant Ambush Protected (MRAP) vehicles that was still intact.

Authorization was obtained from the Fuels Chief to send Killebrew's Marines over uncovered ground east across the X-bus road towards the enemy's last known locations.

Parker and other Marines walked, following the line, and cut the feed from the BFI to the fuel pits. Enemy fire was quiet as the cryo lab smoke from the fire billowed up in the sky. The Marines cut the line again, using special tools. No additional feast for the fires now.

•••

A lot of coordination happened in ten to fifteen minutes after McDonald arrived at VMA headquarters. The Sergeant of the Guard ran in from outside, adrenaline pumping, "There's a guy right outside one of our positions lying on the ground. He is in an Army uniform."

Quick as a bullet, McDonald ran outside and saw a Taliban attacker lying on his side, moving, but it was a bit far away. McDonald called for cover and jogged towards the guy. He scoped him with the ACOG on his rifle. With four-power magnification, McDonald could see he was in an Army uniform, but he had a beard. He was obviously Afghan, wearing white running shoes, and gripping an AK-47 in one hand. The attacker was wearing a foreign body armor harness, and his other hand cocooned a grenade.

The bearded Taliban was alive and looked right at McDonald, but he didn't raise his rifle. McDonald didn't know why, other than he may have wanted McDonald to think he was dead.

It's not that McDonald had any problem pulling a trigger on the attacker. VMA's acting CO was sure he made his shot, but it wasn't lethal, as he saw the guy moving.

McDonald jogged back to headquarters and issued an order, "Don't shoot him, unless he does something aggressive, because we might want to turn him over to intel when this is over. Leave this guy where he is. He's injured. Keep an eye on him."

His eyes darted around the room. "Report back to me if anything changes."

Over the next fifteen minutes or so, more than once, Marines reported, "Hey, he moved. He crawled. Now he's hiding behind this barricade."

"Okay—just sit on it. Keep guarding," reiterated McDonald, adding, "Don't draw attention to exactly where we are."

McDonald surmised there were other Taliban in Army fatigues rampaging the flight line approximately a hundred meters from where this loser was. Situational awareness was elusive, and they would have to pluck them off as they encountered them in their aggressive searches to dominate on this imposed battleground.

Smalley broke into the administrative VMA shop and got rosters.

Another Marine kept a timeline on a whiteboard. The headcount was pretty solidified.

Suddenly, McDonald was aware of the quiet. He knew enemy fighters were out there and figured they discovered the Marines weren't in the hangar anymore. He didn't want some mad suicide charge into their position at the headquarters building. He had an idea and needed someone to watch his back.

Knowing the character of Marines, he presented, "I need three volunteers to go with me."

The group had to be very small. He told Maj Chambless they were going to go out and count the jets. He didn't want everyone in the room to hear him say, *"I'm going to go out there and try to kill these guys so nothing else happens."*

"If I'm not back in ten minutes, then you are in charge," he said to Chambless.

"I need to go find what's out there," he said, and grabbed Jenkins, Weekly, and Colburn.

The group was on task despite any reservations.

McDonald took three Maintenance Marines outside and instructed them. LCpl Weekly was an Air Frames Marine who worked on the skin/control surface of the aircraft. SSgt Colburn, an ejection seat mechanic, and LCpl Jenkins, maintenance control admin. He needed them to do what they were told regardless of their rifle proficiency, as he wanted them to hold a sector of fire to his rear. McDonald needed them to squat where he told them to and look where he directed. He trusted that if something happened or the enemy tried to get them from behind, they knew how to shoot. Off to each side and towards his back are the places he posted the three.

The instructions were, "No matter what happens, when the shooting starts, don't turn around. Keep your sector, because other people might hear the shooting and run up behind us." McDonald's mind was like a computer processor whirring, thinking of not only the moment, but a myriad of "what ifs."

After a sixty-second brief, the fire team understood the plan and did a brass check to ensure a round was in their rifle chamber. Once they pulled the charging handle back and saw a little bit of brass from the shell casing peeking out, they knew they were set to fight. Each Marine then grabbed an extra magazine. McDonald gave one of the Marines, clad in a T-shirt, his Kevlar, and to another Marine gave his protective flak jacket, because the body armor had run out.

McDonald stepped out on the flight line to be met with BAH-JING rifle fire from the attackers. He quickly looked south around a corner of a T-wall and saw a Conex (transporter) box in front of the Authorized Military Overhaul Facility (AMOF) with four Taliban lined up alongside it.

A Conex box is a rigid steel corrugated container developed by the U.S. Army Transportation Corps to carry 9,000 pounds. It was 8 feet, 6 inches (2.59 meters) long, 6 feet, 3 inches (1.91 meters) wide, and 6 feet, 10 inches (2.08 meters) high, with double doors on one end. Now, it was being used as a makeshift hideout for the Taliban invaders, like snakes who crawl up under rocks and then strike.

Defying four of the armed enemy, McDonald committed and leapt out, locking eyes on one Taliban leaning forward at the waist, holding a Pulemyot Kalashnikova Modernizirovany (PKM) machine gun with a bipod. For a brief second, McDonald and the attacker made eye contact. It's a look you have nightmares about for life. McDonald had the drop on him, pulled his weapon up, and shot the Taliban in the face. It was a fast fall to the ground.

One fewer attacker who met the wrath of a U.S. Marine, which is something no one in their right mind should do.

When their buddy got shot, the Taliban moved from the Conex box. McDonald saw them squatting in a gap at the bottom of twelve-foot-wide, eighteen-foot-high T-wall barriers that were pushed together. The barriers provided concealment from the sides. A Taliban fighter looked over at McDonald, as McDonald fired into the group of armed attackers.

Wounded, startled voices sounded out. One of the Taliban reached out from his position, pulled the slain fighter's PKM machine gun over, and held the trigger down, firing a long burst of ammunition toward McDonald. The bullets landed close enough to kick concrete up in McDonald's face. He fired back again, but the angles were bad.

Lance Corporal Weekly ran forward towards McDonald, stopping short of his position to unload his weapon in the back of the T-wall barriers. He was at a worse angle than McDonald and could not hit the attackers.

Yet it was BOOM, BOOM, BOOM suppressive machine gun fire that meant business. McDonald struggled to get a clear shot, but to no avail. He knew the remaining Taliban were injured badly and that he'd killed one of them for sure. He looked over at Weekly and waved his hand in front of his face to cease fire. Weekly complied, and McDonald said, "Let's go."

McDonald, Weekly, and the others headed back to the headquarters building. The Taliban continued to deliver machine gun fire at McDonald's old position, but then started shooting towards the headquarters building.

McDonald was puzzled. Did the Taliban gunner think the Marines' rapid fire was coming at them from both places? Perhaps bleeding wounds and pain blurred perceptions. Because they were hurt, McDonald assessed they would stay put, and if they did leave, it would be slow moving. McDonald ran into headquarters and got on the phone with OPSO Marvel at HMLA headquarters. He knew Marvel from his first helicopter deployment and counted on helicopters being overhead, a trained response to troops in combat. He didn't know who was up there, how many aircraft, or where all the close air support hotspots across the base were, but he was ordering a gunship to come to finish the job he started.

McDonald told Marvel to tell the helicopter pilots to get ahold of him on VMA-211 base frequency. Base radio communicates to pilots while flying. As a former JTAC, McDonald knew typical aviation chatter like the back of his hand, like "Aircraft zero-one, outbound," "Aircraft zero-one's ten minutes out," or "Aircraft zero-one's landed."

Yet, the radio talk that night had a lot of disconnected urgent information and some confusion. It came through a big squawk box speaker, so everyone in the room heard it. He was well aware of the challenges for pilots in identifying threats and making the right decisions. McDonald, focused on his emergent and imminent situation of four Taliban pinned in their midst, was going to help that helo pilot find them.

•••

After Coker refueled at FOB Price, he returned to the overhead approximately thirty-five minutes later, just after 0200. While establishing in the overhead of Bastion once again, Coker was advised that multiple attackers remained in positions on the VMA flight line, and although the QRF was maneuvering to engage the enemy, they were getting hit with small arms fire and RPGs. Coker received a call on HMLA-469 internal base frequency, telling him *Major McDonald intended to utilize the VMA-211 base radio to talk to him about the Taliban positions on the VMA flight line.*

Coker had his three radios back up. He exchanged information with HMLA-469 Base, counting on getting back-briefed.

The second time on station, Coker heard Marvel's voice, "Part, you up?"

"Yep, I'm up," said Coker.

"I've got a guy at the Harrier squadron. He was a former MARSOC JTAC. He has PID insurgents on his flight line," said Marvel.

"Roger, what is his frequency?" asked Coker.

Marvel gave Coker the VMA-211 base freq. Coker relayed to Weingart, "MOG just told me there's a JTAC from a Harrier squadron with PID-insurgents on his flight line. Here's his base freq."

Weingart only had two radios, so he would not be able to hear any forthcoming conversation from VMA-211. Weingart was up on base defense (with Rugger) and interflight while Coker went over to VMA-211 frequency. Coker didn't know who the JTAC was and had to figure out fast what to call him.

"Heat Actual, this is Righteous 55," relayed Coker.

22
NO REWIND, ONLY RETRIBUTION

HELD UP FOR TOO long at the crash barn, at 0200, Phelps responded to the fuel pit fire for the second time, determined. He manned the turret on a firefighting vehicle, delivering a high-powered master stream of water and foam that was instrumental in extinguishing a 50,000-gallon jet propulsion fuel fire.

At 0230 SSgt Wilson, Sgt Morales and crew returned to the fuel pits where the 119,000-gallon fuel fire was burning out of control. He parked his P19 fire truck and quickly led his crew with hand lines into the fire to extinguish the burning fuels equipment. LCpl Williams was in the mix, spraying three 50,000-gallon fuel bags on fire, shooting 9,000 gallons of water and foam out like a rocket on the Taliban's handiwork. Williams and the others were fighting like hell to prevent the other three 50,000-gallon fuel bags from going up in flames. Morales was called to resupply his fire truck with water and compressed air.

•••

As McDonald and Coker were talking, Sturdevant called Smalley, asking, "Hey, can you confirm that your CO's dead?"

Smalley replied, "Yes, he's dead."

Gurganus had asked Sturdevant to confirm, so he could provide an update to higher headquarters in Afghanistan.

Then Smalley called Yuma and got a hold of the remain-behind element.

"I need you to go into your CACO files and to pull the last half of the alphabet and bring it to the MAG CO," said Smalley.

"Uhhh, okay—everything okay over there?" asked a Marine.

"No, everything's not okay. I just need you to fucking do this."

"Okay, sir, I'll go get it."

The Casualty Assistance Calls Officer (CACO) had access to information that needed to be in hand to notify Raible's wife and family. For that officer, it would be a gut-wrenching task.

• • •

McDonald exuded confidence, giving the ground side talk to Coker. Both pilots had combat flight experience, and that welded them together. Missing the mark that night was not an option.

"Righteous, yeah, I've got guys on my flight line. Can you take a lat, long position?" asked McDonald.

"I can, but I'm currently 200 feet over your head. Just talk me on, brother," replied Coker.

"Okay, I'm in the hangar. There are some T-walls right there. The Taliban are at the base of them," said McDonald.

McDonald described the exact T-wall barrier location in between the AV-8B enclosure and another maintenance hangar. The bases of the T-walls are fatter than the tops. There's a forty-five-degree cutout where the base comes out.

Four Taliban were sitting down on the west side of that T-wall, having found shelter in the cutouts that come up above the shoulders, providing effective protection from the fires coming from the south. Yet, the attackers had a false sense of security. There was no place good enough to hide. Could they get their last kills before the last stand? They were trying.

If they can grow a beard, they're old enough to carry a rifle. The ages and names of these recruits are not publicly known. Jihad brainwashing begins early, and human rights are not a factor, as they send their fighters out to die a violent death, but not before they inflict it.

Now informed, Gianelloni worked the sensor to pick up the enemy location.

"Roger, I'm tally, I'm tally," confirmed Coker to McDonald.

An injured Taliban in the northernmost position was on his back, possibly dead. Coker confirmed with McDonald that he was approved to engage on his flight line. McDonald assured Righteous Flight 55 that all his VMA personnel were inside the hangar. Any person outside the hangar was hostile.

With the sensor locked on, Coker could see the four individuals had cammies on—gray Army uniforms. Most everyone on the flight line wore flight suits or maintenance coveralls. Some Marines wore MARPATs (Marine cammies), and he could tell the difference looking into the FLIR.

Coker observed all four Taliban had white tennis shoes, and some had beards. One had an AK-47 in hand, and one had a PKM, the same as what McDonald faced before he dropped one of the attackers.

Just a bit north from the western side of the T-walls, Coker could see the injured Taliban lying on the ground (with something in his hand). Again, the same guy McDonald shot earlier. They could see the other three Taliban with rifles moving in the crevices. One of the surviving Harriers was right in front of them.

"Yes, we do have four individuals on the west side of the T-wall," confirmed Weingart.

Coker radioed Rugger at Base Defense to get approval to attack. Both Coker and Weingart updated Base Defense with the FLIR images, waiting for a green light to engage. The Taliban engaged Coker with small arms each time he did a fly-by. He saw the hot brass leaving their weapons in his sensor footage. *When would it be his turn?* Coker thought. VMA Marines underneath him were still at risk. A British MRAP vehicle pulled up near the T-walls and tried to engage the attackers.

"What are they doing? Get them out of there," yelled Coker over base defense radio.

The Taliban started shooting the MRAP, and the Brits fired back. The vehicle itself was smaller than an American version, and no MK-19 turret gun was on top. Instead, the MK-19 was inside the MRAP, and the Brits couldn't get it to depress down far enough to target the attackers. If they could have, the belt-fed, fully automatic weapon could do some real damage, firing 40mm grenades at a practical rate of fire of sixty (rapid) rounds per minute and forty (sustained) rounds per minute.

Poorly positioned, the Brits posed a lethal threat to the Marines on the other side of the T-walls they were firing at. The hangar McDonald and his squadron were in was right behind the T-walls.

"Get them to stop shooting, abort," Coker yelled. The Brits kept shooting a little longer, then stopped and started backing away.

RS 54 coordinated with BDOC's Theater Air Defense (TAD) to move the QRFs from the engagement area, due to danger close considerations. Weingart decided to use Coker's crew-served weapons rather than Cobra's 20mm to shoot at the Taliban. Even though the Marines were confirmed to be inside the buildings or in IDF bunkers, the close proximity of those structures, as well as the remaining AV-8B Harriers on the flight line, created a risk of collateral damage. Plus, Weingart knew the 20mm's bore sight was slightly off.

"You have TAAC lead, don't worry about me, I'll stay out of your way," Weingart told Coker.

23

TERMINATING MORTAL DANGER

THE HUEY HAD THE best weapon-to-target match. The Taliban continued to shoot directly at Coker (with no tracers). Luckily, Coker could see the hot brass coming off their rifles.

He didn't worry about himself, and he couldn't allow thoughts of home or his family. He zeroed in on what was in front of him. Coker felt great concern for Hebert on the left gun side exposed to the enemy while waiting for orders. Coker jinked the helo, suddenly changing direction to dodge his pursuers. He came back around. Flying at a hundred knots, there was only one way to get to the Taliban, without shooting the friendlies right behind them.

Coker planned to come into a hover and deliver ordnance, so there'd be no ricochets. At about 200 feet, he could shoot off the side, straight down, sitting still. A hover over an armed enemy is a supremely risky move.

The only time helo pilots ever did it was during family days. Pilots flew the helicopters for their loved ones, eager to see the skills of their Marines. Pilots descended into a hover and shot off the side in front of them. He remembered telling people, "We don't ever want to do that." It was for show then, and now it was for the greater good. The attackers were injured and trapped—it was a perfect opportunity to take them out.

Coker needed clearance as quickly as possible. He radioed McDonald at 0230, "I understand I am approved to engage on your flight line."

"Absolutely. Cleared to engage," said Heat Actual.

Coker called up Rugger, "Righteous 55 is in 060-030."

"Cleared hot," responded Rugger.

Coker maneuvered the aircraft into position. "Left gun open fire," Coker said to Hebert.

The .50 caliber let loose on the Taliban. Although Hebert's impacts were well-placed in the T-walls, some of the insurgents kept moving. Watching the sensor, the crew determined they were still alive, and an immediate reattack was approved. Hebert opened up the .50 caliber again.

Rugger passed on that the Predator Drone was still seeing movement and wanted Coker to re-attack. Righteous 55 came back around. At 0236, he ordered Wise to engage with the GAU-17.

"Hey, the Harrier still looks good. Do not hit that Harrier," Coker said to Wise.

Coker maneuvered his aircraft to do *what they never do*. He expertly piloted the Huey into a stable hover; this helped shed the worry about bullets ricocheting. That was no easy task, as the Taliban was still moving approximately ten meters from the Harrier jet.

The Huey was amazingly suspended in a hundred-foot hover as in previous attacks that night. He was not moving forward when Wise engaged his gun. Hell-bent on neutralizing the last of the four Taliban, he was at point-blank range from the target. Wise shot straight down, exactly where it was supposed to go. They did not hear any more small arms sounding off—no RAT-a-TAT after that engagement. As far as Coker knew, the four attackers in the T-walls were dead. He didn't know that was the last of them—all except one injured, Mohammed Nazeer, who remained alive in an undisclosed location.

• • •

At 0300, after resupply, Sgt Morales was called back to the cryo lab with Wilson, Phelps, and others to attack the fire inside a fifty-foot shipping container that stored fifteen metal wall lockers each filled with various unidentified HAZMAT. The shipping container was surrounded by fifty-five-gallon drums filled with flammable liquids and compressed gas cylinders.

Morales deployed his crew to the first container, where they discovered multiple lockers filled with burning hazardous materials. He and Phelps entered the container only to be faced with cans of exploding HAZMAT. Phelps pushed forward to the rear of the container, allowing him and other Marines to begin removing wall lockers to reach the seat of the fire. Phelps and Morales began to pull six lockers, weighing 200 pounds each, out of the containers, which made it even more difficult due to the burning floor of the container that kept giving way. That prevented the firefighters from dragging the lockers, forcing them to lift and carry the lockers out of containers. Active fire, intense heat, and physical exhaustion did not deter them. Morales continued to fight the container fire until he was forced to return to resupply his equipment with water and compressed air.

At 0400, Morales and his crew went back to the container fire at the cryo compound to relieve the crew. Once again, he and his crew began removing 200-pound hazardous material lockers. Morales had depleted his water supply to help extinguish the fire and was directed to cut a ventilation hole through the steel container. He grabbed a rescue saw and, with the help of another Marine, cut an eight-foot triangle through three-sixteenths of steel, successfully ventilating the container. Morales and the crew continued to do this backbreaking labor for at least an hour under the greatest risk possible, until they were once again forced to resupply.

At 0600, LCpl Williams relieved the crew at the cryo container fire. He, with Cpl Harvilla, then began removing eight of the 200-pound hazardous material lockers over a floor that was burnt and lacked any structural integrity. This required Williams and Harvilla to lift and carry the heavy lockers out of the shipping container. The container fire was later declared over at 1000 the next morning.

That night, Sgt Morales had spent a total of eight hours of continuous firefighting operations extinguishing fires caused by the Taliban attackers.

LCpl Phelps worked in fire ground operations for five continuous hours without relief.

LCpl Williams spent a total of four hours of continuous firefighting operations.

Cpl Harvilla spent an exhausting four hours of continuous firefighting.

To put this in perspective, civilian firefighters in the same situation would be replaced every thirty to forty-five minutes due to the strenuous activities performed and the cumbersome gear worn while fighting a fire. ARFF-373 firefighters prevented a total loss at the cryogenics compound and surrounding area. They saved millions of gallons of fuel, keeping the enemy and fires away from the BFI installation. These Marines fearlessly stopped the further loss of airfield equipment and ended the potential spread of the fire onto other areas of the airfield.

•••

Coker and Weingart saw tactical vehicles at the north end of the runway using IR (laser) pointers to the south. Pilots use IR pointers to show the crew chiefs where to shoot on their attacks. Laser pointers can only be seen with NVDs.

A bunch of guys had put their lasers at the same southern location, which could indicate *no comms*. In close air, *no comms* procedure is not standardized, but protocol still exists. If the IR flashes and then goes steady, it means, "We want you to shoot there." Coker thought that might be what they were asking.

CAMP BASTION, Afghanistan. 2012. Marines with Marine Wing Support Squadron 373 at Camp Bastion airfield fuel farm. (Photo courtesy of Sgt Michael Doman)

Rugger found out the tactical vehicles were just telling the aircraft, "Don't shoot the guys moving south."

After the battle ended, Coker flew to get gas and returned to Bastion. RS 54 and 55 flights continued to provide CAS on station until just past sunrise on September 15. They reconnoitered fence lines, rolling terrain, and compounds on the base, looking for any enemy fighters.

Righteous flights heard a couple of reports that indicated something else was going on. Coker supported overhead, not wanting to see anything else but ready to engage if he did.

They looked in the LSAs and made sure there was no one else hiding. They flew around the perimeter as convoys were going in, searching for people and the location of the Taliban breach. Multiple suspicious vehicles were observed within proximity to the base and

CAMP BASTION, Afghanistan. September 15, 2012. One of six AV-8B Harrier jets destroyed in Taliban attack September 14, 2012. Two other AV-8B Harrier jets were severely damaged, and five sunshades destroyed with damage to the VMA hangar/maintenance facility. (HMLA/VMA Camp Bastion Attack Presentation 2015)

were stopped by the RS sections. The vehicles were searched by Marine vehicular patrols roaming the eastern desert. The reports turned out to be nothing.

The fuels compound was still burning. The Harriers were sickening, melted heaps of metal and ash.

Raible and Atwell were in undisclosed locations to receive sacred honors, their bodies being prepared to be sent home.

Coker and Weingart were the last on station. At 0630, RS 54 and 55 were told to go to Dwyer, a base to the south, and Shukvani, respectively. They flew there and shut down, both aircraft having flown 13.6 hours in a day.

It took a while—but everybody finally got to sleep. They remained at Dwyer and Shukvani until the late afternoon of September 15. Coker flew back to Bastion.

When the sun came up, Capt Seth Jordan helped some troops in a convoy drive around outside the wire, trying to find anything else. The convoy did find caches to the east right outside the wire. The caches contained ammunition, weapons, dates and almonds, and green spray paint.

When Gurganus and Sturdevant walked the battlefield that next morning, they saw where the Taliban had been huffing green paint underneath their masks. Intel received some information the Taliban were planning a second attack of indirect fire on the base.

A controlled det of confiscated weapons and ammo happened later that afternoon that no one knew about. EOD forgot to notify. Everyone thought an attack was starting up again.

The day after, the base took two rockets on the British side, one hitting the chow hall. Nobody got hurt, but everyone was on a high-octane edge.

Coker remembered sitting in the maintenance spaces, thinking a rocket could come through and hit them at any time. It was nerve-wracking because they kept getting Intel the Taliban were regrouping.

CAMP BASTION, Afghanistan. October 28, 2012. Secretary of the Navy Ray Mabus (left) tours bullet-ridden T-walls damaged in Marines' counter attack to Taliban destruction. Mabus met with MajGen Charles Mark Gurganus (right) and other senior leaders. (Photo by Chief Mass Communication Specialist Sam Shavers, Wikimedia Commons)

The next day, Coker walked by the cryo facility, ghostly and charred by battle. A Marine was in the cryo lab at the time of Coker's strike on the attackers hiding in the makeshift bunker—separate from his location. When he found out who was in the helo overhead, he asked, "Sir, can I have a picture with you . . . you saved my life."

Colonel Bew's sense of purpose going out amongst the Marines that morning was to make clear that there was a path forward, that there was some stability, and that there was direction. They all experienced a cataclysmic crisis.

"We'll mourn the dead. We'll assess the impact on the airfield and set a trajectory for recovery of operations," Bew summarized in the gloomy aftermath. "We have to get back to conducting operations as soon as possible."

CAMP BASTION, Afghanistan. September 15, 2012. Capt Adam Coker (right) and (unnamed) Marine who thanked Capt Coker for saving his life at the cryo lab when said Marine was overrun by five of fifteen Taliban attackers. (Photo courtesy of LtCol Adam Coker)

The Marines did not have the luxury of what Bew called "security theater."

"You just need to pay attention to how people are reacting to the surprise battle. At the end of the day, you have a mission to accomplish."

"Out of the ten [attackers] that chose to go through the middle by the fuels compound and by the cryo facility, every one of them were killed long before they ever got to the [other] flight lines," recalls Gurganus. "The next day, I walked every inch of the ground, and the bodies were still there . . . I know where every one of them died."

"Not a pretty sight," recalled Sturdevant, who accompanied Gurganus.

His guys pulled the dead insurgents out of the fight zones and laid them out to be picked up later. One insurgent killed in front of the shipping boxes died with a growl look on his face, unnerving Killebrew. The attackers' false idea of glory lay in pieces.

Killebrew and his team reconstructed a forward arming and refueling point (FARP) with 970 trucks, so they could refuel aircraft (still flying missions). He personally put three burned-up Harriers in a box. They got all six that were destroyed cleaned up in four days. He didn't sleep for a week—an hour here, an hour there. Killebrew's team rebuilt the entire fuels compound area and cleaned up the entire bloody battle mess. (See insurgent actions map in front of the book.)

Miraculously, the fuels building was still standing after the brutal attack, with not that much damage. And by it flew the American flag that Sgt Rihn had raised. The flag survived the raging fuel pits fire and did not burn.

CAMP BASTION, Afghanistan, September 14-15, 2012. Collected evidence showing the visual intent of Taliban attackers. (Image from Operational Learning Account and After Action Review – Complex Attack on Camp Bastion on 14-15 Sep 12, 5FPJ3OLAAR/01/16 Sep 12, ISAF, released)

•••

It was a heroic fight in the dark of night and a testament to deeply embedded training, steely grit, overcoming danger to save lives and property, and loving one's brother or sister over self. This battle during the war in Afghanistan is a legacy for Marines to pass on to other Marines—a hard, courageous, and ultimate triumph over the Taliban that goes down in history as one of the Marine Corps' finest.

We forever honor those who gave their lives so others can be free from terror.

LtCol Christopher "Otis" Raible received a Bronze Star, Air Medal, and Purple Heart.

CAMP BASTION, Afghanistan. September 25, 2012. Coalition memorial service to honor LtCol Christopher K. Raible, commanding officer of Marine Attack Squadron (VMA) 211, 3rd Marine Aircraft Wing (Forward). Raible was killed in action while repealing an enemy attack on the Camp Bastion airfield, September 14, 2012. Maj John "Strut" Havener, VMA-211 XO, flew in from Qatar to take over the squadron from Maj Robb T. McDonald (who was acting for one day). Havener then passed command to LtCol Troy Pherson. (DVIDS photo Sgt Keonaona Paulo)

Sgt Bradley Atwell received the Purple Heart.

CAMP BASTION, Afghanistan. September 20, 2012. U.S. Marines pay tribute to Sgt Bradley W. Atwell, an aircraft electrical, instrument, and flight control technician with 3rd Marine Aircraft Wing (Fwd), killed in action five days earlier while repelling an enemy attack on Camp Bastion. (DVIDS photo by Sgt Keonaona Paulo)

AFTERMATH

Major General Charles Mark Gurganus

"Afghanistan was the hardest command because number one, you're the guy at the end of the day that's on the dart board. It was a period when there was a lot of change—the drawdowns, resurgence of the Taliban.

"It was a daily challenge trying to help rebuild a government when Marines aren't trained to rebuild governments. Instead, they are working with the provisional reconstruction team and other civilians that were also trying to do those things.

"But you knew you were making a small difference. That's a credit to those guys I was lucky enough to have around me. On the U.S. side, the Brit side, and on the Dane side.

"We weren't asking them to do easy things. We asked them to do mission impossible on some occasions. If you take care of them, they take care of you and more importantly, they take care of the mission.

"If the guys in charge think they're the smartest people in the group, they've already failed. They may have good ideas, but it takes everyone all the way down . . . to make stuff happen. And if you don't trust them, you're not going to succeed.

"Everything I earned in my life was earned on the backs of my Marines."

AFTERMATH

Major General Gregg Sturdevant

"Mark Gurganus did amazing things with the other three sides of the base . . . the sides he could control. The area to the east where the poppies grew was protected by the politicians. Mark asked multiple times to bulldoze down the plants in the field that were growing right up to the fence line. The first time, 'You have to wait until after the harvest.' The second time (harvest complete), 'We have to put an Afghan face on this; Afghan soldiers have to go house by house to let people know they have to move.' By now more poppy is growing. The third time, 'We have to use Afghan labor to drive the bulldozers to destroy the fields.' Then the attack came.

"Individuals at all levels took responsibility for themselves and whether they liked it or not, they rose to the occasion. They fell into leadership roles up and down the flight line.

"After the attack we were allowed to bulldoze down the poppy fields and open clear fields of view where we could see any threat that approached from the east."

It took months for RC(SW) to get approval from higher headquarters to conduct an attack on the Taliban training camp, Bahrām Chāh, on the Helmand Province/Pakistan border. The Marines from 3rd MAW pounded them for two days with AV-8 Harriers and a KC-130 Harvest Hawk. When they were finished—there was nothing left of the training camp.

The mention of the 3rd MAW flight line barrier plan submitted to the Joint Staff Integrated Vulnerability Assessment (JISVA) on May 11, 2012, was included in a March 20, 2014 letter from Sturdevant to the Secretary of the Navy while fighting a "letter of censure" and to retain his two-star ranking.

Despite the fact his staff identified egregious flight line vulnerabilities months before the attack and submitted a request for improvements, only to be turned down by the ESG, he and Gurganus would suffer the sole and very public blame for the breach. That would be ingrained in the skewed history of the attack, instead of the truth.

"If only they had listened," says Sturdevant looking back.

"To my dying day, I will be proud of the Aviation Combat Element's response that night."

Major General Gregg Sturdevant is the founder and CEO of Mission Critical Leadership Solutions.

In 2021, Sturdevant published a book titled: *Mission Critical Leadership: Marine Corps Leadership Principles to Transform, Motivate, and Lead Your Teams to Success.*

Lieutenant Colonel Stephen Lightfoot

"Getting the aircraft swiftly in the air during the attack allowed HMLA-469 to roll right into flying missions the next day. The mechanics that picked up rifles in the night and then picked up their wrenches the next morning to inspect aircraft, looked at everything. No one even knew if there were unexploded ordnances out there, so it was a bit dangerous.

"One-by-one the mechanics were able to say, 'Yeah, this aircraft can fly, and that aircraft can fly.'

"I am extremely proud to serve with such high-caliber men and women, who, in the face of enemy fire, dropped their wrenches, grabbed their rifles, defended our compound from a heavily armed enemy attack, and launched multiple aircraft into the moonless night to locate, close with, and successfully destroy the enemy forces through combined ground and air power."

Brigadier General Stephen L. Lightfoot is now Director of Capabilities Development at Headquarters United States Marine Corps, Combat and Integration.

Major Robb T. McDonald

"A Marine is a Marine for life. The Marine Corps gives you a discipline and mindset that drives you towards accomplishment of your goals. It makes you realize what you are capable of. To the point where you feel like you are capable of anything if you do it right.

"It's made me feel that I can run as far as I want to run or swim as far as I want to swim. I can't really put it into words. It's given me confidence—a 'can do' type of attitude.

"When you look at the Marines I hang out with, associate with, they have a positive attitude. There's a smile on your face in miserable conditions. You can't take it too seriously when you're physically or emotionally uncomfortable, because it's a passing thing. It's doable. The Marines have taught me all those things."

Colonel Robb T. McDonald was awarded a Silver Star for his heroic role at Camp Bastion. He now serves as the Executive Officer to the NORAD & USNORTHCOM Commander.

CAMP PENDLETON, Calif. December 09, 2013. Maj Robb. T. McDonald received the Silver Star "for conspicuous gallantry and intrepidity in action against the enemy as Executive Officer, Marine Attack Squadron TWO HUNDRED ELEVEN (VMA-211), Third Marine Aircraft Wing (Forward) in support of Operation ENDURING FREEDOM." (From Citation). (Photo courtesy of Col Robb T. McDonald)[65]

65 Home of Heroes, "Silver Star Recipients—Global War on Terror (Marine Corps)," Home of Heroes, accessed January 18, 2024, https://homeofheroes.com/silver-star/global-war-on-terror/marine-corps/.

Chief Warrant Officer 2 Timothy Killebrew

"There were many things I saw that night that made me proud to be a Marine. There was a roundabout excitement, not fear. Hey, we're being attacked, and we're acting correctly. The Fuels and ARFF Marines all moved to their spots. Four lance corporals headed up a search for missing TCNs and ended up killing an insurgent inside the boxes. I remember seeing one of my Fuels Marines coming out of there, and he relayed, 'We just killed this guy in the box,' and I said, 'Good job.'

"They were determined to do what they were trained to do and were very proud they held the line. Nobody thought about leaving. We gave each other magazines of ammunition, and everybody was checking everybody and making sure the people that came up were who they were supposed to be.

"Our guiding principle in the Marine Corps is to 'never get complacent.' What I took from the attack was *no matter where you go, no matter what you do—have a plan to fight*. Have a plan to defend wherever you are at.

"My biggest accomplishment was not losing a Marine and having all my Marines ready to fight.

"No one ran or shirked their duty. I was very proud of my Marines. The biggest disappointment came after when everything seemed to get closed in a rush and forgotten about. I have Marines that did very brave things and got no recognition for it . . . not even a combat ribbon. This led to a bunch of other servicemen claiming to do the things my Marines did, and nobody seemed to care. It haunts me to this day."

Timothy W. Killebrew advanced rank to Chief Warrant Officer 3 before retiring from the Marine Corps in 2018. He is currently a facilities planner and lives in Texas.

Captain Adam Coker

"I never knew anyone to fly more than 13.6 hours in one shift. To this day, I can still see the Taliban faces in the FLIR. In the daylight, I saw where Wise's rounds hit the T-walls and Taliban blood spattered all over. The day after, EOD safe'd the grenade in the hand of the last moving Taliban in the T-walls. With the pin back in, it would not explode as the area was assessed and searched.

"The biggest disappointment of the night was when I heard we lost two good Marines in the attack. Yeah, we lost a lot of very expensive aircraft, but those Marines were much more valuable. The biggest accomplishment was that we eliminated the threat, and no one else was hurt. It could have been much worse.

"I regret we couldn't have done something earlier to save Sgt Atwell and LtCol Raible. I still pray for their families. It does stand out in my mind as one of the most important events in my life and in my Marine Corps career. I do wish my Marines were more properly recognized for what they did. I have seen other pilots and aircrew get much higher awards and recognition for doing far less."

Lieutenant Colonel Adam Coker serves as the Executive Officer for the 24th Marine Expeditionary Force (MEU).

Captain Kevin Smalley

In 2015, Capt Smalley joined LtCol Lightfoot and Majs Havener, Weingart, Gunnels, and Marvel in attending a Marine Air Corps Association Awards event. They presented a slide show brief explaining what happened at their end.

"I'm most proud of being part of the story that makes Robb T. a legend. McDonald did a lot of the right things. I regret that Raible died, as he was trying to do the right thing, too, by leading his troops into combat.

"We had been stone-walled time and time again about getting more defensive perimeters. And it took people dying to get them to listen to us. There were all kinds of funding issues, but we kept asking and asking. And they kept telling us no. What really struck me was what I learned after the fact—that they [the Taliban] had been inside the wire before.

"The hardest thing of the night for Smalley was not answering his wife's emails. Marines were not supposed to talk after a casualty. It would be unfair to other families for me to tell my wife 'I was okay' before officials told the families about their casualties."

Major Kevin Smalley is an instructor pilot at VT-21.

CAMP BASTION, Afghanistan. September 01, 2012. Capt Kevin T. Smalley, launches AV-8B Harrier in support of ground combat operations. (DVIDS photo by Sgt Keonaona Paulo)

Captain Bryan Yerger

"It was weird, because we did our outlook. ISAF Joint Command did an investigation. Everything seemed fine, no issues. He [Gurganus] got selected for his third star, and it wasn't really until we got back in March/April timeframe, when this whole thing got brought up again. And I don't know who initiated that or if it was some senator, some congressman. Then another investigation was launched, and things kind of went downhill from there.

"He [Gurganus] wrote every single family member a handwritten letter every time someone was killed in action. Just watching him, the type of person he is, how he reacts to things . . . if I could only just be a fraction of the type of man he is . . . extremely caring. He listens to people. It doesn't matter if you're a private or a four-star general, he's going to listen to your input, consider it, and make a decision from there."

Captain Bryan Yerger left the Marine Corps in 2016. He is currently a family law attorney practicing in San Diego, California.

Captain Brian Jordan

"Freedom doesn't come free. It's our responsibility to remember those who have fallen and gave their lives for our country, so that we may live free.

"It was a very somber experience which led to everyone being on high alert for the rest of the deployment.

"The Camp Bastion attack reminded me that life can be taken away at any moment and to do the best I can at everything. And not to worry about the small stuff."

When Jordan returned to the U.S. to instruct future pilots at HMLAT-303, his hair-raising flight with a makeshift crew at Camp Bastion was ingrained forever. This led him to push the importance

CAMP BASTION, Afghanistan. June 26, 2012. Battle ready Combat Crew. (Left to right) SSgt Steven Seay, LCpl Joshua Martinez, GySgt Andrew Bond, Capt Joshua Miller, Capt Brian Jordan. (Photo courtesy of Maj Brian Jordan)

of effective crew resource management within the cockpit. A team, he knew assuredly, is stronger working together than individually.

"Marines who were not there became benefactors from those who were."

Major Brian Jordan is now at MATSG-21 instructing new helicopter pilots in the TH-73 (new training helicopter) at Pensacola, Florida.

Sergeant Jon Cudo

Sergeant Cudo had major surgery in Afghanistan to remove shrapnel. He remembers being stitched up in all the places where he had larger lacerations. The doctors put a quick treatment on his head and wrapped it, but it caused burning everywhere. It was miserable, like pouring lemon juice all over open cuts.

"It felt like my whole body had been dipped in acid after that explosion," remembers Cudo.

"I'm not gonna lie. I was very upset, obviously changed from the attack. Looking back and reflecting, what upset me the most? It wasn't gunfire. Loud noises don't bother me. Being in the gunfire was completely normal, in a weird sense. It was watching my commanding officer sacrificing his life for us, seeing him bleed out on the ground. I still remember when the Taliban fired the RPG, I was fighting right next to Maj Chambless."

For injuries sustained at Camp Bastion fighting the Taliban, Sgt Jonathan Cudo received a Purple Heart award. He was also recommended for a Navy Commendation Medal with Valor, but he did not receive it for reasons unknown. Also receiving the Purple Heart award were LCpl Cole Collums, and (former Cpl) Maj Matthew Eason. In addition, Maj Greer Chambless was also a Purple Heart recipient for injuries sustained through actions at Camp Bastion.

Sergeant Jon Cudo was honorably discharged after serving five years. He is currently continuing an active role in the aviation community.

Sergeant Michael Doman

"I'm glad I was with the Marines that I was with. Everyone's quick thinking and actions are the reason the night went the way it did. I am proud to have served with each and every one of them."

Staff Sergeant Michael Doman was medically retired in 2017.

Major Matthew McBride, Operations Officer, MWSS-273

"Gurganus was given an impossibly hard job to cut back a lot of paxs [personnel]. You couldn't man the wire like you used to. The manpower available to complete a job was unbearable. I came in with about 712 Marines and sailors and was replaced with about 106. They were cut back so much that there's absolutely no way that they could have done what we were doing. It was the most horrible thing. We did good assessments; we increased flight line security. But if you don't have wire covered by fire, then it's no longer an obstacle."

Major Matthew McBride retired from the Marine Corps in 2020. He is currently a project manager at United States Space and Rocket Center.

• • •

For years, the Taliban have been blowing off troops' body parts with their bombs, leaving shards of dirty shrapnel as a reminder, and they caused many brain injuries for a send-off back home. Their bullets streamed steadily from secret hiding places, penetrating, paralyzing, and pummeling our finest American warfighters. While these enemies of freedom later boasted of their bloody handiwork, others like them flocked to their riotous ranks.

The night of September 14, 2012, quickly became payback time on a grand scale, despite the unfavorable element of surprise. The Marines of 3rd MAW won their fight across the battlespace they called a temporary home. It was a shame to degrade those victories by targeting blame and punishment to stalwart leaders they looked up to . . . and to cloak each Marine's valor in obscurity for years to come.

The noisy flying machines the insurgents hated were not their greatest adversary. It was the men on the ground getting them up in the air and the aviators flying them. Every mission that flew out of Camp Bastion was an effort to bring security to the region. Every drop of fuel in the tanks for close air support, another day of protecting the forces.

"Every Marine a rifleman" held true. The Marines did what Marines do and fought back with indomitable force. Importantly, they sent a loud message to the enemy, who thought it easy to defeat them by simply cutting the wire.

AUTHOR'S NOTE

MAJOR GENERALS CHARLES MARK Gurganus and Gregg A. Sturdevant were the ones standing watch for their Marines and America, with over six and a half decades of service between them. They were out there on the battleground, in the skies above, or on the vast seas. They were in the planning rooms and classrooms, training the next generations of warfighters to ensure they were ready and prepared for any conflict America would face. They most certainly deserved better from their superiors, from their president, than what they got in the prickly and premature end.

What they could never take from these two fine USMC officers was their honor, courage, loyalty, duty, service, love, and sacrifice that lives on—all for the greater good of this world. Their extraordinary service is a U.S. Marine Corps legacy.

APPENDIX A

COLONEL BEW'S DEFENSE, COMMANDANT AMOS'S SENTENCE

POST-ATTACK, CHIEF OF Staff Colonel "Otter" Bew got into a heated conversation with the Marine Expeditionary Force (MEF) Chief, when forced to reorient their posture to make up for the lack of perimeter security not provided by the Brits. The MEF Chief was aware of the settlements and poppy fields right next to the wire, which were allowed to flourish pre-attack.

Bew was frustrated that, more than thirty-eight hours after the attack, there was still no clarity from the MEF about how they were going to ensure the perimeter was secure. "The wing had over 1,900 [after drawdown] Marines, and we can sure as hell secure the wire if the MEF can't, so I just needed to know if that was now our job too," said Bew at the time.

"Do you want us to fly airplanes or do you want us to guard Camp Bastion?" Bew fired at the MEF Chief, "I thought you wanted us to fly airplanes. Right now, I've got six fucking squadrons laying in guns facing East, not heads-down fixing airplanes to fight."

As Chief of Staff for the air wing, Bew heard everyone's story immediately afterwards. Yet they were not invited to participate in the initial investigation. He recalled finding out about an investigation meeting from the staff secretary for the MEF, and when he grabbed a couple of operators to join the meeting, it was abruptly canceled and rescheduled to a time Bew was not aware. The initial inquiry by the MEF never made it anywhere. Risk decisions had to be made based on resource constraints. Bew believed MajGen Gurganus made the right ones.

• • •

When the second investigation arose ten months after the Camp Bastion attack, Col Bew knew Sturdevant was going to be asked to retire. He had come back from Afghanistan and was called to Washington, D.C., to work at Headquarters Marine Corps. When he was interviewed by Army LTG Garrett for the second and final investigation, Bew said it felt more "like an interrogation, not really an interview."

One thing that frustrated Bew is the Taliban's release of a video they made pre-attack showing the training and planning for the September 14 breach.[66]

"It debunks one of the fucking biggest frustrations I have with this, and it will be stuck in my head forever," says Bew.

It all crystallized during the Army interrogation at Quantico. LTG Garrett questioned him, while Gen "Razor" Murray from the Marine Corps sat there, haplessly watching. Bew assumed he was there to make sure it was an actual investigation, rather than check all the boxes to roll out a narrative.

---

66 Al Jazeera, "Video shows Afghan base attack 'well-planned,'" September 24, 2012, https://www.aljazeera.com/news/2012/9/24/video-shows-afghan-base-attack-well-planned.

Garrett was obviously not interested in the answers to Bew's questions.

"He was just going to frame questions in a way that he could find something in what I said to support that narrative," said Bew.

The general generally criticized the base reaction to the attack and the posture and preparation for an attack, while casually glancing and glossing over the Brits' responsibility for the wire and for perimeter security. But then Garrett said, "insider information," and Bew wanted to stop the interview, challenging Garrett's insider claim that a secret "collaborator" had delivered leaked information about the Bastion airfield layout to the attackers. They hadn't even looked at the Taliban planning material.

Garrett then threw the hardball: "We have information superiority over you."

"I'll never forget that quote, he said, 'information superiority' as if I were an enemy."

Bew offered a screenshot of the material the Taliban used to plan the attack, pointing out its pitfalls. "It was clear that once they [the Taliban] got inside the base, they really didn't know where they were going," informed Bew. "They knew generally where the Harriers were located. Because you can see them approach, hear them taxiing, and hear where the runups are from outside the wire. You could, from outside the base gate, get some idea of where the aircraft were located. The helicopters lifted out of the same spot all the time. But they did not have on their planning materials, the single most significant geographic feature on the base, which is the flight line [X-bus] road. If you're on the base, that's how you get around. It's the thing you see, no matter who you are."

His point to LTG Garrett: "There was a lack of insider information for their planning." And although there may have been some, it didn't come from a leaked detailed layout of their spaces otherwise the Taliban would have gotten a lot more right on their mapping.

"You're pinning that failure of the perimeter security on the air wing," Bew told Garrett, "Our job was to secure our spaces, and we did."

•••

A year after the attack, Commandant James Amos issued the following *Memorandum for the Record* on September 30, 2013. The subject was the accountability determination of U.S. Commanders for the attack on Camp Bastion. Despite and because of the statements in the *official U.S. investigations*, he tried to mix praise with punishment. It did not mix. Amos assigned no accountability to the British, though he would have known if he had read the American and U.K. investigations, but chose the briar path for his own generals with mixed messages:

> "As the Regional Command (Southwest) RC(SW) and I MEF (FWD) Commander, MajGen Gurganus's focus was broad, and his mission was complex. He and his Marines faced an evolving and determined enemy in places like Marjah, Kajaki, and Musa Qal'ah. MajGen Gurganus's area of responsibility spanned approximately 36,000 square miles and encompassed 196 combat outposts and forward operating bases within 19 districts. Our Corps excelled on this complex battlefield under MajGen Gurganus' leadership despite the tragedy on 14-15 September 2012."
>
> "Major General Gurganus made an error in judgment when conducting his risk analysis regarding the requirements to achieve a unified force protection posture within the BLS Complex."

Amos then admits that Gurganus "addressed many aspects of these requirements with his higher headquarters and was often turned down."

In the end, Amos stated, "He could and should have done more." How about in the beginning, higher-up should have listened to

Gurganus, the local commander, who was intimately involved in the combat environment of Bastion in Helmand Province. Instead, Gurganus received no credit for what he did achieve and baseless chastisement and degradation for the security posture he attempted to achieve but was denied by higher-up chain of command and the ESG on Bastion.

Amos' words were no less stinging and life-changing for Sturdevant, "He and his staff unreasonably minimized the force protection threats which, in turn, exposed his command to unnecessary risk." Amos accused Sturdevant, the air wing commander, of failure "to fully engage with coalition partners in the important force protection decision-making process," contravening he stated, "trust and confidence I had in him as a commander."

What happened, on the flip side, to the trust Gurganus and Sturdevant had in Amos and those above them "to watch their backs," and "tell the truth of security matters." Should that trust span the chain of command, at all costs, to provide what was necessary for the protection and security of those sent to an active war zone? Rather than impede officers from doing the job they unequivocally needed to do. It took two deaths by Taliban hands to change all former naysayers' rejections and put action to Gurganus and Sturdevant's pre-attack security force measures. It was a time of war. Yet someone had to pay even though accusations were untrue, and facts ignored. The denial of truth was clear that there existed a diverse list of contributing factors and people that led to the Taliban breach, not in Gurganus, nor Sturdevant's control.

"As such, I have recommended to the Secretary of the Navy that the President rescind MajGen Gurganus's nomination for promotion to the grade of Lieutenant General, and I have requested his retirement. In addition, I have personally counseled MajGen Sturdevant and recommended to the Secretary of the Navy that he issue a Secretarial letter of censure to MajGen Sturdevant.

I have also requested the retirement of MajGen Sturdevant. This action effectively ends the promising careers of two of our General Officers."[67]

Signed by James F. Amos.
Commandant of the Marine Corps

67 Amos, James F. "Memorandum for the Record," Department of the Navy, September 30th, 2013, https://www.hqmc.marines.mil/Portals/142/Docs/CMC%20Memo%20 for%20the%20Record%20in%20Bastion%20Investigation.PDF.

APPENDIX B

HOUSE OF COMMONS, U.K. ACCOUNTABILITY

AS COMMANDANT AMOS LEVIED sole blame on his generals for the Taliban getting through that wire, based on lies and omissions about what led up to it, the U.K. Defense Committee dug the truth out of more lies and accusations coming from Capewell. The Committee Members finally trained a proper light on the failures of their own. Much heated scrutiny was put on the "why" about things no one could change, now the damage was done. It was war. Little to no attention was given to the Marines who fought undauntedly, heroically, at great peril and won over the enemy. A multitude of uncounted lives were saved that night.

House of Commons 17 December 2013 Defence Committee Evidence Session:[68]

---

68 House of Commons Defence Committee, "Afghanistan—Camp Bastion Attack," *The Stationery Office*, April 16, 2014, Ev. 2-3, https://publications.parliament.uk/pa/cm201314/cmselect/cmdfence/830/830vw.pdf.

The deputy commander of ISAF, Lieutenant General Bradshaw, was an appointed U.K. national contingent commander to lead a "contingent" of British forces in the Afghanistan theater. He was ordered to do a post-attack administrative review by Commander ISAF, U.S. Gen John R. Allen. The review was completed on September 27, 2012, thirteen days after the attack.

It took less than two weeks to assess all the vulnerabilities of the airfield: "The recommendations focused on 'force protection, command and control, manning, communications and internal personnel procedures,'" stated Capewell.

"Regional Command (SW) also conducted specific Camp Bastion force protection reviews in October 2012 and February 2013. The ISAF staffing process concluded in March 2013 . . . On the formal conclusion of the ISAF process, Commander ISAF wrote to his British deputy commander requesting that the UK review the reports with a view to taking appropriate action. This request was subsequently referred to me, with the formal documentation, by the deputy commander at the end of March 2013. Subsequently, I [Capewell] directed that a review be conducted within my headquarters to identify any further lessons to be learned from the existing report which had not already been taken into account."

The layered review process itself finally acknowledged that there was a list of security problems that needed fixing pre-attack. One didn't have to look too far. None of it was really news—more like shelved recommendations presented by Gurganus and Sturdevant who both were ultimately and wrongly punished for other's failures.

• • •

Concluding Statements from the U.K. Ministry of Defence (MOD) Investigative Committee (post-attack) are listed in the following text published by the U.K. parliament under parliamentary business/ publications and records.[69]

Afghanistan – Camp Bastion – Defence Committee Contents:

UK ACCOUNTABILITY

14. "In oral evidence, Lieutenant General Capewell, Chief of Joint Operations, acknowledged that errors had been made by UK personnel, but that 'they were not culpable errors.'"

THE BURNING MAN INCIDENT

23. "We were not satisfied by the responses we received and asked further questions about the MOU following the evidence session. In its response, the MoD told us that the principal differences between the 2011 MOU and the revised MOU are now in force related to command relationships and organization which had been streamlined under Commander Regional Command (SW). Specifically, the Bastion-Leatherneck-Shorabak complex now operates under the command of the US Marine Corps Commander of RC(SW)."

24. "At the time of the attack, the Memorandum of Understanding between USCENTCOM and PJHQ had not been revised, despite the fact that all parties appeared to agree on the necessity to make revisions in the aftermath of the 'burning man incident' . . . The delays to the process of revision allowed weaknesses in command and control arrangements for force protection to persist . . . ISAF

69 "Accountability review," U.K. Parliament, April 16, 2014, https://publications.parliament.uk/pa/cm201314/cmselect/cmdfence/830/83005.htm.

personnel were exposed to unnecessary risk. In response to our report the MoD must explain why the failure to revise the MOU prior to the September 2012 attack should not be regarded as an act of omission."

SECURITY INCIDENTS RECORDED IN
HELMAND PROVINCE

26. "The inference we drew from the Chief of Joint Operation's evidence was that the number of security incidents was unusually high in Helmand Province in 2012. Unfortunately, the MoD declined to provide us with comparable details of the level of security incidents recorded in Helmand for previous years as this information was classified. This would have allowed us to make an informed assessment of the relative threat levels in the area at the time."

SECURITY AND FORCE PROTECTION
OPERATIONS IN CAMP BASTION

28. "Asked to clarify who was in overall charge of security and force protection for Camp Bastion and the airfield at the time of the attack, the MoD told us: In accordance with the then extant MOU (dated January 2011), Commander Leatherneck was designated as the Battlespace owner of Area of Operations Belleau Wood and a Security Force Commander (US Marine Corps officer) was responsible for executing security operations in Area of Operations Belleau Wood [outside the wire]. . . . The Bastion Force Protection Commander (a UK officer) was responsible for providing perimeter and on base Force Protection of Bastion, including Bastion Airfield."

CAMP BASTION GUARD TOWERS

31. "Eleven of the twenty-four guard towers on Camp Bastion were manned at the time of the attack. The UK 5 FP Wing did not employ a dedicated security force on the Camp Bastion perimeter."

33. "The arrangements for manning of the guard towers around the perimeter of Camp Bastion were exposed by the attack as inadequate. The decision not to man Tower 16 on the night of 14-15 September 2014 contributed directly to the failure to detect the insurgents at an early stage which might have limited the impact of their assault. We note that all guard towers are now manned constantly."

PERIMETER SECURITY

34. ". . . a breach of the perimeter fence in the Camp Leatherneck sector near Tower 40 or 41 that occurred in late June 2012 and three breaches that occurred in the Camp Bastion perimeter in July-August 2012, [were] identified by UK patrols after the breaches occurred. The cause or purpose of the breaches was unknown, but the [British] 5 FP Wing had assessed them as 'scrapping' activity by individuals who would try to come near the base to take or steal metal to sell. Statements by US personnel suggested that on at least one occasion intruders were able to enter unoccupied guard posts. The US Army also released, as one of the exhibits associated with the investigation report, surveillance video footage dated 18 July 2012 of a nighttime breach of the perimeter by two individuals who moved near the cryogenics lab by the airfield and then departed out of the same breach."

35. "The MoD told us that there had been approximately nine breaches in 2011 and 12 breaches in 2012 in both the UK and US sectors. The breaches were considered by UK personnel to be

low-level scrapping and criminal activity and any identified breaches had been repaired."

36. "Several US personnel, including Major General Gurganus and Major General Sturdevant, expressed concerns they had about encroachment on the southeast side of the base by poppy farmers. Major General Sturdevant, interviewed as part of the US investigation following the attack, stated:

'We literally had poppy growing right up against the perimeter fence. That was another thing that MajGen Gurganus tried to take action on, but he wasn't able to accomplish that. It was because the Afghans had to do it. We weren't allowed to. The biggest external threat to the base came from there, and Task Force Belleau Wood was down there running patrols every single day.'"

37. "In oral evidence, Lieutenant General Capewell characterized the decision to allow poppy cultivation close to the perimeter fence as a 'minor tactical error' which had contributed to the enemy's success."

38. "We were concerned to learn of the number of breaches of the perimeter fence of Camp Bastion in the two years prior to the attack and the apparent tolerance of poppy cultivation immediately outside the fence. We consider that the failure to take concerted action to prevent these activities increased the risk of surveillance and intelligence gathering by Afghan nationals which could have assisted insurgent planning for an attack on the base."

APPENDIX C

MRS. MOON'S LESSONS LEARNED

HOUSE OF COMMONS 17 December 2013 Defence Committee Evidence Session:[70]

(Q53) Mrs. Moon: "Can I start right at the beginning? Lieutenant-General, you said heavily armed individuals attacked on a moonless night. I have watched lots of films about cowboys and Indians, and that is usually when these things happen—on a moonless night heavily armed insurgents try to get into the fort. . . . Let us take things right from the start and work our way through what we could have done, should have done and, perhaps in retrospect, were wrong not to have done. We are told throughout the report that people coming in and out of the camp were seen as 'scrappers.' Has the U.K. learned a major lesson in terms of allowing potential access to exterior fence lines, allowing close access to the fence line, allowing incursions through the fence line and failing to respond to

70 House of Commons Defence Committee, "Afghanistan—Camp Bastion Attack," *The Stationery Office*, April 16, 2014, Ev. 12, 18, https://publications.parliament.uk/pa/cm201314/cmselect/cmdfence/830/830vw.pdf.

known incursions through the fence line? Were we wrong not to have addressed those things?"

Lt. Gen. Capewell: "I think that question strikes at the very heart of a counter-insurgency campaign, which is what we are conducting in Afghanistan. It is an excellent question because it describes how difficult operations in those conditions are."

Capewell later admits, ". . . if I thought that there was nothing to learn from this, we would not have made some changes in the aftermath collectively as a coalition and from some of our national perspectives in terms of lessons learned."

Sticking to lies despite the truth revealed by his own country was not a lesson learned for Capewell. After reams of investigations and documented facts saying otherwise, he insisted that "Generals Gurganus and Sturdevant were accused of failing to take adequate force protection measures."

•••

Across the ocean, on a big, damp foggy island, a promotion followed the attack on Bastion. Lt. Gen. Sir David Andrew Capewell was appointed Knight Commander of the Order of the Bath in the 2014 New Year Honors for commanding U.K. Global Operations during a period of unprecedented volatility.[71]

---

71 Wikipedia contributors, "David Capewell," *Wikipedia, Wikimedia Foundation,* Accessed January 30, 2024, https://en.wikipedia.org/w/index.php?title=David_Capewell&oldid=1186092413.

APPENDIX D

ATTACK FACTS, NAZEER WHEREABOUTS

AT NO PLACE IN the Amos letter, the CENTCOM or Dept. of the Army investigations, Capewell's remarks, or the British MOD's conclusions is any detailed account of the valor of the night by 3rd MAW Marines distinctly loyal to and operating under the command and trust of their leaders Major Generals Gurganus and Sturdevant.

USMC Bastion Attack Narrative Summary report:

"Throughout the attack, HMLA-469 aircraft were able to provide near constant overhead coverage in defense of the flight line and Camp Bastion. The incredible efforts of the squadron's Marines also ensured that aircraft maintenance readiness did not suffer over the following days. The Marines swept the compound for unexploded ordnance, while the Maintenance Department initiated conditional inspections to ensure that the squadron's aircraft did not receive damage during the assault. This allowed the squadron to support the next day's flight schedule without interruption. Even under small arms and RPG fire, HMLA-469 Marines armed and launched aircraft, then defended the squadron compound without suffering any casualties or damage to aircraft.

"The strong force protection measures, in the form of T-wall, HESCO, and concertina wire barriers, initiated by previous HMLAs and reinforced by HMLA-469, played a significant role in deterring a direct enemy assault upon the HMLA compound. The high degree of professionalism and devotion to duty, displayed by every Marine, ensured that everyone did their job despite the physical dangers they were subjected to.

"On the night of 14 September 2012, the quick thinking, courage under fire, and devotion to duty of every Righteous Marine proved that they are deserving of the fine legacy established by their Marine Aviation predecessors during battles such as those at Henderson Field, Guadalcanal, proving that every Marine is a rifleman."[72]

The U.S. suffered two casualties due to the courageous sacrifices of LtCol Christopher Raible and Sgt Bradley Atwell. These Marines died fighting in battle with a determined enemy and will be forever remembered as heroes standing with their fellow Marines they fought alongside. There was no other U.S. loss of life. The U.K. MOD reported no casualties in February 2013.

U.S. CENTCOM Bastion Attack Summary:[73]

"The resulting friendly casualties and damage included two US personnel killed in action (KIA), eight US personnel wounded in action (WIA), eight UK personnel WIA, one civilian contractor WIA, six AV-8B Harriers destroyed, two AV-8B Harriers severely

---

72 "OEF Enemy Attack on Camp Bastion, 14 September 2012, NARRATIVE SUMMARY, HMLA 469" (Private source)

73 Garrett, William B., Murray, Thomas M., "USCENTCOM Bastion Attack Investigation Executive Summary," Accessed November 29, 2023, Pg. 1, https://www.hqmc.marines.mil/Portals/142/Docs/USCENTCOM%20Bastion%20Attack%20Investigation%20Executive%20Summary.pdf.

damaged, one C-12 damaged, three MV-22B minor damaged, one C-130E severely damaged, one UK SKASaC (Sea King) minor damaged, two UK Jackal vehicles significantly damaged, three fuel bags destroyed, five sun shades destroyed, one sun shade with structural and fire damage, three sun shades with fabric damage, extensive concrete damage, and damage to the VMA-211 hangar/maintenance facility. Fourteen of the Taliban attackers were killed and one remaining attacker wounded who was detained and interrogated."

...

A Taliban propaganda video made well in advance of the attack, which outlined their plans and movement on the base, was released after the attack on September 14. This, to claim credit and look powerful to the people they controlled with lies and exploitation. It is speculated that the Taliban announced Captain Wales was the target of the attack only after they learned through U.S./U.K./International reporting that Prince Harry was at Bastion/Leatherneck.

The Washington Post reported Sept. 12, 2014, "Only one of the armed attackers involved in that Sept. 14, 2012, attack on Camp Bastion survived, military officials said. Mohammed Nazeer, [then] twenty-four, was convicted and sentenced to death by an Afghan court, said Maj John Caldwell, a Marine Corps spokesman at the Pentagon. But it still isn't certain the punishment will stand. An Afghan appellate court affirmed the death penalty July 6, but the case is now before the Afghan Supreme Court for additional review, Caldwell said."[74]

---

74 Lamonthe, Dan, "A Taliban fighter survived the attack on Afghanistan's Camp Bastion. Will he get the death penalty?" *Washington Post*, September 12, 2014, https://www.washingtonpost.com/news/checkpoint/wp/2014/09/12/one-taliban-insurgent-survived-the-attack-on-afghanistans-camp-bastion-will-he-get-the-death-penalty/.

Wounded attacker Mohammed Nazeer was treated at the Role 3 hospital on Bastion. Despite extensive research, his known whereabouts or outcome are unknown to this author.

The Hill wrote on September 18, 2012,[75] "The Obama administration plans to pull all U.S. troops out of Afghanistan by 2014. However, that plan is predicated upon Afghan military and police units being able to shoulder the load for the country's security operations once American forces leave."

Anyone can write history. Only the great ones live it.

75 Muñoz, Carlos, "US captures Taliban leader tied to Camp Bastion attack," *The Hill*, September 18, 2012, https://thehill.com/policy/defense/125723-us-captures-taliban-leader-tied-to-camp-bastion-attack/.

BIBLIOGRAPHY

March 2019, June 2020, MajGen Charles Mark Gurganus, personal interview

December 2019, MajGen Gregg Sturdevant, personal interview

May/December 2014, BGen Stephen L. Lightfoot, personal interview

October 2015, Col Robb T. McDonald, personal interview

October 2021, Col Richard Bew, personal interview

October 2016, LtCol Adam Coker, personal interview

March/April 2017, August 2018, CW3 Timothy W. Killebrew, personal interview

February 2015, February 2016, June 2019, Maj Brian Jordan, personal interview

May 2020, Maj Kevin Smalley, personal interview

April/May/September 2019, Capt Bryan Yerger, personal interview

August 2021, Sgt Michael Doman, personal interview

September 2021, Sgt Jon Cudo, personal interview

September 2022, Maj Matthew McBride, personal interview

ACKNOWLEDGMENTS

I WISH TO THANK everyone who contributed to this book—for their enduring patience and faith in my mission. They are fantastic people you will get to know through these courageous actions. I'm especially humbled and honored to have talked to Major Generals Charles Mark Gurganus and Gregg Sturdevant, who took the brunt of unrighteous blame for the breach with dignity and continuing love for the Marines they led. All the Marines I interviewed for this book have gone above and beyond to tell this story with the highest integrity and dedication to sharing the battle to save Camp Bastion as it really happened. All were driven to recognize and give credit to their fellow Marines they fought alongside to eliminate the enemy on their turf. They have given me countless hours of direction and answered innumerable questions with kindness and generosity. I am forever indebted to them all and have grown to love them and feel deeply honored to tell their stories.

For the Marines of 3rd MAW, I was not able to interview personally, your meritorious actions are an achievement to be noted. Many of you risked your lives taking the fight to the enemy and were not recognized. But your legacy is written in the successful counter attack of which you played a critical role.

From BGen Stephen Lightfoot, September 26, 2021: "Many Marines who received gunfire were NOT awarded the Combat Action Ribbon because they did not fire back. Some of those Marines were running towards or launching aircraft while receiving gunfire, while others along the perimeter could not see exactly where the rounds were coming from, so didn't just 'spray and pray' in the darkness when the entire fight was within friendly lines. I'm quite proud that there were zero friendly fire incidents on that chaotic night, and it is because of the fire discipline of our Marines and officers who were not chasing ribbons or medals."

I also wish to thank my husband, Dave McKinney, who encouraged me to write this book and has given me every freedom to do it. I'd like to thank my sister, Penny Burd, who supports my passion to honor our U.S. military members.

We are a nation of strangers bound together by these friends who defend our gift of freedom, our opportunities, and our very lives and the lives of others around the world. The men and women of our active-duty United States military are real people from all walks of life, like us, but with a crucial difference. Their daily universe is war, crisis, and chaos of every kind. Their job is to be ready and act when called upon and leave a footprint of freedom, bound by an oath to serve in the best and worst situations.

My respect knows no bounds for our warriors and heroes that not only keep this country from falling prey to terrorists, tyrants, and dictators, but rescue other nations as well. They serve faithfully and are fully committed to "the mission."

ABOUT THE AUTHOR

JEANNE MCKINNEY IS AN award-winning military journalist as well as a military documentary filmmaker. She is currently in the final stages of writing, directing, and producing *Ronin 3: The Battle for Sangin*—a three-part documentary series that follows 3rd Battalion, 5th Marines through a labyrinth of murder holes and IEDs in a heavily entrenched Taliban stronghold, on their mission to restore security to the local Afghan people.

Her focus and passion are telling the legendary stories about United States active-duty military members in their fight to keep America and her allies safe and free. McKinney offers an inside look at men and women who do the hard and very dangerous job of counterinsurgency to stop and disrupt the plans of the world's most notorious terrorist groups. She shines a light on America's amazing warfighters, telling their stories as if you were there with them on combat missions throughout Afghanistan, Iraq, Africa, Syria, or wherever the next global hotspot erupts. You'll get to know the people who watch our backs, on the ground, in the air, and on the seas.

One-on-one interviews are McKinney's signature style, getting news directly from the source. She's spoken with troops from all U.S. Armed Services, in all kinds of roles with varying ranks, doing their country's work in many parts of the world. McKinney has also covered (on site) the U.S. southern border illegal immigration crisis. In January 2019, U.S. Customs and Border Patrol offered her a personal tour of the San Diego Sector to show the public how they work and the hard challenges they face to stop illegal immigration. Additionally, she has written and published dozens of investigative articles in her ongoing fight to preserve America, the Republic, and its Constitution.

McKinney has won multiple San Diego Press Club Excellence in Journalism Awards, including eight First-Place honors. The President's Own Marine Band performed an original score for her film series at a World Premiere in August 2022.

•••

In personal interviews, thirteen Marines from the 3rd Marine Aircraft Wing who fought at Camp Bastion on September 14, 2012, gave McKinney both the ground and air perspectives to write *Triumph Over the Taliban*. Hours of lengthy and candid conversations and hundreds of email exchanges enabled her to reconstruct the entire Battle story, which she was honored to do. In researching this book, she acquired a critical understanding of both U.S. and U.K. post-attack investigations (declassified) that led to the discovery of misrepresentations, including lies and omissions kept dark. She also has studied dozens of articles and reports on the history of the volatile region as well as the politics surrounding it. In doing so, McKinney got a deep look into what it takes to be a U.S. Marine fighting an enemy that is out to kill them because they are a roadblock to terror, opening a pathway to freedom and stability. The book and film *13 Hours* inspired her to write *Triumph Over the Taliban,* describing a battle where Americans once again stood as mighty Spartans against the wrath of extremist Islamic insurgents.

Connect with Jeanne McKinney through her website at: **www. patriotprofiles.com.**

Printed in Great Britain
by Amazon

41159155R00165